KEY STATUTES

CRIMINAL LAW

2008–2009 EDITION

DAMIAN WARBURTON LLB LLM

PART OF HACHETTE LIVRE UK

Orders: please contact Bookpoint Ltd, 130 Milton Park, Abingdon, Oxon OX14 4SB.
Telephone: (44) 01235 827720. Fax: (44) 01235 400454. Lines are open from 9.00–5.00,
Monday to Saturday, with a 24 hour message answering service. You can also order
through our website www.hoddereducation.co.uk

If you have any comments to make about this, or any of our other titles, please send
them to educationenquiries@hodder.co.uk

British Library Cataloguing in Publication Data

A catalogue record for this title is available from the British Library

ISBN: 978 0 340 97238 0

First Edition Published 2008
Impression number   10 9 8 7 6 5 4 3 2 1
Year   2012 2011 2010 2009 2008

This selection © 2008 Damian Warburton

© Crown copyright material is reproduced with permission of the Controller of HMSO.

All rights reserved. No part of this publication may be reproduced or transmitted in any form or by any means, electronic or mechanical, including photocopy, recording, or any information storage and retrieval system, without permission in writing from the publisher or under licence from the Copyright Licensing Agency Limited. Further details of such licences (for reprographic reproduction) may be obtained from the Copyright Licensing Agency Limited, Saffron House, 6-10 Kirby Street, London EC1N 8TS.

Hachette Livre UK's policy is to use papers that are natural, renewable and recyclable products and made from wood grown in sustainable forests. The logging and manufacturing processes are expected to conform to the environmental regulations of the country of origin.

Typeset by Transet Limited, Coventry, England
Printed in Malta for Hodder Education, a part of Hachette Livre UK, 338 Euston Road, London NW1 3BH

CONTENTS

CHRONOLOGICAL LIST OF ACTS	v
PREFACE	vii
PART 1 ▌ ACTS	1
Abortion Act 1967, ss.1–2 , 4–6	2
Accessories and Abettors Act 1861, s.8	3
Animal Welfare Act 2006, ss.1–9	3
Anti-terrorism, Crime and Security Act 2001, ss.113–115	7
Aviation Security Act 1982, ss.1–4, 38	9
Bail Act 1976, s.6	13
Broadcasting Act 1990, s.202	13
Child Abduction Act 1984, ss.1–3	13
Children Act 2004, s.58	15
Children and Young Persons Act 1933, ss.1, 50	15
Communications Act 2003, s.127	16
Computer Misuse Act 1990, ss.1–10, 17	17
Contempt of Court Act 1981, ss.1–9	21
Corporate Manslaughter and Homicide Act 2007, ss.1–8, 18–20	23
Crime and Disorder Act 1998, ss.1, 28–32, 34	28
Criminal Appeal Act 1968, ss.1–7, 12, 20, 33	31
Criminal Attempts Act 1981, ss.1, 1A, 3, 4, 6, 8, 9	34
Criminal Damage Act 1971, ss.1–5, 10	36
Criminal Justice Act 1925, s.47	38
Criminal Justice Act 1967, ss.8, 91	38
Criminal Justice Act 1988, ss.39, 134, 139, 139A, 160, 160A	39
Criminal Justice and Immigration Act 2008, ss.63–67, 76, 79	41
Criminal Justice and Public Order Act 1994, ss.51, 68–69	44
Criminal Law Act 1967, ss.1, 3–6	47
Criminal Law Act 1977, ss.1–3	49
Criminal Procedure (Insanity) Act 1964, s.5	51
Criminal Procedure (Insanity and Unfitness to Plead) Act 1991, ss.1, 6	51
Dangerous Dogs Act 1991, ss.1–4, 7, 10	52
Dealing in Cultural Objects Act 2003, ss.1–3, 5	55
Dogs Act 1871, s.2	56
Domestic Violence, Crime and Victims Act 2004, s.5	56
Education Act 1996, s.4	57
Explosives Act 1875, s.3	58
Explosive Substances Act 1883, ss.2–5, 9	58
Female Genital Mutilation Act 2003, ss.1–6	59
Finance Act 2000, s.144	60
Firearms Act 1968, ss.1–5A, 7, 16–25, 57–58, Schedule 1	60
Firearms (Amendment) Act 1988, ss.5–8	70
Firearms (Amendment) Act 1997, ss.2–8	71
Football Offences Act 1991, ss.1–4	72
Forgery and Counterfeiting Act 1981, ss.1–5, 8–10	73
Fraud Act 2006, ss.1–9, 11–12	76
Gambling Act 2005, ss.42–43	78
Gender Recognition Act 2004, ss.9, 20	79
Health Act 2006, ss.1–3, 6–8	80

Homicide Act 1957, ss.1–4	80
Human Fertilisation and Embryology Act 1990, ss.1–4, 41	84
Human Rights Act 1998, ss.1–4, Schedule 1	87
Hunting Act 2004, ss.1–6, 11, Schedule 1	91
Identity Cards Act 2006, ss.25–26	95
Infant Life (Preservation) Act 1929, ss.1, 2	98
Infanticide Act 1938, s.1	99
Interpretation Act 1978, ss.5–6, 15, 16, 18, Schedule 1	99
Intoxicating Substances (Supply) Act 1985, s.1	100
Knives Act 1997, ss.1–4, 9–10	101
Law Reform (Year and a Day Rule) Act 1996, ss.1–3	103
Licensing Act 2003, ss.141–142	103
Magistrates Courts Act 1980, s.44	104
Malicious Communications Act 1988, s.1	104
Mental Capacity Act 2005, ss.2, 3, 44, 62	105
Misuse of Drugs Act 1971, ss.2–9A, 28, 37, Schedule 2	106
Mobile Telephone (Re-programming Act) 2002, ss.1–2	114
Murder (Abolition of Death Penalty) Act 1965, s.1	115
Offences Against the Person Act 1861, ss.4, 9, 16, 18, 20–24, 28–30, 32–33, 38, 47, 57–60, 64	115
Perjury Act 1911, ss.1–1A, 7, 13	118
Police Act 1996, ss.89–91	119
Prevention of Crime Act 1953, s.1	120
Protection from Harassment Act 1997, ss.1–2, 4, 7	121
Protection of Children Act 1978, ss.1–2, 6, 7	122
Public Order Act 1986, ss.1–8, 17–19, 29A–G; J–N	124
Serious Crime Act 2007, ss. 44–50, 55–59, 64–66, Schedule 1 (part 1), Schedule 3 (part 1)	130
Serious Organised Crime and Police Act 2005, ss.128, 132, 138, 145–49	139
Sexual Offences Act 1956, ss.33–36	142
Sexual Offences Act 1967, s.6	143
Sexual Offences Act 1985, ss.1–2, 4	144
Sexual Offences Act 1993, s.1	144
Sexual Offences Act 2003, ss.1–15, 30–33, 47–51, 61–63, 72–79, Schedule 2	144
Street Offences Act 1959, s.1	155
Suicide Act 1961, ss.1, 2	156
Suppression of Terrorism Act 1978, ss.4, 8, Schedule 1	156
Taking of Hostages Act 1982, s.1	157
Terrorism Act 2000, ss.1, 3, 11–19, 21–21H, 39, 48–49, 51–52, 54–59, 62, 1117–18, 121, Schedule 2	158
Terrorism Act 2006, ss.1–6, 8–11, 17–20	172
Theft Act 1968, ss.1–10, 12–13, 17–25, 30, 34	180
Theft Act 1978, ss.3, 4	187
Treasure Act 1996, s.8	188
Trial of Lunatics Act 1883, s.2	188
UK Borders Act 2007, s.2	189
Violent Crime Reduction Act 2006, ss.28, 36–38, 55	189
Water Resources Act 1991, ss.85, 89	193
Wireless Telegraphy Act 2006, s.47	194

PART 2 | BILLS BEFORE PARLIAMENT (2007–2008 SESSION)   195

Counter Terrorism Bill 2006–07, cl 1–3, 83–84, 98–99	196
Drugs (Reclassification) Bill 2007–08, cl.1–2	198
Illegally Logged Timber (Prohibition of Sale and Distribution) Bill 2007–08, cl.1–3	198
Human Fertilisation and Embryology Bill [HL] 2007–08, cl.3–4	190
Statute Law (Repeals) Bill [HL] 2007-08, Schedule 1, Part 3	201

CHRONOLOGICAL LIST OF ACTS

Accessories and Abettors Act 1861, s.8	3
Offences Against the Person Act 1861, ss.4, 9, 16, 18, 20–24, 28–30, 32–33, 38, 47, 57–60, 64	115
Dogs Act 1871, s.2	56
Explosives Act 1875, s. 3	58
Explosive Substances Act 1883, ss.2–5, 9	58
Trial of Lunatics Act 1883, s.2	188
Perjury Act 1911, ss.1–2, 7, 13	118
Criminal Justice Act 1925, s.47	38
Infant Life (Preservation) Act 1929, ss.1, 2	98
Children and Young Persons Act 1933, ss.1, 50	15
Infanticide Act 1938, s.1	99
Prevention of Crime Act 1953, s.1	120
Sexual Offences Act 1956 ss.33–36	142
Homicide Act 1957, ss.1–4	83
Street Offences Act 1959, s.1	155
Suicide Act 1961, ss.1, 2	156
Criminal Procedure (Insanity) Act 1964, s.5	51
Murder (Abolition of Death Penalty) Act 1965, s.1	115
Abortion Act 1967, ss.1–2 , 4–6	2
Criminal Justice Act 1967, ss.8, 91	38
Criminal Law Act 1967, ss.1, 3–6	47
Sexual Offences Act 1967, s.6	143
Criminal Appeal Act 1968, ss.1–7, 12, 20, 33	31
Firearms Act 1968, ss.1–5A, 7, 16–25, 57–58, Schedule 1	60
Theft Act 1968 ss.1–10, 12–13, 17–25, 30, 34	180
Criminal Damage Act 1971, ss.1–5, 10	36
Misuse of Drugs Act 1971, ss.2–9A, 28, 37, Schedule 2	106
Bail Act 1976, s.6	13
Criminal Law Act 1977, ss.1–3	49
Interpretation Act 1978, ss.5–6, 15, 16, 18, Schedule 1	99
Protection of Children Act 1978, ss.1–2, 6, 7	122
Suppression of Terrorism Act 1978, ss.4, 8, Schedule 1	156
Theft Act 1978 ss.3, 4	187
Magistrates Courts Act 1980, s.44	104
Contempt of Court Act 1981, ss.1–9	21
Criminal Attempts Act 1981, ss.1, 1A, 3, 4, 6, 8, 9	34
Forgery and Counterfeiting Act 1981, ss.1–5, 8–10	73
Aviation Security Act 1982, ss.1–4, 38	9
Taking of Hostages Act 1982, s.1	158
Child Abduction Act 1984, ss.1–3	13
Intoxicating Substances (Supply) Act 1985, s.1	100
Sexual Offences Act 1985, ss.1–2, 4	144
Public Order Act 1986, ss.1–8, 17–19, 29A–G ; J–N	124
Criminal Justice Act 1988, ss.39, 134, 139, 139A, 160, 160A	39
Firearms (Amendment) Act 1988, ss.5–8	70
Malicious Communications Act 1988, s.1	104
Broadcasting Act 1990, s.202	13
Computer Misuse Act 1990, ss.1–10, 17	17
Human Fertilisation and Embryology Act 1990, ss.1–4, 41	84
Criminal Procedure (Insanity and Unfitness to Plead) Act 1991, ss.1, 6	51
Dangerous Dogs Act 1991, ss.1–4, 7, 10	52
Football Offences Act 1991, ss.1–4	72

Water Resources Act 1991, ss.85, 89	193
Sexual Offences Act 1993 s.1	144
Criminal Justice and Public Order Act 1994, ss.51, 68–69	44
Education Act 1996, s. 4	57
Law Reform (Year and a Day Rule) Act 1996, ss.1–3	103
Police Act 1996, ss.89–91	119
Treasure Act 1996, s.8	188
Firearms (Amendment) Act 1997, ss.2–8	71
Knives Act 1997, ss.1–4, 9–10	101
Protection from Harassment Act 1997, ss.1–2, 4, 7	121
Crime and Disorder Act 1998, ss.1, 28–32, 34	28
Human Rights Act 1998, ss.1–4, Schedule 1	87
Finance Act 2000, s.144	60
Terrorism Act 2000, ss.1, 3, 11–19, 21–21H, 39, 48–49, 51–52, 54–59, 62, 117–118, 121, Schedule 2	158
Anti-terrorism, Crime and Security Act 2001, ss.113–15	7
Mobile Telephone (Re-programming Act) 2002, ss.1–2	114
Communications Act 2003, s.127	16
Dealing in Cultural Objects Act 2003, ss.1–3, 5	55
Female Genital Mutilation Act 2003, ss.1–6	59
Licensing Act 2003, ss.141–142	103
Sexual Offences Act 2003, ss. 1–15, 30–33, 47–51, 61–63, 72–79, Schedule 2	144
Children Act 2004, s.58	15
Domestic Violence, Crime and Victims Act 2004, s.5	56
Gender Recognition Act 2004, ss.9, 20	79
Hunting Act 2004, ss.1–6, 11, Schedule 1	91
Gambling Act 2005, ss.42–43	78
Mental Capacity Act 2005, ss.2, 3, 44, 62	105
Serious Organised Crime and Police Act 2005, ss.128, 132, 138, 145–49	139
Animal Welfare Act 2006, ss.1–9	3
Fraud Act 2006, ss.1–9, 11–12	76
Health Act 2006, ss.1–3, 6–8	80
Identity Cards Act 2006, ss.25–26	95
Terrorism Act 2006, ss.1–6, 8–11, 17–20	172
Violent Crime Reduction Act 2006, ss.28, 36–38, 55	189
Wireless Telegraphy Act 2006, s.47	194
Corporate Manslaughter and Homicide Act 2007, ss.1–8, 18–20	23
Serious Crime Act 2007, ss. 44–50, 55–59, 64–66, Schedule 1 (part 1), Schedule 3 (part 1)	130
UK Borders Act 2007, s.2	189
Criminal Justice and Immigration Act 2008, ss.63–67, 76, 79	41

PREFACE

The purpose of this book is to provide degree students with a collection of the most relevant sections of the statutes that usually feature or impact upon under- and post-graduate law courses in English and Welsh universities, and to do so in as succinct form as possible for swift referencing to just those sections of Acts that most matter. The task of preparing it has not presented problems with what to include, but indeed with what to *exclude* so as not to overburden the wallet and shoulder of those who use it. However, this is the first edition of this work, and in selecting those key statutes, while careful attention has been paid to the contents of the law degrees at institutions other than my own, it is impossible to ensure that nothing that would be of value at all law departments has been overlooked. As such, tutor suggestions for inclusions or omissions in future editions would be welcome.

With something approaching 10,000 offences in English law, and roughly ten per cent of those only being created since the Labour Party came to government in 1997, the criminal law has certainly moved at a pace that is perhaps unrivalled by any other area of English law, and it continues to do so. Hence, while it has been possible to include recent amendments to existing Acts, and the provisions of some Bills that are at the time of writing still working their way through Parliament, it is not possible to determine if those Bills will survive beyond the current session, or if indeed as yet unknown amendments will appear. The accompanying website to this Key Statutes title will provide periodic updates during the coming year.

It has not been possible to include the following change into the text of the book itself, but merely to add this note that the Statute Law Repeals Bill 2007–2008 received Royal Assent on 21st July 2008 and became the Statute Law Repeals Act 2008. The provisions of the Bill as included in this book on p203 have survived into the 2008 Act unchanged, and the commencement of the 2008 Act is date of Royal Assent. Therefore, the relevant sections of the Sexual Offences Act 1956 as included in this book should be read as now amended.

Great care has been taken to ensure not just the appropriateness of the content and its accuracy, but also its timeliness. There have been some recent, and some not so recent, amendments to current statute that have yet to come into force. For example, schedule 26 of the Criminal Justice Act 2003 amends s69 of the Criminal Justice and Public Order Act 1994, and yet after five years the provisions of the 2003 Act still have no date set for when they will come into force, thus the section remains unamended for the present time. In much greater quantity, a similar effect exists with the Computer Misuse Act 1990, as amended by the Police and Justice Act 2006 – and yet the amendments have so far only taken place in Scotland with no date set for an English commencement. Indeed, it makes one wonder *why do they both pass these amendments*?!

There is a general precursor that must be read in relation to the penalties included in the sections. It is that until s154(1) of the Criminal Justice Act 2003 comes into force, a date for which is not yet set, but which will increase the sentencing power of magistrates from six to twelve months, then any reference to summary conviction that reads twelve months must for now be read as six months.

Where (NYIF) appears after the entry for a statute section, this means that the section is not yet in force. If a bracketed date follows this, then that is the date that the section is currently due to come into force. If no date appears then the date at which the section is due to come into force is not known at the time of publication, but will be updated on the accompanying website when that information becomes available.

My grateful thanks go to Colin Goodlad and Matthew Sullivan at Hodder Education for their endless patience, and to the anonymous reviewers for their diligence in proofreading the final manuscript. Any errors of course remain my own.

Damian Warburton

Part 1

ACTS

ABORTION ACT 1967

1. Medical termination of pregnancy

(1) Subject to the provisions of this section, a person shall not be guilty of an offence under the law relating to abortion when a pregnancy is terminated by a registered medical practitioner if two medical practitioners are of the opinion, formed in good faith—
   (a) that the pregnancy has not exceeded its twenty-fourth week and that the continuance of the pregnancy would involve risk, greater than if the pregnancy were terminated, of injury to the physical or mental health of the pregnant woman, or any existing children of her family; or
   (b) that the termination is necessary to prevent grave permanent injury to the physical or mental health of the pregnant woman; or
   (c) that the continuance of the pregnancy would involve risk to the life of the pregnant woman, greater than if the pregnancy were terminated; or
   (d) that there is a substantial risk that if the child were born it would suffer from physical or mental abnormalities as to be seriously handicapped.

(2) In determining whether the continuance of a pregnancy would involve such risk of injury to health as is mentioned in paragraph (a) of subsection (1) of this section, account may be taken of the pregnant woman's actual or reasonably foreseeable environment.

(3) Except as provided by subsection (4) of this section, any treatment for the termination of pregnancy must be carried out in a hospital vested in the Secretary of State for the purpose of his function under the National Health Service Act 2006 or the National Health Service(Scotland) Act 1978 or in a hospital vested in a Primary Care Trust or a National Health Service trust, or an NHS foundation trust, or in a place for the time being approved for the purposes of this section by the Secretary of State.

(3A)…

(4) Subsection (3) of this section, and so much of subsection (1) as relates to the opinion of two registered medical practitioners, shall not apply to the termination of a pregnancy by a registered medical practitioner in a case where he is of the opinion, formed in good faith, that the termination is immediately necessary to save the life or to prevent grave permanent injury to the physical or mental health of the pregnant woman.

2. Notification

(1) The Minister of Health in respect of England and Wales, and the Secretary of State in respect of Scotland, shall by statutory instrument make regulations to provide—
   (a) for requiring any such opinion as is referred to in section 1 of this Act to be certified by the practitioners or practitioner concerned in such form and at such time as may be prescribed by the regulations, and for requiring the preservation and disposal of certificates made for the purposes of the regulations;
   (b) for requiring any registered medical practitioner who terminates a pregnancy to give notice of the termination and such other information relating to the termination as may be so prescribed;
   (c) for prohibiting the disclosure, except to such persons or for such purposes as may be so prescribed, of notices given or information furnished pursuant to the regulations.

4. Conscientious objection to participation in treatment

(1) Subject to subsection (2) of this section, no person shall be under any duty, whether by contract or by any statutory or other legal requirement, to participate in any treatment authorised by this Act to which he has a conscientious objection:

Provided that in any legal proceedings the burden of proof of conscientious objection shall rest on the person claiming to rely on it.

(2) Nothing in subsection (1) of this section shall affect any duty to participate in treatment which is necessary to save the life or to prevent grave permanent injury to the physical or mental health of a pregnant woman.

5. Supplementary provisions

(1) No offence under the Infant Life (Preservation) Act 1929 (Protecting the life of the viable foetus) shall be committed by a registered medical practitioner who terminates a pregnancy in accordance with the provisions of this Act.
(2) For the purposes of the law relating to abortion, anything done with intent to procure the miscarriage of a woman (or, in the case of a woman carrying more than one foetus, her miscarriage of any foetus) is unlawfully done unless authorised by section 1 of this Act, and in the case of a woman carrying more than one foetus, anything done with intent to procure her miscarriage of any foetus is authorised by this section if—
    (a) the ground for termination of pregnancy specified in subsection (1)(d) of that section applies in relation to any foetus and the thing is done for the purpose of procuring the miscarriage of that foetus; or
    (b) any of the other grounds for termination of the pregnancy specified in that section applies.

6. Interpretation

In this Act, the following expressions have meanings hereby assigned to them:—
'the law relating to abortion' means sections 58 and 59 of the Offences against the Person Act 1861, and any rule of law relating to the procurement of abortion;

ACCESSORIES AND ABETTORS ACT 1861

8. Abettors

Whosoever shall aid, abet, counsel, or procure the commission of any indictable offence, whether the same be an offence at common law or by virtue of any Act passed or to be passed, shall be liable to be tried, indicted, and punished as a principal offender.

ANIMAL WELFARE ACT 2006

1. Animals to which the Act applies

(1) In this Act, except subsections (4) and (5), 'animal' means a vertebrate other than man.
(2) Nothing in this Act applies to an animal while it is in its foetal or embryonic form.
(3) The appropriate national authority may by regulations for all or any of the purposes of this Act—
    (a) extend the definition of 'animal' so as to include invertebrates of any description;
    (b) make provision in lieu of subsection (2) as respects any invertebrates included in the definition of 'animal';
    (c) amend subsection (2) to extend the application of this Act to an animal from such earlier stage of its development as may be specified in the regulations.
(4) The power under subsection (3)(a) or (c) may only be exercised if the appropriate national authority is satisfied, on the basis of scientific evidence, that animals of the kind concerned are capable of experiencing pain or suffering.
(5) In this section, 'vertebrate' means any animal of the Sub-phylum Vertebrata of the Phylum Chordata and 'invertebrate' means any animal not of that Sub-phylum.

2. 'Protected animal'

An animal is a 'protected animal' for the purposes of this Act if—
    (a) it is of a kind which is commonly domesticated in the British Islands,
    (b) it is under the control of man whether on a permanent or temporary basis, or
    (c) it is not living in a wild state.

3. Responsibility for animals

(1) In this Act, references to a person responsible for an animal are to a person responsible for an animal whether on a permanent or temporary basis.
(2) In this Act, references to being responsible for an animal include being in charge of it.
(3) For the purposes of this Act, a person who owns an animal shall always be regarded as being a person who is responsible for it.
(4) For the purposes of this Act, a person shall be treated as responsible for any animal for which a person under the age of 16 years of whom he has actual care and control is responsible.

4. Unnecessary suffering

(1) A person commits an offence if—
   (a) an act of his, or a failure of his to act, causes an animal to suffer,
   (b) he knew, or ought reasonably to have known, that the act, or failure to act, would have that effect or be likely to do so,
   (c) the animal is a protected animal, and
   (d) the suffering is unnecessary.
(2) A person commits an offence if—
   (a) he is responsible for an animal,
   (b) an act, or failure to act, of another person causes the animal to suffer,
   (c) he permitted that to happen or failed to take such steps (whether by way of supervising the other person or otherwise) as were reasonable in all the circumstances to prevent that happening, and
   (d) the suffering is unnecessary.
(3) The considerations to which it is relevant to have regard when determining for the purposes of this section whether suffering is unnecessary include—
   (a) whether the suffering could reasonably have been avoided or reduced;
   (b) whether the conduct which caused the suffering was in compliance with any relevant enactment or any relevant provisions of a licence or code of practice issued under an enactment;
   (c) whether the conduct which caused the suffering was for a legitimate purpose, such as—
      (i) the purpose of benefiting the animal, or
      (ii) the purpose of protecting a person, property or another animal;
   (d) whether the suffering was proportionate to the purpose of the conduct concerned;
   (e) whether the conduct concerned was in all the circumstances that of a reasonably competent and humane person.
(4) Nothing in this section applies to the destruction of an animal in an appropriate and humane manner.

5. Mutilation

(1) A person commits an offence if—
   (a) he carries out a prohibited procedure on a protected animal;
   (b) he causes such a procedure to be carried out on such an animal.
(2) A person commits an offence if—
   (a) he is responsible for an animal,
   (b) another person carries out a prohibited procedure on the animal, and
   (c) he permitted that to happen or failed to take such steps (whether by way of supervising the other person or otherwise) as were reasonable in all the circumstances to prevent that happening.
(3) References in this section to the carrying out of a prohibited procedure on an animal are to the carrying out of a procedure which involves interference with the sensitive tissues or bone structure of the animal, otherwise than for the purpose of its medical treatment.
(4) Subsections (1) and (2) do not apply in such circumstances as the appropriate national authority may specify by regulations.
(5) Before making regulations under subsection (4), the appropriate national authority shall consult such persons appearing to the authority to represent any interests concerned as the authority considers appropriate.

(6) Nothing in this section applies to the removal of the whole or any part of a dog's tail.

6. Docking of dogs' tails

(1) A person commits an offence if—
   (a) he removes the whole or any part of a dog's tail, otherwise than for the purpose of its medical treatment;
   (b) he causes the whole or any part of a dog's tail to be removed by another person, otherwise than for the purpose of its medical treatment.
(2) A person commits an offence if—
   (a) he is responsible for a dog,
   (b) another person removes the whole or any part of the dog's tail, otherwise than for the purpose of its medical treatment, and
   (c) he permitted that to happen or failed to take such steps (whether by way of supervising the other person or otherwise) as were reasonable in all the circumstances to prevent that happening.
(3) Subsections (1) and (2) do not apply if the dog is a certified working dog that is not more than 5 days old.
(4) For the purposes of subsection (3), a dog is a certified working dog if a veterinary surgeon has certified, in accordance with regulations made by the appropriate national authority, that the first and second conditions mentioned below are met.
(5) The first condition referred to in subsection (4) is that there has been produced to the veterinary surgeon such evidence as the appropriate national authority may by regulations require for the purpose of showing that the dog is likely to be used for work in connection with—
   (a) law enforcement,
   (b) activities of Her Majesty's armed forces,
   (c) emergency rescue,
   (d) lawful pest control, or
   (e) the lawful shooting of animals.
(6) The second condition referred to in subsection (4) is that the dog is of a type specified for the purposes of this subsection by regulations made by the appropriate national authority.
(7) It is a defence for a person accused of an offence under subsection (1) or (2) to show that he reasonably believed that the dog was one in relation to which subsection (3) applies.
(8) A person commits an offence if—
   (a) he owns a subsection (3) dog, and
   (b) fails to take reasonable steps to secure that, before the dog is 3 months old, it is identified as a subsection (3) dog in accordance with regulations made by the appropriate national authority.
(9) A person commits an offence if—
   (a) he shows a dog at an event to which members of the public are admitted on payment of a fee,
   (b) the dog's tail has been wholly or partly removed (in England and Wales or elsewhere), and
   (c) removal took place on or after the commencement day.
(10) Where a dog is shown only for the purpose of demonstrating its working ability, subsection (9) does not apply if the dog is a subsection (3) dog.
(11) It is a defence for a person accused of an offence under subsection (9) to show that he reasonably believed—
   (a) that the event was not one to which members of the public were admitted on payment of an entrance fee,
   (b) that the removal took place before the commencement day, or
   (c) that the dog was one in relation to which subsection (10) applies.
(12) A person commits an offence if he knowingly gives false information to a veterinary surgeon in connection with the giving of a certificate for the purposes of this section.
(13) The appropriate national authority may by regulations make provision about the functions of inspectors in relation to—
   (a) certificates for the purposes of this section, and
   (b) the identification of dogs as subsection (3) dogs.

(14) Power to make regulations under this section includes power—
   (a) to make different provision for different cases, and
   (b) to make incidental, supplementary, consequential or transitional provision or savings.
(15) Before making regulations under this section, the appropriate national authority shall consult such persons appearing to the authority to represent any interests concerned as the authority considers appropriate.
(16) In this section—
   'commencement day' means the day on which this section comes into force;
   'subsection (3) dog' means a dog whose tail has, on or after the commencement day, been wholly or partly removed without contravening subsection (1), because of the application of subsection (3).

7. Administration of poisons etc.
(1) A person commits an offence if, without lawful authority or reasonable excuse, he—
   (a) administers any poisonous or injurious drug or substance to a protected animal, knowing it to be poisonous or injurious, or
   (b) causes any poisonous or injurious drug or substance to be taken by a protected animal, knowing it to be poisonous or injurious.
(2) A person commits an offence if—
   (a) he is responsible for an animal,
   (b) without lawful authority or reasonable excuse, another person administers a poisonous or injurious drug or substance to the animal or causes the animal to take such a drug or substance, and
   (c) he permitted that to happen or, knowing the drug or substance to be poisonous or injurious, he failed to take such steps (whether by way of supervising the other person or otherwise) as were reasonable in all the circumstances to prevent that happening.
(3) In this section, references to a poisonous or injurious drug or substance include a drug or substance which, by virtue of the quantity or manner in which it is administered or taken, has the effect of a poisonous or injurious drug or substance.

8. Fighting etc.
(1) A person commits an offence if he—
   (a) causes an animal fight to take place, or attempts to do so;
   (b) knowingly receives money for admission to an animal fight;
   (c) knowingly publicises a proposed animal fight;
   (d) provides information about an animal fight to another with the intention of enabling or encouraging attendance at the fight;
   (e) makes or accepts a bet on the outcome of an animal fight or on the likelihood of anything occurring or not occurring in the course of an animal fight;
   (f) takes part in an animal fight;
   (g) has in his possession anything designed or adapted for use in connection with an animal fight with the intention of its being so used;
   (h) keeps or trains an animal for use for in connection with an animal fight;
   (i) keeps any premises for use for an animal fight.
(2) A person commits an offence if, without lawful authority or reasonable excuse, he is present at an animal fight.
(3) A person commits an offence if, without lawful authority or reasonable excuse, he—
   (a) knowingly supplies a video recording of an animal fight,
   (b) knowingly publishes a video recording of an animal fight,
   (c) knowingly shows a video recording of an animal fight to another, or
   (d) possesses a video recording of an animal fight, knowing it to be such a recording, with the intention of supplying it.
(4) Subsection (3) does not apply if the video recording is of an animal fight that took place—
   (a) outside Great Britain, or
   (b) before the commencement date.
(5) Subsection (3) does not apply—

(a) in the case of paragraph (a), to the supply of a video recording for inclusion in a programme service;
(b) in the case of paragraph (b) or (c), to the publication or showing of a video recording by means of its inclusion in a programme service;
(c) in the case of paragraph (d), by virtue of intention to supply for inclusion in a programme service.

(6) Provision extending the application of an offence under subsection (3), so far as relating to the provision of information society services, may be made under section 2(2) of the European Communities Act 1972 (powers to implement Community obligations by regulations) notwithstanding the limits imposed by paragraph 1(1)(d) of Schedule 2 to that Act on the penalties with which an offence may be punishable on summary conviction.

(7) In this section—

'animal fight' means an occasion on which a protected animal is placed with an animal, or with a human, for the purpose of fighting, wrestling or baiting;

'commencement date' means the date on which subsection (3) comes into force;

'information society services' has the meaning given in Article 2(a) of Directive 2000/31/EC of the European Parliament and of the Council of 8 June 2000 on certain legal aspects of information society services, in particular electronic commerce in the Internal Market (Directive on electronic commerce);

'programme service' has the same meaning as in the Communications Act 2003;

'video recording' means a recording, in any form, from which a moving image may by any means be reproduced and includes data stored on a computer disc or by other electronic means which is capable of conversion into a moving image.

(8) In this section—
(a) references to supplying or publishing a video recording are to supplying or publishing a video recording in any manner, including, in relation to a video recording in the form of data stored electronically, by means of transmitting such data;
(b) references to showing a video recording are to showing a moving image reproduced from a video recording by any means.

9. Duty of person responsible for animal to ensure welfare

(1) A person commits an offence if he does not take such steps as are reasonable in all the circumstances to ensure that the needs of an animal for which he is responsible are met to the extent required by good practice.
(2) For the purposes of this Act, an animal's needs shall be taken to include—
(a) its need for a suitable environment,
(b) its need for a suitable diet,
(c) its need to be able to exhibit normal behaviour patterns,
(d) any need it has to be housed with, or apart from, other animals, and
(e) its need to be protected from pain, suffering, injury and disease.
(3) The circumstances to which it is relevant to have regard when applying subsection (1) include, in particular—
(a) any lawful purpose for which the animal is kept, and
(b) any lawful activity undertaken in relation to the animal.
(4) Nothing in this section applies to the destruction of an animal in an appropriate and humane manner.

❙ ANTI-TERRORISM, CRIME AND SECURITY ACT 2001

113. Use of noxious substances or things to cause harm and intimidate

(1) A person who takes any action which—

(a) involves the use of a noxious substance or other noxious thing;
   (b) has or is likely to have an effect falling within subsection (2); and
   (c) is designed to influence the government or to intimidate the public or section of the public,
   is guilty of an offence.
(2) Action has an effect falling within this subsection if it—
   (a) causes serious violence against a person anywhere in the world;
   (b) causes serious damage to real or personal property anywhere in the world;
   (c) endangers human life or creates a serious risk to the health or safety of the public or a section of the public; or
   (d) induces in members of the public the fear that the action is likely to endanger their lives or create a serious risk to their health or safety;
   but any effect on the person taking the action is to be disregarded.
(3) A person who—
   (a) makes a threat that he or another will take any action which constitutes an offence under subsection (1); and
   (b) intends thereby to induce in a person anywhere in the world the fear that the threat is likely to be carried out,
   is guilty of an offence.
(4) A person guilty of an offence under this section is liable—
   (a) on summary conviction, to imprisonment for a term not exceeding six months or a fine not exceeding the statutory maximum (or both); and
   (b) on conviction on indictment, to imprisonment for a term not exceeding fourteen years or a fine (or both).
(5) In this section—
   'the government' means the government of the United Kingdom, of a part of the United Kingdom or of a country other than the United Kingdom; and
   'the public' includes the public of a country other than the United Kingdom.

113A. Application of section 113
(1) Section 113 applies to conduct done—
   (a) in the United Kingdom; or
   (b) outside the United Kingdom which satisfies the following two conditions.
(2) The first condition is that the conduct is done for the purpose of advancing a political, religious or ideological cause.
(3) The second condition is that the conduct is—
   (a) by a United Kingdom national or a United Kingdom resident;
   (b) by any person done to, or in relation to, a United Kingdom national, a United Kingdom resident or a protected person; or
   (c) by any person done in circumstances which fall within section 63D(1)(b) and (c) or (3)(b) and (c) of the Terrorism Act 2000.
(4) The following expressions have the same meaning as they have for the purposes of sections 63C and 63D of that Act—
   (a) 'United Kingdom national';
   (b) 'United Kingdom resident';
   (c) 'protected person'.
(5) For the purposes of this section it is immaterial whether a person knows that another is a United Kingdom national, a United Kingdom resident or a protected person.

113B. Consent to prosecution for offence under section 113
(1) Proceedings for an offence committed under section 113 outside the United Kingdom are not to be started—
   (a) in England and Wales, except by or with the consent of the Attorney General;
   ...
(2) Proceedings for an offence committed under section 113 outside the United Kingdom may be taken, and the offence may for incidental purposes be treated as having been committed, in any part of the United Kingdom.
   ...

114. Hoaxes involving noxious substances or things

(1) A person is guilty of an offence if he—
    (a) places any substance or other thing in any place; or
    (b) sends any substance or other thing from one place to another (by post, rail or any other means whatever);
    with the intention of inducing in a person anywhere in the world a belief that it is likely to be (or contain) a noxious substance or other noxious thing and thereby endanger human life or create a serious risk to human health.

(2) A person is guilty of an offence if he communicates any information which he knows or believes to be false with the intention of inducing in a person anywhere in the world a belief that a noxious substance or other noxious thing is likely to be present (whether at the time the information is communicated or later) in any place and thereby endanger human life or create a serious risk to human health.

(3) A person guilty of an offence under this section is liable—
    (a) on summary conviction, to imprisonment for a term not exceeding six months or a fine not exceeding the statutory maximum (or both); and
    (b) on conviction on indictment, to imprisonment for a term not exceeding seven years or a fine (or both).

115. Sections 113 and 114: supplementary

(1) For the purposes of sections 113 and 114 'substance' includes any biological agent and any other natural or artificial substance (whatever its form, origin or method of production).

(2) For a person to be guilty of an offence under section 113(3) or 114 it is not necessary for him to have any particular person in mind as the person in whom he intends to induce the belief in question.

AVIATION SECURITY ACT 1982

1. Hijacking

(1) A person on board an aircraft in flight who unlawfully, by the use of force or by threats of any kind, seizes the aircraft or exercises control of it commits the offence of hijacking, whatever his nationality, whatever the State in which the aircraft is registered and whether the aircraft is in the United Kingdom or elsewhere, but subject to subsection (2) below.

(2) If—
    (a) the aircraft is used in military, customs or police service, or
    (b) both the place of take-off and the place of landing are in the territory of the State in which the aircraft is registered, subsection (1) above shall not apply unless—
        (i) the person seizing or exercising control of the aircraft is a United Kingdom national; or
        (ii) his act is committed in the United Kingdom; or
        (iii) the aircraft is registered in the United Kingdom or is used in the military or customs service of the United Kingdom or in the service of any police force in the United Kingdom.

(3) A person who commits the offence of hijacking shall be liable, on conviction on indictment, to imprisonment for life.

(4) If the Secretary of State by order made by statutory instrument declares—
    (a) that any two or more States named in the order have established an organisation or agency which operates aircraft; and
    (b) that one of those States has been designated as exercising, for aircraft so operated, the powers of the State of registration, the State declared under paragraph (b) of this subsection shall be deemed for the purposes of this section to be the State in which any aircraft so operated is registered; but in relation to such an aircraft subsection (2)(b) above shall have effect as if it referred to the territory of any one of the States named in the order.

(5) For the purposes of this section the territorial waters of any State shall be treated as part of its territory.

2. Destroying, damaging or endangering safety of aircraft

(1) It shall, subject to subsection (4) below, be an offence for any person unlawfully and intentionally
  (a) to destroy an aircraft in service or so to damage such an aircraft as to render it incapable of flight or as to be likely to endanger its safety in flight; or
  (b) to commit on board an aircraft in flight any act of violence which is likely to endanger the safety of the aircraft.

(2) It shall also, subject to subsection (4) below, be an offence for any person unlawfully and intentionally to place, or cause to be placed, on an aircraft in service any device or substance which is likely to destroy the aircraft, or is likely so to damage it as to render it incapable of flight or as to be likely to endanger its safety in flight; but nothing in this subsection shall be construed as limiting the circumstances in which the comission of any act—
  (a) may constitute an offence under subsection (1) above, or
  (b) may constitute attempting or conspiring to commit, or aiding, abetting, counselling or procuring, or being art and part in, the commission of such an offence.

(3) Except as provided by subsection (4) below, subsections (1) and (2) above shall apply whether any such act as is therein mentioned is committed in the United Kingdom or elsewhere, whatever the nationality of the person committing the act and whatever the State in which the aircraft is registered.

(4) Subsections (1) and (2) above shall not apply to any act committed in relation to an aircraft used in military, customs or police service unless—
  (a) the act is committed in the United Kingdom, or
  (b) where the act is committed outside the United Kingdom, the person committing it is a United Kingdom national.

(5) A person who commits an offence under this section shall be liable, on conviction on indictment, to imprisonment for life.

(6) In this section 'unlawfully'—
  (a) in relation to the commission of an act in the United Kingdom, means so as (apart from this Act) to constitute an offence under the law of the part of the United Kingdom in which the act is committed, and
  (b) in relation to the commission of an act outside the United Kingdom, means so that the commission of the act would (apart from this Act) have been an offence under the law of England and Wales if it had been committed in England and Wales or of Scotland if it had been committed in Scotland.

(7) In this section 'act of violence' means—
  (a) any act done in the United Kingdom which constitutes the offence of murder, attempted murder, manslaughter, culpable homicide or assault or an offence under sections 18, 20, 21, 22, 23, 24, 28 or 29 of the Offences against the Person Act 1861 or under section 2 of the Explosive Substances Act 1883, and
  (b) any act done outside the United Kingdom which, if done in the United Kingdom, would constitute such an offence as is mentioned in paragraph (a) above.

3. Other acts endangering or likely to endanger the safety of the aircraft

(1) It shall, subject to subsections (5) and (6) below, be an offence for any person unlawfully and intentionally to destroy or damage any property to which this subsection applies, or to interfere with the operation of any such property, where the destruction, damage or interference is likely to endanger the safety of aircraft in flight.

(2) Subsection (1) above applies to any property used for the provision of air navigation facilities, including any land, building or ship so used, and including any apparatus or equipment so used, whether it is on board an aircraft or elsewhere.

(3) It shall also, subject to subsections (4) and (5) below, be an offence for any person intentionally to communicate any information which is false, misleading or deceptive in a material particular, where the communication of the information endangers the safety of an aircraft in flight or is likely to endanger the safety of aircraft in flight.

(4) It shall be a defence for a person charged with an offence under subsection (3) above to prove—

(a) that he believed, and had reasonable grounds for believing, that the information was true; or
(b) that, when he communicated the information, he was lawfully employed to perform duties which consisted of or included the communication of information and that he communicated the information in good faith in the performance of those duties.
(5) Subsections (1) and (3) above shall not apply to the commission of any act unless either the act is committed in the United Kingdom, or, where it is committed outside the United Kingdom—
   (a) the person committing it is a United Kingdom national; or
   (b) the commission of the act endangers or is likely to endanger the safety in flight of a civil aircraft registered in the United Kingdom or chartered by demise to a lessee whose principal place of business, or (if he has no place of business) whose permanent residence, is in the United Kingdom; or
   (c) the act is committed on board a civil aircraft which is so registered or so chartered; or
   (d) the act is committed on board a civil aircraft which lands in the United Kingdom with the person who committed the act still on board.
(6) Subsection (1) above shall also not apply to any act committed outside the United Kingdom and so committed in relation to property which is situated outside the United Kingdom and is not used for the provision of air navigation facilities in connection with international air navigation, unless the person committing the act is a United Kingdom national.
(7) A person who commits an offence under this section shall be liable, on conviction on indictment, to imprisonment for life.
(8) In this section 'civil aircraft' means any aircraft other than an aircraft used in military, customs or police service and 'unlawfully' has the same meaning as in section 2 of this Act.

4. Offences in relation to certain dangerous articles

(1) It shall be an offence for any person without lawful authority or reasonable excuse (the proof of which shall lie on him) to have with him—
   (a) in any aircraft registered in the United Kingdom, whether at a time when the aircraft is in the United Kingdom or not, or
   (b) in any other aircraft at a time when it is in, or in flight over, the United Kingdom, or
   (c) in any part of an aerodrome in the United Kingdom, or
   (d) in any air navigation installation in the United Kingdom which does not form part of an aerodrome,
   any article to which this section applies.
(2) This section applies to the following articles, that is to say—
   (a) any firearm, or any article having the appearance of being a firearm, whether capable of being discharged or not;
   (b) any explosive, any article manufactured or adapted (whether in the form of a bomb, grenade or otherwise) so as to have the appearance of being an explosive, whether it is capable of producing a practical effect by explosion or not, or any article marked or labelled so as to indicate that it is or contains an explosive; and
   (c) any article (not falling within either of the preceding paragraphs) made or adapted for use for causing injury to or incapacitating a person or for destroying or damaging property, or intended by the person having it with him for such use, whether by him or by any other person.
(3) For the purposes of this section a person who is for the time being in an aircraft, or in part of an aerodrome, shall be treated as having with him in the aircraft, or in that part of the aerodrome, as the case may be, an article to which this section applies if—
   (a) where he is in an aircraft, the article, or an article in which it is contained, is in the aircraft and has been caused (whether by him or by any other person) to be brought there as being, or as forming part of, his baggage on a flight in the aircraft or has been caused by him to be brought there as being, or as forming part of, any other property to be carried on such a flight, or
   (b) where he is in part of an aerodrome (otherwise than in an aircraft), the article, or an article in which it is contained, is in that or any other part of the aerodrome and has been caused (whether by him or by any other person) to be brought into the aerodrome as being, or as forming part of, his baggage on a flight from that aerodrome or has been caused by him to be brought there as being, or as forming part of, any other property to be carried on such a flight on which he is also to be carried,

notwithstanding that the circumstances may be such that (apart from this subsection) he would not be regarded as having the article with him in the aircraft or in a part of the aerodrome, as the case may be.
(4) A person guilty of an offence under this section shall be liable—
   (a) on summary conviction, to a fine not exceeding the statutory maximum or to imprisonment for a term not exceeding three months or to both;
   (b) on conviction on indictment, to a fine or to imprisonment for a term not exceeding five years or to both.
(5) Nothing in subsection (3) above shall be construed as limiting the circumstances in which a person would, apart from that subsection, be regarded as having an article with him as mentioned in subsection (1) above.

38. Interpretation

(1) In this Act, except in so far as the context otherwise requires—
'aerodrome' means the aggregate of the land, buildings and works comprised in an aerodrome within the meaning of the Civil Aviation Act 1982 and (if and so far as not comprised in an aerodrome as defined in that Act) any land, building or works situated within the boundaries of an area designated, by an order made by the Secretary of State which is for the time being in force, as constituting the area of an aerodrome for the purposes of this Act;
'air navigation installation' means any building, works, apparatus or equipment used wholly or mainly for the purpose of assisting air traffic control or as an aid to air navigation, together with any land contiguous or adjacent to any such building, works, apparatus or equipment and used wholly or mainly for purposes connected therewith;
'aircraft registered or operating in the United Kingdom' means any aircraft which is either—
(a) an aircraft registered in the United Kingdom, or
(b) an aircraft not so registered which is for the time being allocated for use on flights which (otherwise than in exceptional circumstances) include landing at or taking off from one or more aerodromes in the United Kingdom;
   'article' includes any substance, whether in solid or liquid form or in the form of a gas or vapour;
   'constable' includes any person having the powers and privileges of a constable;
   'explosive' means any article manufactured for the purpose of producing a practical effect by explosion, or intended for that purpose by a person having the article with him;
   'firearm' includes an airgun or air pistol;
   'manager', in relation to an aerodrome, means the person (whether the British Airports Authority, the Civil Aviation Authority, a local authority or any other person) by whom the aerodrome is managed;
   'military service' includes naval and air force service;
   'measures' (without prejudice to the generality of that expression) includes the construction, execution, alteration, demolition or removal of buildings or other works and also includes the institution or modification, and the supervision and enforcement, of any practice or procedure;
   'operator' has the same meaning as in the Civil Aviation Act 1982;
   'property' includes any land, buildings or works, any aircraft or vehicle and any baggage, cargo or other article of any description;
   'United Kingdom national' means an individual who is—
(a) a British citizen, a British Dependent Territories citizen, a British National (Overseas) or a British Overseas citizen;
(b) a person who under the British Nationality Act 1981 is a British subject; or
(c) a British protected person (within the meaning of that Act).
(2) For the purposes of this Act—
   (a) in the case of an air navigation installation provided by, or used wholly or mainly by, the Civil Aviation Authority, that Authority, and
   (b) in the case of any other air navigation installation, the manager of an aerodrome by whom it is provided, or by whom it is wholly or mainly used, shall be taken to be the authority responsible for that air navigation installation.

(3) For the purposes of this Act—
   (a) the period during which an aircraft is in flight shall be deemed to include any period from the moment when all its external doors are closed following embarkation until the moment when any such door is opened for disembarkation, and, in the case of a forced landing, any period until the competent authorities take over responsibility for the aircraft and for persons and property on board; and
   (b) an aircraft shall be taken to be in service during the whole of the period which begins with the pre-flight preparation of the aircraft for a flight and ends 24 hours after the aircraft lands having completed that flight, and also at any time (not falling within that period) while, in accordance with the preceding paragraph, the aircraft is in flight, and anything done on board an aircraft while in flight over any part of the United Kingdom shall be treated as done in that part of the United Kingdom.
(4) For the purposes of this Act the territorial waters adjacent to any part of the United Kingdom shall be treated as included in that part of the United Kingdom.

BAIL ACT 1976

6. Absconding whilst on bail

(1) If a person who has been released on bail in criminal proceedings fails without reasonable cause to surrender to custody he shall be guilty of an offence.
(2) If a person who—
   (a) has been released on bail in criminal proceedings, and
   (b) having reasonable cause therefore, has failed to surrender to custody, fails to surrender to custody at the appointed place as soon after the appointed time as is reasonably practicable he shall be guilty of an offence.
(3) It shall be for the accused to prove that he had reasonable cause for his failure to surrender to custody.
(4) A failure to give to a person granted bail in criminal proceedings a copy of the record of the decision shall not constitute a reasonable cause for that person's failure to surrender to custody.
(5) An offence under subsection (1) or (2) above shall be punishable either on summary conviction or as if it were a criminal contempt of court.

BROADCASTING ACT 1990

202. General interpretation

(1) In this Act (unless the context otherwise requires)—
   …'programme' includes an advertisement and, in relation to any service, includes any item included in that service;

CHILD ABDUCTION ACT 1984

1. Offence of abduction of child by parent, etc.

(1) Subject to subsections (5) and (8) below, a person connected with a child under the age of sixteen commits an offence if he takes or sends the child out of the United Kingdom without the appropriate consent.
(2) A person is connected with a child for the purposes of this section if—
   (a) he is a parent of the child; or

(b) in the case of a child whose parents were not married to each other at the time of his birth, there are reasonable grounds for believing that he is the father of the child; or
(c) he is a guardian of the child; or
(d) he is a person in whose favour a residence order is in force with respect to the child; or
(e) he has custody of the child.
(3) In this section 'the appropriate consent', in relation to a child, means—
  (a) the consent of each of the following—
    (i) the child's mother;
    (ii) the child's father, if he has parental responsibility for him;
    (iii) any guardian of the child;
    (iv) any person in whose favour a residence order is in force with respect to the child;
    (v) any person who has custody of the child; or
  (b) the leave of the court granted under or by virtue of any provision of Part II of the Children Act 1989; or
  (c) if any person has custody of the child, the leave of the court which awarded custody to him.
(4) A person does not commit an offence under this section by taking or sending a child out of the United Kingdom without obtaining the appropriate consent if—
  (a) he is a person in whose favour there is a residence order in force with respect to the child, and
  (b) he takes or sends the child out of the United Kingdom for a period of less than one month.
(4A) Subsection (4) above does not apply if the person taking or sending the child out of the United Kingdom does so in breach of an order under Part II of the Children Act 1989.
(5) A person does not commit an offence under this section by doing anything without the consent of another person whose consent is required under the foregoing provisions if—
  (a) he does it in the belief that the other person—
    (i) has consented; or
    (ii) would consent if he was aware of all the relevant circumstances; or
  (b) he has taken all reasonable steps to communicate with the other person but has been unable to communicate with him; or
  (c) the other person has unreasonably refused to consent.
(5A) Subsection (5)(c) above does not apply if—
  (a) the person who refused to consent is a person—
    (i) in whose favour there is a residence order in force with respect to the child; or
    (ii) who has custody of the child; or
  (b) the person taking or sending the child out of the United Kingdom is, by so acting, in breach of an order made by a court in the United Kingdom.
(6) Where, in proceedings for an offence under this section, there is sufficient evidence to raise an issue as to the application of subsection (5) above, it shall be for the prosecution to prove that that subsection does not apply.
(7) For the purposes of this section—
  (a) 'guardian of a child', 'residence order' and 'parental responsibility' have the same meaning as in the Children Act 1989; and
  (b) a person shall be treated as having custody of a child if there is in force an order of a court in the United Kingdom awarding him (whether solely or jointly with another person) custody, legal custody or care and control of the child.
(8) This section shall have effect subject to the provisions of the Schedule to this Act in relation to a child who is in the care of a local authority detained in a place of safety, remanded to a local authority accommodation or the subject of proceedings or an order relating to adoption.

2. Offence of abduction of child by other persons

(1) Subject to subsection (3) below, a person, other than one mentioned in subsection (2) below commits an offence if, without lawful authority or reasonable excuse, he takes or detains a child under the age of sixteen—
  (a) so as to remove him from the lawful control of any person having lawful control of the child; or

(b) so as to keep him out of the lawful control of any person entitled to lawful control of the child.
(2) The persons are—
    (a) where the father and mother of the child in question were married to each other at the time of his birth, the child's father and mother;
    (b) where the father and mother of the child in question were not married to each other at the time of his birth, the child's mother; and
    (c) any other person mentioned in section 1(2)(c) to (e) above.
(3) In proceedings against any person for an offence under this section, it shall be a defence for that person to prove—
    (a) where the father and mother of the child in question were not married to each other at the time of his birth—
        (i) that he is the child's father; or
        (ii) that, at the time of the alleged offence, he believed, on reasonable grounds, that he was the child's father; or
    (b) that, at the time of the alleged offence, he believed that the child had attained the age of sixteen.

3. Construction of references to taking, sending and detaining
For the purposes of this Part of this Act—
    (a) a person shall be regarded as taking a child if he causes or induces the child to accompany him or any other person or causes the child to be taken;
    (b) a person shall be regarded as sending a child if he causes the child to be sent;
    (c) a person shall be regarded as detaining a child if he causes the child to be detained or induces the child to remain with him or any other person; and
    (d) references to a child's parents and to a child whose parents were (or were not) married to each other at the time of his birth shall be construed in accordance with section 1 of the Family Law Reform Act 1987 (which extends their meaning).

CHILDREN ACT 2004

58. Reasonable punishment
(1) In relation to any offence specified in subsection (2), battery of a child cannot be justified on the ground that it constituted reasonable punishment.
(2) The offences referred to in subsection (1) are—
    (a) an offence under section 18 or 20 of the Offences against the Person Act 1861 (wounding and causing grievous bodily harm);
    (b) an offence under section 47 of that Act (assault occasioning actual bodily harm);
    (c) an offence under section 1 of the Children and Young Persons Act 1933 (cruelty to persons under 16).
(3) Battery of a child causing actual bodily harm to the child cannot be justified in any civil proceedings on the ground that it constituted reasonable punishment.
(4) For the purposes of subsection (3) 'actual bodily harm' has the same meaning as it has for the purposes of section 47 of the Offences against the Person Act 1861.

CHILDREN AND YOUNG PERSONS ACT 1933

1. Cruelty to persons under sixteen
(1) If any person who has attained the age of sixteen years and has responsibility for any child or young person under that age, wilfully assaults, ill-treats, neglects, abandons, or exposes him, or causes or procures him to be assaulted, ill-treated, neglected, abandoned, or exposed, in

a manner likely to cause him unnecessary suffering or injury to health (including injury to or loss of sight, or hearing, or limb, or organ of the body, and any mental derangement), that person shall be guilty of an offence, and shall be liable—
  (a) on conviction on indictment, to a fine or alternatively, or in addition thereto, to imprisonment for any term not exceeding ten years;
  (b) on summary conviction, to a fine not exceeding the prescribed sum, or alternatively, or in addition thereto, to imprisonment for any term not exceeding six months.
(2) For the purposes of this section—
  (a) a parent or other person legally liable to maintain a child or young person, or the legal guardian of a child or young person, shall be deemed to have neglected him in a manner likely to cause injury to his health if he has failed to provide adequate food, clothing, medical aid or lodging for him, or if, having been unable otherwise to provide such food, clothing, medical aid or lodging, he has failed to take steps to procure it to be provided under the enactments applicable in that behalf;
  (b) where it is proved that the death of an infant under three years of age was caused by suffocation (not being suffocation caused by disease or the presence of any foreign body in the throat or air passages of the infant) while the infant was in bed with some other person who has attained the age of sixteen years, that other person shall, if he was, when he went to bed, under the influence of drink, be deemed to have neglected the infant in a manner likely to cause injury to its health.
(3) A person may be convicted of an offence under this section—
  (a) notwithstanding that actual suffering or injury to health, or the likelihood of actual suffering or injury to health, was obviated by the action of another person;
  (b) notwithstanding the death of the child or young person in question.
  ...
(7) Nothing in this section shall be construed as affecting the right of any parent, or (subject to section 548 of the Education Act 1996) any other person, having the lawful control or charge of a child or young person to administer punishment to him.

50. Age of criminal responsibility

It shall be conclusively presumed that no child under the age of ten years can be guilty of any offence.

COMMUNICATIONS ACT 2003

127. Improper use of public electronic communications network

(1) A person is guilty of an offence if he—
  (a) sends by means of a public electronic communications network a message or other matter that is grossly offensive or of an indecent, obscene or menacing character; or
  (b) causes any such message or matter to be so sent.
(2) A person is guilty of an offence if, for the purpose of causing annoyance, inconvenience or needless anxiety to another, he—
  (a) sends by means of a public electronic communications network, a message that he knows to be false,
  (b) causes such a message to be sent; or
  (c) persistently makes use of a public electronic communications network.
(3) A person guilty of an offence under this section shall be liable, on summary conviction, to imprisonment for a term not exceeding six months or to a fine not exceeding level 5 on the standard scale, or to both.
(4) Subsections (1) and (2) do not apply to anything done in the course of providing a programme service (within the meaning of the Broadcasting Act 1999 (c42)).

COMPUTER MISUSE ACT 1990

1. Unauthorised access to computer material
(1) A person is guilty of an offence if—
  (a) he causes a computer to perform any function with intent to secure access to any program or data held in any computer;
  (b) the access he intends to secure is unauthorised; and
  (c) he knows at the time when he causes the computer to perform the function that that is the case.
(2) The intent a person has to have to commit an offence under this section need not be directed at—
  (a) any particular program or data;
  (b) a program or data of any particular kind; or
  (c) a program or data held in any particular computer.
(3) A person guilty of an offence under this section shall be liable on summary conviction to imprisonment for a term not exceeding six months or to a fine not exceeding level 5 on the standard scale or to both.

2. Unauthorised access with intent to commit or facilitate commission of further offences
(1) A person is guilty of an offence under this section if he commits an offence under section 1 above ('the unauthorised access offence') with intent—
  (a) to commit an offence to which this section applies; or
  (b) to facilitate the commission of such an offence (whether by himself or by any other person); and the offence he intends to commit or facilitate is referred to below in this section as the further offence.
(2) This section applies to offences—
  (a) for which the sentence is fixed by law; or
  (b) for which a person of twenty-one years of age or over (not previously convicted) may be sentenced to imprisonment for a term of five years (or, in England and Wales, might be so sentenced but for the restrictions imposed by section 33 of the Magistrates' Courts Act 1980).
(3) It is immaterial for the purposes of this section whether the further offence is to be committed on the same occasion as the unauthorised access offence or on any future occasion.
(4) A person may be guilty of an offence under this section even though the facts are such that the commission of the further offence is impossible.
(5) A person guilty of an offence under this section shall be liable—
  (a) on summary conviction, to imprisonment for a term not exceeding six months or to a fine not exceeding the statutory maximum or to both; and
  (b) on conviction on indictment, to imprisonment for a term not exceeding five years or to a fine or to both.

3. Unauthorised modification of computer material
(1) A person is guilty of an offence if—
  (a) he does any act which causes an unauthorised modification of the contents of any computer; and
  (b) at the time when he does the act he has the requisite intent and the requisite knowledge.
(2) For the purposes of subsection (1)(b) above the requisite intent is an intent to cause a modification of the contents of any computer and by so doing—
  (a) to impair the operation of any computer;
  (b) to prevent or hinder access to any program or data held in any computer; or
  (c) to impair the operation of any such program or the reliability of any such data.
(3) The intent need not be directed at—
  (a) any particular computer;
  (b) any particular program or data or a program or data of any particular kind; or

    (c) any particular modification or a modification of any particular kind.
(4) For the purposes of subsection (1)(b) above the requisite knowledge is knowledge that any modification he intends to cause is unauthorised.
(5) It is immaterial for the purposes of this section whether an unauthorised modification or any intended effect of it of a kind mentioned in subsection (2) above is, or is intended to be, permanent or merely temporary.
(6) For the purposes of the Criminal Damage Act 1971 a modification of the contents of a computer shall not be regarded as damaging any computer or computer storage medium unless its effect on that computer or computer storage medium impairs its physical condition.
(7) A person guilty of an offence under this section shall be liable—
    (a) on summary conviction, to imprisonment for a term not exceeding six months or to a fine not exceeding the statutory maximum or to both; and
    (b) on conviction on indictment, to imprisonment for a term not exceeding five years or to a fine or to both.

4. Territorial scope of offences under this Act

(1) Except as provided below in this section, it is immaterial for the purposes of any offence under section 1 or 3 above—
    (a) whether any act or other event proof of which is required for conviction of the offence occurred in the home country concerned; or
    (b) whether the accused was in the home country concerned at the time of any such act or event.
(2) Subject to subsection (3) below, in the case of such an offence at least one significant link with domestic jurisdiction must exist in the circumstances of the case for the offence to be committed.
(3) There is no need for any such link to exist for the commission of an offence under section 1 above to be established in proof of an allegation to that effect in proceedings for an offence under section 2 above.
(4) Subject to section 8 below, where—
    (a) any such link does in fact exist in the case of an offence under section 1 above; and
    (b) commission of that offence is alleged in proceedings for an offence under section 2 above; section 2 above shall apply as if anything the accused intended to do or facilitate in any place outside the home country concerned which would be an offence to which section 2 applies if it took place in the home country concerned were the offence in question.
    ...
(6) References in this Act to the home country concerned are references—
    (a) in the application of this Act to England and Wales, to England and Wales;
    ...

5. Significant links with domestic jurisdiction

(1) The following provisions of this section apply for the interpretation of section 4 above.
(2) In relation to an offence under section 1, either of the following is a significant link with domestic jurisdiction—
    (a) that the accused was in the home country concerned at the time when he did the act which caused the computer to perform the function; or
    (b) that any computer containing any program or data to which the accused secured or intended to secure unauthorised access by doing that act was in the home country concerned at that time.
(3) In relation to an offence under section 3, either of the following is a significant link with domestic jurisdiction—
    (a) that the accused was in the home country concerned at the time when he did the act which caused the unauthorised modification; or
    (b) that the unauthorised modification took place in the home country concerned.

6. Territorial scope of inchoate offences related to offences under this Act

(1) On a charge of conspiracy to commit an offence under this Act the following questions are immaterial to the accused's guilt—

(a) the question where any person became a party to the conspiracy; and
  (b) the question whether any act, omission or other event occurred in the home country concerned.
(2) On a charge of attempting to commit an offence under section 3 above the following questions are immaterial to the accused's guilt—
  (a) the question where the attempt was made; and
  (b) the question whether it had an effect in the home country concerned.
(3) On a charge of incitement to commit an offence under this Act the question where the incitement took place is immaterial to the accused's guilt.

7. Territorial scope of inchoate offences related to offences under external law corresponding to offences under this Act

...

(4) Subject to section 8 below, if any act done by a person in England and Wales would amount to the offence of incitement to commit an offence under this Act but for the fact that what he had in view would not be an offence triable in England and Wales—
  (a) what he had in view shall be treated as an offence under this Act for the purposes of any charge of incitement brought in respect of that act; and
  (b) any such charge shall accordingly be triable in England and Wales.

8. Relevance of external law

(1) A person is guilty of an offence triable by virtue of section 4(4) above only if what he intended to do or facilitate would involve the commission of an offence under the law in force where the whole or any part of it was intended to take place.
(3) A person is guilty of an offence triable by virtue of section 1(1A) of the Criminal Attempts Act 1981 or by virtue of section 7(4) above only if what he had in view would involve the commission of an offence under the law in force where the whole or any part of it was intended to take place.
(4) Conduct punishable under the law in force in any place is an offence under that law for the purposes of this section, however it is described in that law.
(5) Subject to subsection (7) below, a condition specified in any of subsections (1) or (3) above shall be taken to be satisfied unless not later than rules of court may provide the defence serve on the prosecution a notice—
  (a) stating that, on the facts as alleged with respect to the relevant conduct, the condition is not in their opinion satisfied;
  (b) showing their grounds for that opinion; and
  (c) requiring the prosecution to show that it is satisfied.
(6) In subsection (5) above 'the relevant conduct' means—
  (a) where the condition in subsection (1) above is in question, what the accused intended to do or facilitate; and
  (c) where the condition in subsection (3) above is in question, what the accused had in view.
(7) The court, if it thinks fit, may permit the defence to require the prosecution to show that the condition is satisfied without the prior service of a notice under subsection (5) above.
  ...
(9) In the Crown Court the question whether the condition is satisfied shall be decided by the judge alone.

9. British citizenship immaterial

(1) In any proceedings brought in England and Wales in respect of any offence to which this section applies it is immaterial to guilt whether or not the accused was a British citizen at the time of any act, omission or other event proof of which is required for conviction of the offence.
(2) This section applies to the following offences—
  (a) any offence under this Act;
  (c) any attempt to commit an offence under section 3 above; and
  (d) incitement to commit an offence under this Act.

10. Saving for certain law enforcement powers

Section 1(1) above has effect without prejudice to the operation—
   (a) in England and Wales of any enactment relating to powers of inspection, search or seizure; and
   (b) ...
       and nothing designed to indicate a withholding of consent to access to any program or data from persons as enforcement officers shall have effect to make access unauthorised for the purposes of the said section 1(1).

In this section 'enforcement officer' means a constable or other person charged with the duty of investigating offences; and withholding consent from a person 'as' an enforcement officer of any description includes the operation, by the person entitled to control access, of rules whereby enforcement officers of that description are, as such, disqualified from membership of a class of persons who are authorised to have access.

17. Interpretation

(1) The following provisions of this section apply for the interpretation of this Act.
(2) A person secures access to any program or data held in a computer if by causing a computer to perform any function he—
   (a) alters or erases the program or data;
   (b) copies or moves it to any storage medium other than that in which it is held or to a different location in the storage medium in which it is held;
   (c) uses it; or
   (d) has it output from the computer in which it is held (whether by having it displayed or in any other manner); and references to access to a program or data (and to an intent to secure such access) shall be read accordingly.
(3) For the purposes of subsection (2)(c) above a person uses a program if the function he causes the computer to perform—
   (a) causes the program to be executed; or
   (b) is itself a function of the program.
(4) For the purposes of subsection (2)(d) above—
   (a) a program is output if the instructions of which it consists are output; and
   (b) the form in which any such instructions or any other data is output (and in particular whether or not it represents a form in which, in the case of instructions, they are capable of being executed or, in the case of data, it is capable of being processed by a computer) is immaterial.
(5) Access of any kind by any person to any program or data held in a computer is unauthorised if—
   (a) he is not himself entitled to control access of the kind in question to the program or data; and
   (b) he does not have consent to access by him of the kind in question to the program or data from any person who is so entitled but this subsection is subject to section 10.
(6) References to any program or data held in a computer include references to any program or data held in any removable storage medium which is for the time being in the computer; and a computer is to be regarded as containing any program or data held in any such medium.
(7) A modification of the contents of any computer takes place if, by the operation of any function of the computer concerned or any other computer—
   (a) any program or data held in the computer concerned is altered or erased; or
   (b) any program or data is added to its contents; and any act which contributes towards causing such a modification shall be regarded as causing it.
(8) Such a modification is unauthorised if—
   (a) the person whose act causes it is not himself entitled to determine whether the modification should be made; and
   (b) he does not have consent to the modification from any person who is so entitled.
(9) References to the home country concerned shall be read in accordance with section 4(6) above.
(10) References to a program include references to part of a program.

CONTEMPT OF COURT ACT 1981

1. The strict liability rule
In this Act 'the strict liability rule' means the rule of law whereby conduct may be treated as a contempt of court as tending to interfere with the course of justice in particular legal proceedings regardless of intent to do so.

2. Limitation of scope of strict liability
(1) The strict liability rule applies only in relation to publications, and for this purpose 'publication' includes any speech, writing, programme included in a cable programme service or other communication in whatever form, which is addressed to the public at large or any section of the public.
(2) The strict liability rule applies only to a publication which creates a substantial risk that the course of justice in the proceedings in question will be seriously impeded or prejudiced.
(3) The strict liability rule applies to a publication only if the proceedings in question are active within the meaning of this section at the time of the publication.
(4) Schedule 1 applies for determining the times at which proceedings are to be treated as active within the meaning of this section.
(5) In this section 'programme service' has the same meaning as in the Broadcasting Act 1990.

3. Defence of innocent publication or distribution
(1) A person is not guilty of contempt of court under the strict liability rule as the publisher of any matter to which that rule applies if at the time of publication (having taken all reasonable care) he does not know and has no reason to suspect that relevant proceedings are active.
(2) A person is not guilty of contempt of court under the strict liability rule as the distributor of a publication containing any such matter if at the time of distribution (having taken all reasonable care) he does not know that it contains such matter and has no reason to suspect that it is likely to do so.
(3) The burden of proof of any fact tending to a defence afforded by this section to any person lies upon that person.

4. Contemporary reports of proceedings
(1) Subject to this section a person is not guilty of contempt of court under the strict liability rule in respect of a fair and accurate report of legal proceedings held in public, published contemporaneously and in good faith.
(2) In any such proceedings the court may, where it appears to be necessary for avoiding a substantial risk of prejudice to the administration of justice in those proceedings, or in any other proceedings pending or imminent, order that the publication of any report of the proceedings, or any part of the proceedings, be postponed for such period as the court thinks necessary for that purpose.
(2A) Where in proceedings for any offence which is an administration of justice offence for the purposes of section 54 of the Criminal Procedure and Investigations Act 1996 (acquittal tainted by an administration of justice offence) it appears to the court that there is a possibility that (by virtue of that section) proceedings may be taken against a person for an offence of which he has been acquitted, subsection (2) of this section shall apply as if those proceedings were pending or imminent.
(3) For the purposes of subsection (1) of this section a report of proceedings shall be treated as published contemporaneously—
    (a) in the case of a report of which publication is postponed pursuant to an order under subsection (2) of this section, if published as soon as practicable after that order expires;
    (b) in the case of a report of allocation or sending proceedings of which publication is permitted by virtue only of subsection (6) of section 52A of the Crime and Disorder Act 1998 ('The 1998 Act'), if published as soon as practicable after publication is so permitted.
    (c) in the case of a report of an application of which publication is permitted by virtue only of

sub-paragraph (5) or (7) of paragraph 3 of schedule 3 to the 1998 Act, if published as soon as practicable after publication is so permitted.

5. Discussion of public affairs
A publication made as or as part of a discussion in good faith of public affairs or other matters of general public interest is not to be treated as a contempt of court under the strict liability rule if the risk of impediment or prejudice to particular legal proceedings is merely incidental to the discussion.

6. Savings
Nothing in the foregoing provisions of this Act—
- (a) prejudices any defence available at common law to a charge of contempt of court under the strict liability rule;
- (b) implies that any publication is punishable as contempt of court under that rule which would not be so punishable apart from those provisions;
- (c) restricts liability for contempt of court in respect of conduct intended to impede or prejudice the administration of justice.

7. Consent required for institution of proceedings
Proceedings for a contempt of court under the strict liability rule (other than Scottish proceedings) shall not be instituted except by or with the consent of the Attorney General or on the motion of a court having jurisdiction to deal with it.

8. Confidentiality of jury's deliberations
(1) Subject to subsection (2) below, it is a contempt of court to obtain, disclose or solicit any particulars of statements made, opinions expressed, arguments advanced or votes cast by members of a jury in the course of their deliberations in any legal proceedings.

(2) This section does not apply to any disclosure of any particulars—
- (a) in the proceedings in question for the purpose of enabling the jury to arrive at their verdict, or in connection with the delivery of that verdict, or
- (b) in evidence in any subsequent proceedings for an offence alleged to have been committed in relation to the jury in the first mentioned proceedings,

or to the publication of any particulars so disclosed.

9. Use of tape recorders
(1) Subject to subsection (4) below, it is a contempt of court—
- (a) to use in court, or bring into court for use, any tape recorder or other instrument for recording sound, except with the leave of the court;
- (b) to publish a recording of legal proceedings made by means of any such instrument, or any recording derived directly or indirectly from it, by playing it in the hearing of the public or any section of the public, or to dispose of it or any recording so derived, with a view to such publication;
- (c) to use any such recording in contravention of any conditions of leave granted under paragraph (a).

(2) Leave under paragraph (a) of subsection (1) may be granted or refused at the discretion of the court, and if granted may be granted subject to such conditions as the court thinks proper with respect to the use of any recording made pursuant to the leave; and where leave has been granted the court may at the like discretion withdraw or amend it either generally or in relation to any particular part of the proceedings.

(3) Without prejudice to any other power to deal with an act of contempt under paragraph (a) of subsection (1), the court may order the instrument, or any recording made with it, or both, to be forfeited; and any object so forfeited shall (unless the court otherwise determines on application by a person appearing to be the owner) be sold or otherwise disposed of in such manner as the court may direct.

(4) This section does not apply to the making or use of sound recordings for purposes of official transcripts of proceedings.

CORPORATE MANSLAUGHTER AND HOMICIDE ACT 2007

1. The offence

(1) An organisation to which this section applies is guilty of an offence if the way in which its activities are managed or organised—
   (a) causes a person's death, and
   (b) amounts to a gross breach of a relevant duty of care owed by the organisation to the deceased.
(2) The organisations to which this section applies are—
   (a) a corporation;
   (b) a department or other body listed in Schedule 1;
   (c) a police force;
   (d) a partnership, or a trade union or employers' association, that is an employer.
(3) An organisation is guilty of an offence under this section only if the way in which its activities are managed or organised by its senior management is a substantial element in the breach referred to in subsection (1).
(4) For the purposes of this Act—
   (a) 'relevant duty of care' has the meaning given by section 2, read with sections 3 to 7;
   (b) a breach of a duty of care by an organisation is a 'gross' breach if the conduct alleged to amount to a breach of that duty falls far below what can reasonably be expected of the organisation in the circumstances;
   (c) 'senior management', in relation to an organisation, means the persons who play significant roles in—
      (i) the making of decisions about how the whole or a substantial part of its activities are to be managed or organised, or
      (ii) the actual managing or organising of the whole or a substantial part of those activities.
(5) The offence under this section is called—
   (a) corporate manslaughter, in so far as it is an offence under the law of England and Wales or Northern Ireland;
   (b) corporate homicide, in so far as it is an offence under the law of Scotland.
(6) An organisation that is guilty of corporate manslaughter or corporate homicide is liable on conviction on indictment to a fine.
(7) The offence of corporate homicide is indictable only in the High Court of Justiciary.

2. Meaning of 'relevant duty of care'

(1) A 'relevant duty of care', in relation to an organisation, means any of the following duties owed by it under the law of negligence—
   (a) a duty owed to its employees or to other persons working for the organisation or performing services for it;
   (b) a duty owed as occupier of premises;
   (c) a duty owed in connection with—
      (i) the supply by the organisation of goods or services (whether for consideration or not),
      (ii) the carrying on by the organisation of any construction or maintenance operations,
      (iii) the carrying on by the organisation of any other activity on a commercial basis, or
      (iv) the use or keeping by the organisation of any plant, vehicle or other thing;
   (d) a duty owed to a person who, by reason of being a person within subsection (2), is someone for whose safety the organisation is responsible.
(2) A person is within this subsection if—
   (a) he is detained at a custodial institution or in a custody area at a court or police station;
   (b) he is detained at a removal centre or short-term holding facility;
   (c) he is being transported in a vehicle, or being held in any premises, in pursuance of prison escort arrangements or immigration escort arrangements;

(d) he is living in secure accommodation in which he has been placed;
(e) he is a detained patient.
(3) Subsection (1) is subject to sections 3 to 7.
(4) A reference in subsection (1) to a duty owed under the law of negligence includes a reference to a duty that would be owed under the law of negligence but for any statutory provision under which liability is imposed in place of liability under that law.
(5) For the purposes of this Act, whether a particular organisation owes a duty of care to a particular individual is a question of law.
The judge must make any findings of fact necessary to decide that question.
(6) For the purposes of this Act there is to be disregarded—
  (a) any rule of the common law that has the effect of preventing a duty of care from being owed by one person to another by reason of the fact that they are jointly engaged in unlawful conduct;
  (b) any such rule that has the effect of preventing a duty of care from being owed to a person by reason of his acceptance of a risk of harm.
(7) In this section—
'construction or maintenance operations' means operations of any of the following descriptions—
  (a) construction, installation, alteration, extension, improvement, repair, maintenance, decoration, cleaning, demolition or dismantling of—
    (i) any building or structure,
    (ii) anything else that forms, or is to form, part of the land, or
    (iii) any plant, vehicle or other thing;
  (b) operations that form an integral part of, or are preparatory to, or are for rendering complete, any operations within paragraph (a);
'custodial institution' means a prison, a young offender institution, a secure training centre, a young offenders institution, a young offenders centre, a juvenile justice centre or a remand centre;
'detained patient' means—
(a) a person who is detained in any premises under—
  (i) Part 2 or 3 of the Mental Health Act 1983 ('the 1983 Act'), or
  ...
(b) a person who (otherwise than by reason of being detained as mentioned in paragraph (a)) is deemed to be in legal custody by—
  (i) section 137 of the 1983 Act,
  (ii) Article 131 of the 1986 Order, or
  ...
'immigration escort arrangements' means arrangements made under section 156 of the Immigration and Asylum Act 1999;
'the law of negligence' includes—
(a) in relation to England and Wales, the Occupiers' Liability Act 1957, the Defective Premises Act 1972 and the Occupiers' Liability Act 1984;
  ...
'prison escort arrangements' means arrangements made under section 80 of the Criminal Justice Act 1991 or under sections 102 or 118 of the Criminal Justice and Public Order Act 1994;
'removal centre' and 'short-term holding facility' have the meaning given by section 147 of the Immigration and Asylum Act 1999;
'secure accommodation' means accommodation, not consisting of or forming part of a custodial institution, provided for the purpose of restricting the liberty of persons under the age of 18.

3. Public policy decisions, exclusively public functions and statutory inspections
(1) Any duty of care owed by a public authority in respect of a decision as to matters of public policy (including in particular the allocation of public resources or the weighing of competing public interests) is not a 'relevant duty of care'.

(2) Any duty of care owed in respect of things done in the exercise of an exclusively public function is not a 'relevant duty of care' unless it falls within section 2(1)(a), (b) or (d).
(3) Any duty of care owed by a public authority in respect of inspections carried out in the exercise of a statutory function is not a 'relevant duty of care' unless it falls within section 2(1)(a) or (b).
(4) In this section—

'exclusively public function' means a function that falls within the prerogative of the Crown or is, by its nature, exercisable only with authority conferred—
(a) by the exercise of that prerogative, or
(b) by or under a statutory provision;'
statutory function' means a function conferred by or under a statutory provision.

4. Military activities

(1) Any duty of care owed by the Ministry of Defence in respect of—
    (a) operations within subsection (2),
    (b) activities carried on in preparation for, or directly in support of, such operations, or
    (c) training of a hazardous nature, or training carried out in a hazardous way, which it is considered needs to be carried out, or carried out in that way, in order to improve or maintain the effectiveness of the armed forces with respect to such operations,
is not a 'relevant duty of care'.
(2) The operations within this subsection are operations, including peacekeeping operations and operations for dealing with terrorism, civil unrest or serious public disorder, in the course of which members of the armed forces come under attack or face the threat of attack or violent resistance.
(3) Any duty of care owed by the Ministry of Defence in respect of activities carried on by members of the special forces is not a 'relevant duty of care'.
(4) In this section 'the special forces' means those units of the armed forces the maintenance of whose capabilities is the responsibility of the Director of Special Forces or which are for the time being subject to the operational command of that Director.

5. Policing and law enforcement

(1) Any duty of care owed by a public authority in respect of—
    (a) operations within subsection (2),
    (b) activities carried on in preparation for, or directly in support of, such operations, or
    (c) training of a hazardous nature, or training carried out in a hazardous way, which it is considered needs to be carried out, or carried out in that way, in order to improve or maintain the effectiveness of officers or employees of the public authority with respect to such operations,
is not a 'relevant duty of care'.
(2) Operations are within this subsection if—
    (a) they are operations for dealing with terrorism, civil unrest or serious disorder,
    (b) they involve the carrying on of policing or law-enforcement activities, and
    (c) officers or employees of the public authority in question come under attack, or face the threat of attack or violent resistance, in the course of the operations.
(3) Any duty of care owed by a public authority in respect of other policing or law enforcement activities is not a 'relevant duty of care' unless it falls within section 2(1)(a), (b) or (d).
(4) In this section 'policing or law-enforcement activities' includes—
    (a) activities carried on in the exercise of functions that are—
        (i) functions of police forces, or
        (ii) functions of the same or a similar nature exercisable by public authorities other than police forces;
    (b) activities carried on in the exercise of functions of constables employed by a public authority;
    (c) activities carried on in the exercise of functions exercisable under Chapter 4 of Part 2 of the Serious Organised Crime and Police Act 2005 (protection of witnesses and other persons);
    (d) activities carried on to enforce any provision contained in or made under the Immigration Acts.

6. Emergencies

(1) Any duty of care owed by an organisation within subsection (2) in respect of the way in which it responds to emergency circumstances is not a 'relevant duty of care' unless it falls within section 2(1)(a) or (b).
(2) The organisations within this subsection are—
   (a) a fire and rescue authority in England and Wales;
   ...
   (d) any other organisation providing a service of responding to emergency circumstances either—
      (i) in pursuance of arrangements made with an organisation within paragraph (a), (b) or (c), or
      (ii) (if not in pursuance of such arrangements) otherwise than on a commercial basis;
   (e) a relevant NHS body;
   (f) an organisation providing ambulance services in pursuance of arrangements—
      (i) made by, or at the request of, a relevant NHS body, or
      (ii) made with the Secretary of State or with the Welsh Ministers;
   (g) an organisation providing services for the transport of organs, blood, equipment or personnel in pursuance of arrangements of the kind mentioned in paragraph (f);
   (h) an organisation providing a rescue service;
   (i) the armed forces.
(3) For the purposes of subsection (1), the way in which an organisation responds to emergency circumstances does not include the way in which—
   (a) medical treatment is carried out, or
   (b) decisions within subsection (4) are made.
(4) The decisions within this subsection are decisions as to the carrying out of medical treatment, other than decisions as to the order in which persons are to be given such treatment.
(5) Any duty of care owed in respect of the carrying out, or attempted carrying out, of a rescue operation at sea in emergency circumstances is not a 'relevant duty of care' unless it falls within section 2(1)(a) or (b).
(6) Any duty of care owed in respect of action taken—
   (a) in order to comply with a direction under Schedule 3A to the Merchant Shipping Act 1995 (safety directions), or
   (b) by virtue of paragraph 4 of that Schedule (action in lieu of direction),
   is not a 'relevant duty of care' unless it falls within section 2(1)(a) or (b).
(7) In this section—
   'emergency circumstances' means circumstances that are present or imminent and—
   (a) are causing, or are likely to cause, serious harm or a worsening of such harm, or
   (b) are likely to cause the death of a person;
   'medical treatment' includes any treatment or procedure of a medical or similar nature;
   'relevant NHS body' means—
   (a) a Strategic Health Authority, Primary Care Trust, NHS trust, Special Health Authority or NHS foundation trust in England;
   (b) a Local Health Board, NHS trust or Special Health Authority in Wales;
   ...
   'serious harm' means—
   (a) serious injury to or the serious illness (including mental illness) of a person;
   (b) serious harm to the environment (including the life and health of plants and animals);
   (c) serious harm to any building or other property.
(8) A reference in this section to emergency circumstances includes a reference to circumstances that are believed to be emergency circumstances.

7. Child-protection and probation functions

(1) A duty of care to which this section applies is not a 'relevant duty of care' unless it falls within section 2(1)(a), (b) or (d).
(2) This section applies to any duty of care that a local authority or other public authority owes in respect of the exercise by it of functions conferred by or under—

(a) Parts 4 and 5 of the Children Act 1989,
...
(3) This section also applies to any duty of care that a local probation board or other public authority owes in respect of the exercise by it of functions conferred by or under—
(a) Chapter 1 of Part 1 of the Criminal Justice and Court Services Act 2000,
...

8. Factors for jury

(1) This section applies where—
(a) it is established that an organisation owed a relevant duty of care to a person, and
(b) it falls to the jury to decide whether there was a gross breach of that duty.
(2) The jury must consider whether the evidence shows that the organisation failed to comply with any health and safety legislation that relates to the alleged breach, and if so—
(a) how serious that failure was;
(b) how much of a risk of death it posed.
(3) The jury may also—
(a) consider the extent to which the evidence shows that there were attitudes, policies, systems or accepted practices within the organisation that were likely to have encouraged any such failure as is mentioned in subsection (2), or to have produced tolerance of it;
(b) have regard to any health and safety guidance that relates to the alleged breach.
(4) This section does not prevent the jury from having regard to any other matters they consider relevant.
(5) In this section 'health and safety guidance' means any code, guidance, manual or similar publication that is concerned with health and safety matters and is made or issued (under a statutory provision or otherwise) by an authority responsible for the enforcement of any health and safety legislation.

18. No individual liability

(1) An individual cannot be guilty of aiding, abetting, counselling or procuring the commission of an offence of corporate manslaughter.
(1A) An individual cannot be guilty of an offence under Part 2 of the Serious Crime Act 2007 (encouraging or assisting crime) by reference to an offence of corporate manslaughter.
(2) An individual cannot be guilty of aiding, abetting, counselling or procuring, or being art and part in, the commission of an offence of corporate homicide.

19. Convictions under this Act and under health and safety legislation

(1) Where in the same proceedings there is—
(a) a charge of corporate manslaughter or corporate homicide arising out of a particular set of circumstances, and
(b) a charge against the same defendant of a health and safety offence arising out of some or all of those circumstances,
the jury may, if the interests of justice so require, be invited to return a verdict on each charge.
(2) An organisation that has been convicted of corporate manslaughter or corporate homicide arising out of a particular set of circumstances may, if the interests of justice so require, be charged with a health and safety offence arising out of some or all of those circumstances.
(3) In this section 'health and safety offence' means an offence under any health and safety legislation.

20. Abolition of liability of corporations for manslaughter at common law

The common law offence of manslaughter by gross negligence is abolished in its application to corporations, and in any application it has to other organisations to which section 1 applies.

CRIME AND DISORDER ACT 1998

1. Anti-social behaviour orders
(1) An application for an order under this section may be made by a relevant authority if it appears to the authority that the following conditions are fulfilled with respect to any person aged 10 or over, namely—
- (a) that the person has acted, since the commencement date, in an anti-social manner, that is to say, in a manner that caused or was likely to cause harassment, alarm or distress to one or more persons not of the same household as himself; and
- (b) that such an order is necessary to protect relevant persons from further anti-social acts by him;

...

(1A) In this section ... 'relevant authority' means—
- (a) the council for a local government area;
- (aa) in relation to England, a county council;
- (b) the chief officer of police of any police force maintained for a police area;
- (c) the chief constable of the British Transport Police Force; or
- (d) any person registered under section 1 of the Housing Act 1996 as a social landlord who provides or manages any houses or hostel in a local government area; or
- (e) a housing action trust established by order in pursuance of section 62 of the Housing Act 1988.

(1B) In this section 'relevant persons' means—
- (a) in relation to a relevant authority falling within paragraph (a) of subsection (1A), persons within the local government area of that council;
- (aa) in relation to a relevant authority falling within paragraph (aa) of subsection (1A), persons within the county of the county council;
- (b) in relation to a relevant authority falling within paragraph (b) of that subsection, persons within the police area;
- (c) in relation to a relevant authority falling within paragraph (c) of that subsection—
  - (i) persons who are on or likely to be on policed premises in a local government area; or
  - (ii) persons who are in the vicinity of or likely to be in the vicinity of such premises;
- (d) in relation to a relevant authority falling within paragraph (d) of that subsection—
  - (i) persons who are within or likely to be within a place specified in section 3A(1)(a) of the Railways and Transport Safety Act 2003 in a local government area; or
  - (ii) persons who are in the vicinity of or likely to be in the vicinity of such premises.

(2) ...

(3) Such an application shall be made by complaint to a magistrates' court.

(4) If, on such an application, it is proved that the conditions mentioned in subsection (1) above are fulfilled, the magistrates' court may make an order under this section (an 'anti-social behaviour order') which prohibits the defendant from doing anything described in the order.

(5) For the purpose of determining whether the condition mentioned in subsection (1)(a) above is fulfilled, the court shall disregard any act of the defendant which he shows was reasonable in the circumstances.

(5A) Nothing in this section affects the operation of section 127 of the Magistrates Court Act 1980 (limitation of time in respect of information laid or complaints made in magistrates' courts).

(6) The prohibitions that may be imposed by an anti-social behaviour order are those necessary for the purpose of protecting persons (whether relevant persons or persons elsewhere in England and Wales) from further anti-social acts by the defendant.

(7) An anti-social behaviour order shall have effect for a period (not less than two years) specified in the order or until further order.

(8) Subject to subsection (9) below, the applicant or the defendant may apply by complaint to the court which made an anti-social behaviour order for it to be varied or discharged by a further order.

(9) Except with the consent of both parties, no anti-social behaviour order shall be discharged before the end of the period of two years beginning with the date of service of the order.
(10) If without reasonable excuse a person does anything which he is prohibited from doing by an anti-social behaviour order, he is guilty of an offence and liable—
    (a) on summary conviction, to imprisonment for a term not exceeding six months or to a fine not exceeding the statutory maximum, or to both; or
    (b) on conviction on indictment, to imprisonment for a term not exceeding five years or to a fine, or to both.
    ...
(11) Where a person is convicted of an offence under subsection (10) above, it shall not be open to the court by or before which he is so convicted to make an order under subsection (1)(b) (conditional discharge) of section 12 of the Powers of Criminal Courts Sentencing Act 2000 in respect of the offence.
(12) In this section—
    British Transport Police Force means the force of constables appointed under section 53 of the British Transport Commission Act 1949;
    'child' and 'young person' shall have the same meaning as in the Children and Young Persons Act 1933;
    'the commencement date' means the date of the commencement of this section;
    'local government area' means—
    (a) in relation to England, a district or London borough, the City of London, the Isle of Wight and the Isles of Scilly;
    (b) in relation to Wales, a county or county borough.
        'policed premises' has the same meaning given by section 53(3) of the British Transport Commission Act 1949.
    ...

28. Meaning of 'racially or religiously aggravated'

(1) An offence is racially or religiously aggravated for the purposes of sections 29 to 32 below if—
    (a) at the time of committing the offence, or immediately before or after doing so, the offender demonstrates towards the victim of the offence hostility based on the victim's membership (or presumed membership) of a racial or religious group; or
    (b) the offence is motivated (wholly or partly) by hostility towards members of a racial or religious group based on their membership of that group.
(2) In subsection (1)(a) above—
    'membership', in relation to a racial or religious group, includes association with members of that group;
    'presumed' means presumed by the offender.
(3) It is immaterial for the purposes of paragraph (a) or (b) of subsection (1) above whether or not the offender's hostility is also based, to any extent, on any other factor not mentioned in that paragraph.
(4) In this section 'racial group' means a group of persons defined by reference to race, colour, nationality (including citizenship) or ethnic or national origins.
(5) In this section 'religious group' means a group of persons defined by reference to religious belief or lack of religious belief.

29. Racially or religiously aggravated assaults

(1) A person is guilty of an offence under this section if he commits—
    (a) an offence under section 20 of the Offences Against the Person Act 1861 (malicious wounding or grievous bodily harm);
    (b) an offence under section 47 of that Act (actual bodily harm); or
    (c) common assault,
    which is racially or religiously aggravated for the purposes of this section.
(2) A person guilty of an offence falling within subsection (1)(a) or (b) above shall be liable—
    (a) on summary conviction, to imprisonment for a term not exceeding six months or to a fine not exceeding the statutory maximum, or to both;

(b) on conviction on indictment, to imprisonment for a term not exceeding seven years or to a fine, or to both.
(3) A person guilty of an offence falling within subsection (1)(c) above shall be liable—
   (a) on summary conviction, to imprisonment for a term not exceeding six months or to a fine not exceeding the statutory maximum, or to both;
   (b) on conviction on indictment, to imprisonment for a term not exceeding two years or to a fine, or to both.

30. Racially or religiously aggravated criminal damage
(1) A person is guilty of an offence under this section if he commits an offence under section 1(1) of the Criminal Damage Act 1971 (destroying or damaging property belonging to another) which is racially or religiously aggravated for the purposes of this section.
(2) A person guilty of an offence under this section shall be liable—
   (a) on summary conviction, to imprisonment for a term not exceeding six months or to a fine not exceeding the statutory maximum, or to both;
   (b) on conviction on indictment, to imprisonment for a term not exceeding fourteen years or to a fine, or to both.
(3) For the purposes of this section, section 28(1)(a) above shall have effect as if the person to whom the property belongs or is treated as belonging for the purposes of that Act were the victim of the offence.

31. Racially or religiously aggravated public order offences
(1) A person is guilty of an offence under this section if he commits—
   (a) an offence under section 4 of the Public Order Act 1986 (fear or provocation of violence);
   (b) an offence under section 4A of that Act (intentional harassment, alarm or distress); or
   (c) an offence under section 5 of that Act (harassment, alarm or distress),
   which is racially or religiously aggravated for the purposes of this section.
   ...
(4) A person guilty of an offence falling within subsection (1)(a) or (b) above shall be liable—
   (a) on summary conviction, to imprisonment for a term not exceeding six months or to a fine not exceeding the statutory maximum, or to both;
   (b) on conviction on indictment, to imprisonment for a term not exceeding two years or to a fine, or to both.
(5) A person guilty of an offence falling within subsection (1)(c) above shall be liable on summary conviction to a fine not exceeding level 4 on the standard scale.
(6) If, on the trial on indictment of a person charged with an offence falling within subsection (1)(a) or (b) above, the jury find him not guilty of the offence charged, they may find him guilty of the basic offence mentioned in that provision.
(7) For the purposes of subsection (1)(c) above, section 28(1)(a) above shall have effect as if the person likely to be caused harassment, alarm or distress were the victim of the offence.

32. Racially or religiously aggravated harassment etc.
(1) A person is guilty of an offence under this section if he commits—
   (a) an offence under section 2 of the Protection from Harassment Act 1997 (offence of harassment); or
   (b) an offence under section 4 of that Act (putting people in fear of violence),
   which is racially or religiously aggravated for the purposes of this section.
   ...
(3) A person guilty of an offence falling within subsection (1)(a) above shall be liable—
   (a) on summary conviction, to imprisonment for a term not exceeding six months or to a fine not exceeding the statutory maximum, or to both;
   (b) on conviction on indictment, to imprisonment for a term not exceeding two years or to a fine, or to both.
(4) A person guilty of an offence falling within subsection (1)(b) above shall be liable—
   (a) on summary conviction, to imprisonment for a term not exceeding six months or to a fine not exceeding the statutory maximum, or to both;

(b) on conviction on indictment, to imprisonment for a term not exceeding seven years or to a fine, or to both.
(5) If, on the trial on indictment of a person charged with an offence falling within subsection (1)(a) above, the jury find him not guilty of the offence charged, they may find him guilty of the basic offence mentioned in that provision.
(6) If, on the trial on indictment of a person charged with an offence falling within subsection (1)(b) above, the jury find him not guilty of the offence charged, they may find him guilty of an offence falling within subsection (1)(a) above.
(7) Section 5 of the Protection from Harassment Act 1997 (restraining orders) shall have effect in relation to a person convicted of an offence under this section as if the reference in subsection (1) of that section to an offence under section 2 or 4 included a reference to an offence under this section.

34. Abolition of rebuttable presumption that a child is doli incapax
The rebuttable presumption of criminal law that a child aged 10 or over is incapable of committing an offence is hereby abolished.

CRIMINAL APPEAL ACT 1968

1. Right of appeal
(l) Subject to subsection (3) below a person convicted of an offence on indictment may appeal to the Court of Appeal against his conviction.
(2) An appeal under this section lies only —
 (a) with the leave of the Court of Appeal, or
 (b) if the judge of the court of trial grants a certificate that the case is fit for appeal.
(3) Where a person is convicted before the Crown Court of a scheduled offence it shall not be open to him to appeal to the Court of Appeal against the conviction on the ground that the decision of the court which sent him to the Crown Court for trial as to the value involved was mistaken.
(4) In subsection (3) above 'scheduled offence' and 'the value involved' have the same meanings as they have in section 22 of the Magistrates Court Act 1980 (certain offences against property to be tried summarily if the value of property or damage is small).

2. Grounds for allowing an appeal under section 1
(1) Subject to the provisions of this Act, the Court of Appeal —
 (a) shall allow an appeal against conviction if they think that the conviction is unsafe; and
 (b) shall dismiss such an appeal in any other case.
(2) In the case of an appeal against conviction the Court shall, if they allow the appeal, quash the conviction.
(3) An order of the Court of Appeal quashing a conviction shall, except when under section 7 below the appellant is ordered to be retried, operate as a direction to the court of trial to enter, instead of the record of conviction, a judgment and verdict of acquittal.

3. Power to substitute conviction of alternative offence
(l) This section applies on an appeal against conviction, where the appellant has been convicted of an offence and the jury could on the indictment have found him guilty of some other offence, and on the finding of the jury it appears to the Court of Appeal that the jury must have been satisfied of facts which proved him guilty of the other offence.
(2) The Court may, instead of allowing or dismissing the appeal, substitute for the verdict found by the jury a verdict of guilty of the other offence, and pass such sentence in substitution for the sentence passed at the trial as may be authorised by law for the other offence, not being a sentence of greater severity.

3A. Power to substitute conviction of alternative offence after guilty plea

(1) This section applies on an appeal against conviction where —
 (a) an appellant has been convicted of an offence to which he pleaded guilty,
 (b) if he had not pleaded, he could on the indictment have pleaded, or been found, guilty of some other offence, and
 (c) it appears to the Court of Appeal that the plea of guilty indicates an admission by the appellant of facts which prove him guilty of the other offence.

(2) The Court of Appeal may, instead of allowing or dismissing the appeal, substitute for the appellant's plea of guilty a plea of guilty of the other offence and pass such sentence in substitution for the sentence passed at the trial as may be authorised by law for the other offence, not being a sentence of greater severity.

4. Sentence when plea allowed on part of an indictment

(1) This section applies where—
 (a) two or more related sentences are passed,
 (b) the Court of Appeal allow an appeal against conviction in respect of one or more of the offences for which the sentences were passed ('the related offences'), but
 (c) the appellant remains convicted of one or more of those offences.

(2) Except as provided by subsection (3) below, the Court may in respect of any related offence of which the appellant remains convicted pass such sentence, in substitution for any sentence passed thereon at the trial, as they think proper and is authorised by law.

(3) The Court shall not under this section pass any sentence such that the appellant's sentence on the indictment as a whole will, in consequence of the appeal, be of greater severity than the sentence (taken as a whole) which was passed at the trial for all the related offences.

(4) For the purposes of subsection (1)(a), two or more sentences are related if—
 (a) they are passed on the same day,
 (b) they are passed on different days but the court in passing any one of them states that it is treating that one together with the other or others as substantially one sentence, or
 (c) they are passed on different days but in respect of counts on the same indictment.

(5) Where—
 (a) two or more sentences are related to each other by virtue of subsection (4)(a) or (b), and
 (b) any one or more of those sentences is related to one or more other sentences by virtue of subsection (4)(c),

all the sentences are to be treated as related for the purposes of subsection (1)(a).

5. Disposal of appeal against conviction on special verdict

(1) This section applies on an appeal against conviction in a case where the jury have found a special verdict.

(2) If the Court of Appeal consider that a wrong conclusion has been arrived at by the court of trial on the effect of the jury's verdict they may, instead of allowing the appeal, order such conclusion to be recorded as appears to them to be in law required by the verdict, and pass such sentence in substitution for the sentence passed at the trial as may be authorised by law.

6. Substitution of finding of insanity or finding of unfitness to plead, etc.

(1) This subsection applies where, on an appeal against conviction, the Court of Appeal on the written or oral evidence of two or more registered medical practitioners at least one of whom is duly approved, are of opinion—
 (a) that the proper verdict would have been one of not guilty by reason of insanity; or
 (b) that the case is not one where there should have been a verdict of acquittal, but that there should have been a finding that the accused was under a disability and that he did the act or made the omission charged against him

(2) The Court of Appeal shall make in respect of the accused —
 (a) an hospital order (with or without a restriction order);
 (b) a supervision order; or
 (c) an order for his absolute discharge

(3) Where —
 (a) the offence to which the appeal relates is an offence the sentence for which is fixed by law, and
 (b) the court have power to make a hospital order,
 the court shall make a hospital order with a restriction order (whether or not they would have power to make a restriction order apart from this subsection).
(4) Schedule 5A of the Criminal Procedure (Insanity) Act 1964 ('the 1964 Act') applies in relation to this section as it applies in relation to section 5 of that Act
(5) Where the Court of Appeal makes an interim hospital order by virtue of this section —
 (a) the power of renewing or terminating it and of dealing with the appellant on its termination shall be exercisable by the court below and not by the Court of Appeal; and
 (b) the court below shall be treated for the purpose of section 38(7) of the Mental Health Act 1983 (absconding offenders) as the court that made the order.
(6) Where the Court of Appeal make a supervision order by virtue of this section, any power of revoking or amending it shall be exercisable as if the order had been made by the court below.
(7) In this section —
'hospital order' has the meaning given in section 37 of the Mental Health Act 1983.
'interim hospital order' has the meaning given in section 38 of that Act;
'restriction order' has the meaning given in section 41 of that Act.
'supervision order' has the meaning given in Part 1 of Schedule 1A to the 1964 Act.

7. Power to order retrial

(1) Where the Court of Appeal allow an appeal against conviction and it appears to the Court that the interests of justice so require, they may order the appellant to be retried.
(2) A person shall not under this section be ordered to be retried for any offence other than—
 (a) the offence of which he was convicted at the original trial and in respect of which his appeal is allowed as mentioned in subsection (1) above;
 (b) an offence of which he could have been convicted at the original trial on an indictment for the first mentioned offence; or
 (c) an offence charged in an alternative count of the indictment in respect of which the jury were discharged from giving a verdict in consequence of convicting him of the first-mentioned offence.

12. Appeal against verdict of not guilty by reason of insanity

A person in whose case there is returned a verdict of not guilty by reason of insanity may appeal to the Court of Appeal against the verdict —
 (a) with the leave of the Court of Appeal, or
 (b) if the judge of the court of trial grants a certificate that the case is fit for appeal.

20. Disposal of groundless appeal or application of leave to appeal

If it appears to the registrar that a notice of appeal or application for leave does not show any substantial ground of appeal, he may refer the appeal or application for leave to the Court for summary determination; and where the case is so referred the Court may, if they consider that the appeal or application for leave is frivolous or vexatious, and can be determined without adjourning it for a full hearing, dismiss the appeal or application for leave summarily, without calling on anyone to attend the hearing or to appear for the Crown thereon.

33. Right of appeal to the House of Lords

(1) An appeal lies to the House of Lords, at the instance of the defendant or the prosecutor, from any decision of the Court of Appeal on an appeal to that court under Part I of this Act or Part 9 of the Criminal Justice Act 2003 or section 9 (preparatory hearings) of the Criminal Justice Act 1987 or section 35 of the Criminal Procedure and Investigations Act 1996 or section 47 of the Criminal Justice Act 2003.
(1A) In subsection (1) above the references to the prosecutor include a reference to the Director of Assets Recovery Agency in a case where (and to the extent that) he is party to the appeal to the Court of Appeal.

(1B) An appeal lies to the House of Lords, at the instance of the acquitted person or the prosecutor, from any decision of the Court of Appeal on an application under section 76(1) or (2) of the Criminal Justice Act 2003 (retrial for serious offences).
(2) The appeal lies only with the leave of the Court of Appeal or the House of Lords; and leave shall not be granted unless it is certified by the Court of Appeal that a point of law of general public importance is involved in the decision and it appears to the Court of Appeal or the House of Lords (as the case may be) that the point is one which ought to be considered by that House.
(3) Except as provided by this Part of the Act and section 13 of the Administration of Justice Act 1960 (appeal in cases of contempt of court), no appeal shall lie from any decision of the criminal division of the Court of Appeal.
(4) In relation to an appeal under subsection (1B), references in this Part to a defendant are references to the acquitted person.

CRIMINAL ATTEMPTS ACT 1981

1. Attempting to commit an offence
(1) If, with intent to commit an offence to which this section applies, a person does an act which is more than merely preparatory to the commission of the offence, he is guilty of attempting to commit the offence.
(1A) Subject to section 8 of the Computer Misuse Act 1990 (relevance of external law), if this subsection applies to an act, what the person doing it had in view shall be treated as an offence to which this section applies.
(1B) Subsection (1A) above applies to an act if—
   (a) it is done in England and Wales;
   (b) it would fall within subsection (1) above as more than merely preparatory to the commission of an offence under section 3 of the Computer Misuse Act 1990 but for the fact that the offence, if completed, would not be an offence triable in England and Wales.
(2) A person may be guilty of attempting to commit an offence to which this section applies even though the facts are such that the commission of the offence is impossible.
(3) In any case where—
   (a) apart from this subsection a person's intention would not be regarded as having amounted to an intent to commit an offence; but
   (b) if the facts of the case had been as he believed them to be, his intention would be so regarded,
then, for the purposes of subsection (1) above, he shall be regarded as having had an intent to commit that offence.
(4) This section applies to any offence which, if it were completed, would be triable in England and Wales as an indictable offence, other than—
   (a) conspiracy (at common law or under section 1 of the Criminal Law Act 1977 or any other enactment);
   (b) aiding, abetting, counselling, procuring or suborning the commission of an offence;
   (c) offences under section 4(1) (assisting offenders) or 5(1) (accepting or agreeing to accept consideration for not disclosing information about a relevant offence) of the Criminal Law Act 1967.

1A. Extended jurisdiction in relation to certain offences
(1) If this section applies to an act, what the person doing the act had in view shall be treated as an offence to which this section 1(1) above applies.
(2) This section applies to an act if—
   (a) it is done in England and Wales; and
   (b) it would fall within section 1(1) above as more than merely preparatory to the commission of a Group A offence but for the fact that that offence, if completed, would not have been an offence triable in England and Wales.

(3) In this section 'Group A offence' has the same meaning as in Part 1 of the Criminal Justice Act 1993.
(4) Subsection 1 above is subject to the provisions of section 6 of the Act of 1993 (relevance of external law).
(5) Where a person does an act to which this section applies, the offence which he commits shall for all purposes be treated as the offence of attempting the relevant Group A offence.

3. Offences of attempt under other enactments

(1) Subsections (2) to (5) below shall have effect, subject to subsection (6) below and to any inconsistent provision in any other enactment, for the purpose of determining whether a person is guilty of an attempt under a special statutory provision.
(2) For the purposes of this Act an attempt under a special statutory provision is an offence which—
   (a) is created by an enactment other than section 1 above, including an enactment passed after this Act; and
   (b) is expressed as an offence of attempting to commit another offence (in this section referred to as 'the relevant full offence').
(3) A person is guilty of an attempt under a special statutory provision if, with intent to commit the relevant full offence, he does an act which is more than merely preparatory to the commission of that offence.
(4) A person may be guilty of an attempt under a special statutory provision even though the facts are such that the commission of the relevant full offence is impossible.
(5) In any case where—
   (a) apart from this subsection a person's intention would not be regarded as having amounted to an intent to commit the relevant full offence ; but
   (b) if the facts of the case had been as he believed them to be, his intention would be so regarded,
   then, for the purposes of subsection (3) above, he shall be regarded as having had an intent to commit that offence.
(6) Subsections (2) to (5) above shall not have effect in relation to an act done before the commencement of this Act.

4. Trial and penalties

(1) A person guilty by virtue of section 1 above of attempting to commit an offence shall—
   (a) if the offence attempted is murder or any other offence the sentence for which is fixed by law, be liable on conviction on indictment to imprisonment for life; and
   (b) if the offence attempted is indictable but does not fall within paragraph (a) above, be liable on conviction on indictment to any penalty to which he would have been liable on conviction on indictment of that offence; and
   (c) if the offence attempted is triable either way, be liable on summary conviction to any penalty to which he would have been liable on summary conviction of that offence.
(2) In any case in which a court may proceed to summary trial of an information charging a person with an offence and an information charging him with an offence under section 1 above of attempting to commit it or an attempt under a special statutory provision, the court may, without his consent, try the informations together.
(3) Where, in proceedings against a person for an offence under section 1 above, there is evidence sufficient in law to support a finding that he did an act falling within subsection (1) of that section, the question whether or not his act fell within that subsection is a question of fact.
(4) Where, in proceedings against a person for an attempt under a special statutory provision, there is evidence sufficient in law to support a finding that he did an act falling within subsection (3) of section 3 above, the question whether or not his act fell within that subsection is a question of fact.
(5) Subsection (1) above shall have effect—
   (b) notwithstanding anything—
      (i) in section 32(1) (no limit to fine on conviction on indictment) of the Criminal Law Act 1977; or

(ii) in section 78(1) and (2) (maximum of six months' imprisonment on summary conviction unless express provision made to the contrary) of the Powers of Criminal Courts (Sentencing) Act 2000.

6. Effect of Part 1 on common law
(1) The offence of attempt at common law and any offence at common law of procuring materials for crime are hereby abolished for all purposes not relating to acts done before the commencement of this Act.
(2) Except as regards offences committed before the commencement of this Act, references in any enactment passed before this Act which fall to be construed as references to the offence of attempt at common law shall be construed as references to the offence under section 1 above.

8. Abolition of offence of loitering, etc. with intent
The provisions of section 4 of the Vagrancy Act 1824 which apply to suspected persons and reputed thieves frequenting or loitering about the places described in that section with the intent there specified shall cease to have effect.

9. Interference with vehicles
(1) A person is guilty of the offence of vehicle interference with vehicles, if he interferes with a motor vehicle or trailer or with anything carried in or on a motor vehicle or trailer with the intention that an offence specified in subsection (2) below shall be committed by himself or some other person.
(2) The offences mentioned in subsection (1) above are—
   (a) theft of the motor vehicle or trailer or part of it;
   (b) theft of anything carried in or on the motor vehicle or trailer; and
   (c) an offence under section 12(1) of the Theft Act 1968 (taking and driving away without consent);
   and, if it is shown that a person accused of an offence under this section intended that one of those offences should be committed, it is immaterial that it cannot be shown which it was.
(3) A person guilty of an offence under this section shall be liable on summary conviction to imprisonment for a term not exceeding three months or to a fine not exceeding level 4 on the standard scale or to both.
   ...
(5) In this section 'motor vehicle' and 'trailer' have the meanings assigned to them by section 185(1) of the Road Traffic Act 1988.

CRIMINAL DAMAGE ACT 1971

1. Destroying or damaging property
(1) A person who without lawful excuse destroys or damages any property belonging to another intending to destroy or damage any such property or being reckless as to whether any such property would be destroyed or damaged shall be guilty of an offence.
(2) A person who without lawful excuse destroys or damages any property, whether belonging to himself or another—
   (a) intending to destroy or damage any property or being reckless as to whether any property would be destroyed or damaged; and
   (b) intending by the destruction or damage to endanger the life of another or being reckless as to whether the life of another would be thereby endangered;
   shall be guilty of an offence.
(3) An offence committed under this section by destroying or damaging property by fire shall be charged as arson.

2. Threats to destroy or damage property

A person who without lawful excuse makes to another a threat, intending that that other would fear it would be carried out, —
  (a) to destroy or damage any property belonging to that other or a third person; or
  (b) to destroy or damage his own property in a way which he knows is likely to endanger the life of that other or a third person;
shall be guilty of an offence.

3. Possessing anything with intent to destroy or damage property

A person who has anything in his custody or under his control intending without lawful excuse to use it or cause or permit another to use it—
  (a) to destroy or damage any property belonging to some other person; or
  (b) to destroy damage his own or the user's property in a way which he knows is likely to endanger the life of some other person;
shall be guilty of an offence.

4. Punishment of offences

(1) A person guilty of arson under section 1 above or of an offence under section 1(2) above (whether arson or not) shall on conviction on indictment be liable to imprisonment for life.
(2) A person guilty of any other offence under this Act shall on conviction on indictment be liable to imprisonment for a term not exceeding ten years.

5. 'Without lawful excuse'

(1) This section applies to any offence under section 1(1) above and any offence under section 2 or 3 above other than one involving a threat by the person charged to destroy or damage property in a way which he knows is likely to endanger the life of another or involving an intent by the person charged to use or cause or permit the use of something in his custody or under his control so to destroy or damage property.
(2) A person charged with an offence to which this section applies shall, whether or not he would be treated for the purposes of this Act as having a lawful excuse apart from this subsection, be treated for those purposes as having a lawful excuse—
  (a) if at the time of the act or acts alleged to constitute the offence he believed that the person or persons whom he believed to be entitled to consent to the destruction of or damage to the property in question had so consented, or would have so consented to it if he or they had known of the destruction or damage and its circumstances; or
  (b) if he destroyed or damaged or threatened to destroy or damage the property in question or, in the case of a charge of an offence under section 3 above, intended to use or cause or permit the use of something to destroy or damage it, in order to protect property belonging to himself or another or a right or interest in property which was or which he believed to be vested in himself or another, and at the time of the act or acts alleged to constitute the offence he believed—
    (i) that the property, right or interest was in immediate need of protection; and
    (ii) that the means of protection adopted or proposed to be adopted were or would be reasonable having regard to all the circumstances.
(3) For the purposes of this section it is immaterial whether a belief is justified or not if it is honestly held.
(4) For the purposes of subsection (2) above a right or interest in property includes any right or privilege in or over land, whether created by grant, licence or otherwise.
(5) This section shall not be construed as casting doubt on any defence recognised by law as a defence to criminal charges.

10. Interpretation

(l) In this Act 'property' means property of a tangible nature, whether real or personal, including money and—
  (a) including wild creatures which have been tamed or are ordinarily kept in captivity, and any other wild creatures or their carcasses if, but only if, they have been reduced into possession

which has not been lost or abandoned or are in the course of being reduced into possession; but
  (b) not including mushrooms growing wild on any land or flowers, fruit or foliage of a plant growing wild on any land.
For the purposes of this subsection 'mushroom' includes any fungus and 'plant' includes any shrub or tree.
(2) Property shall be treated for the purposes of this Act as belonging to any person—
  (a) having the custody or control of it;
  (b) having in it any proprietary right or interest (not being an equitable interest arising only from an agreement to transfer or grant an interest); or
  (c) having a charge on it.
(3) Where property is subject to a trust, the persons to whom it belongs shall be so treated as including any person having a right to enforce the trust.
(4) Property of a corporation sole shall be so treated as belonging to the corporation notwithstanding a vacancy in the corporation.
(5) For the purposes of this Act a modification of the contents of a computer shall not be regarded as damaging any computer or computer storage medium unless its effect on that computer or computer storage medium impairs its physical condition.

CRIMINAL JUSTICE ACT 1925

47. Abolition of presumption of coercion of married woman by husband
Any presumption that an offence committed by a wife in the presence of her husband is committed under the coercion of her husband is hereby abolished, but on a charge against a wife for any offence other than treason or murder it shall be a good defence to prove that the offence was committed in the presence of, and under, the coercion of the husband.

CRIMINAL JUSTICE ACT 1967

8. Proof of criminal intent
A court or jury, in determining whether a person has committed an offence, —
  (a) shall not be bound in law to infer that he intended or foresaw a result of his actions by reason only of its being a natural and probable consequence of those actions; but
  (b) shall decide whether he did foresee that result by reference to all the evidence, drawing such inferences from the evidence as appear proper in the circumstances.

91. Drunkenness in a public place
(1) Any person who in any public place is guilty, while drunk, of disorderly behaviour may be arrested without warrant by any person and shall be liable on summary conviction to a fine not exceeding level 3 on the standard scale.
  ...
(4) In this section 'public place' includes any highway and any other premises or place to which at the material time the public have or are permitted to have access, whether on payment or otherwise.

CRIMINAL JUSTICE ACT 1988

39. Common assault and battery to be summary offences
Common assault and battery shall be summary offences and a person guilty of either of them shall be liable to a fine not exceeding level 5 on the standard scale, to imprisonment for a term not exceeding six months, or to both.

134. Torture
(1) A public official or person acting in an official capacity, whatever his nationality, commits the offence of torture if in the United Kingdom or elsewhere he intentionally inflicts severe pain or suffering on another in the performance or purported performance of his official duties.
(2) A person not falling within subsection (1) above commits the offence of torture, whatever his nationality, if—
   (a) in the United Kingdom or elsewhere he intentionally inflicts severe pain or suffering on another at the instigation or with the consent or acquiescence—
      (i) of a public official; or
      (ii) of a person acting in an official capacity; and
   (b) the official or other person is performing or purporting to perform his official duties when he instigates the commission of the offence or consents to or acquiesces in it.
(3) It is immaterial whether the pain or suffering is physical or mental and whether it is caused by an act or an omission.
(4) It shall be a defence for a person charged with an offence under this section in respect of any conduct of his to prove that he had lawful authority, justification or excuse for that conduct.
(5) For the purposes of this section 'lawful authority, justification or excuse' means—
   (a) in relation to pain or suffering inflicted in the United Kingdom, lawful authority, justification or excuse under the law of the part of the United Kingdom where it was inflicted;
   (b) in relation to pain or suffering inflicted outside the United Kingdom—
      (i) if it was inflicted by a United Kingdom official acting under the law of the United Kingdom or by a person acting in an official capacity under that law, lawful authority, justification or excuse under that law;
      (ii) if it was inflicted by a United Kingdom official acting under the law of any part of the United Kingdom or by a person acting in an official capacity under such law, lawful authority, justification or excuse under the law of the part of the United Kingdom under whose law he was acting; and
      (iii) in any other case, lawful authority, justification or excuse under the law of the place where it was inflicted.
(6) A person who commits the offence of torture shall be liable on conviction on indictment to imprisonment for life.

139. Offence of having article with blade or point in public place
(1) Subject to subsections (4) and (5) below, any person who has an article to which this section applies with him in a public place shall be guilty of an offence.
(2) Subject to subsection (3) below, this section applies to any article which has a blade or is sharply pointed except a folding pocketknife.
(3) This section applies to a folding pocketknife if the cutting edge of its blade exceeds 3 inches.
(4) It shall be a defence for a person charged with an offence under this section to prove that he had good reason or lawful authority for having the article with him in a public place.
(5) Without prejudice to the generality of subsection (4) above, it shall be a defence for a person charged with an offence under this section to prove that he had the article with him—
   (a) for use at work;
   (b) for religious reasons; or
   (c) as part of any national costume.

(6) A person guilty of an offence under subsection (1) above shall be liable—
   (a) on summary conviction to imprisonment for a term not exceeding six months, or a fine not exceeding the statutory maximum, or both;
   (b) on conviction on indictment, to imprisonment for a term not exceeding four years, or a fine or both.
(7) In this section 'public place' includes any place to which at the material time the public have or are permitted access, whether on payment or otherwise.
(8) This section shall not have effect in relation to anything done before it comes into force.

139A. Offence of having article with blade or point (or offensive weapon) on school premises

(1) Any person who has an article to which section 139 of this Act applies with him on school premises shall be guilty of an offence.
(2) Any person who has an offensive weapon within the meaning of section 1 of the Prevention of Crime Act 1953 with him on school premises shall be guilty of an offence.
(3) It shall be a defence for a person charged with an offence under subsection 1 or 2 above to prove that he had good reason or lawful authority for having the article or weapon with him on the premises in question.
(4) Without prejudice to the generality of subsection (3) above, it shall be a defence for a person charged with an offence under subsection 1 or 2 above to prove that he had the article or weapon in question with him—
   (a) for use at work;
   (b) for educational purposes;
   (c) for religious reasons; or
   (d) as part of any national costume.
(5) A person guilty of an offence—
   (a) under subsection (1) above shall be liable—
      (i) on summary conviction to imprisonment for a term not exceeding six months, or a fine not exceeding the statutory maximum, or both;
      (ii) on conviction on indictment, to imprisonment for a term not exceeding four years, or a fine, or both
   (b) under subsection (2) above shall be liable—
      (i) on summary conviction, to imprisonment for a term not exceeding six months, or a fine not exceeding the statutory maximum, or both;
      (ii) on conviction on indictment, to imprisonment for a term not exceeding four years, or a fine, or both.
(6) In this section and section 139B, 'school premises' means land used for the purpose of a school excluding any land occupied solely as a dwelling by a person employed at the school; and 'school' has the meaning given by section 4 of the Education Act 1996.

160. Possession of indecent photograph of child

(1) Subject to section 160A it is an offence for a person to have any indecent photograph or pseudo-photograph of a child (meaning in this section a person under the age of 18) in his possession.
(2) Where a person is charged with an offence under subsection (1) above, it shall be a defence for him to prove—
   (a) that he had a legitimate reason for having the photograph or pseudo-photograph in his possession; or
   (b) that he had not himself seen the photograph or pseudo-photograph and did not know, nor had any cause to suspect, it to be indecent; or
   (c) that the photograph or pseudo-photograph was sent to him without any prior request made by him or on his behalf and that he did not keep it for an unreasonable time.
(2A) A person shall be liable on conviction on indictment of an offence under this section to imprisonment for a term not exceeding five years or a fine, or both.
(4) Sections 1(3), 2(3), 3 and 7 of the Protection of Children Act 1978 shall have effect as if any reference in them to that Act included a reference to this section.
(5) Possession before this section comes into force is not an offence.

160A. Marriage or other relationships

(1) This section applies where, in proceedings for an offence under section 160 relating to an indecent photograph of a child, the defendant proves that the photograph was of the child aged 16 or over, and at the time of the offence charged the child and he—
(a) were married or civil partners of each other; or
(b) lived together as partners in an enduring family relationship.

(2) This section also applies where, in proceedings for an offence under section 160 relating to an indecent photograph of a child, the defendant proves that the photograph was of the child aged 16 or over, and at the time when he obtained it the child and he—
(a) were married or civil partners of each other; or
(b) lived together as partners in an enduring family relationship.

(3) This section applies whether the photograph showed the child alone or with the defendant, but not if it showed any other person.

(4) If sufficient evidence is adduced to raise an issue as to whether the child consented to the photograph being in the defendant's possession, or as to whether the defendant reasonably believed that the child so consented, the defendant is not guilty of the offence unless it is proved that the child did not so consent and that the defendant did not reasonably believe that the child so consented.

CRIMINAL JUSTICE AND IMMIGRATION ACT 2008

63. Possession of extreme pornographic images (NYIF)

(1) It is an offence for a person to be in possession of an extreme pornographic image.

(2) An 'extreme pornographic image' is an image which is both—
(a) pornographic, and
(b) an extreme image.

(3) An image is 'pornographic' if it is of such a nature that it must reasonably be assumed to have been produced solely or principally for the purpose of sexual arousal.

(4) Where (as found in the person's possession) an image forms part of a series of images, the question whether the image is of such a nature as is mentioned in subsection (3) is to be determined by reference to—
(a) the image itself, and
(b) (if the series of images is such as to be capable of providing a context for the image) the context in which it occurs in the series of images.

(5) So, for example, where—
(a) an image forms an integral part of a narrative constituted by a series of images, and
(b) having regard to those images as a whole, they are not of such a nature that they must reasonably be assumed to have been produced solely or principally for the purpose of sexual arousal,
the image may, by virtue of being part of that narrative, be found not to be pornographic, even though it might have been found to be pornographic if taken by itself.

(6) An 'extreme image' is an image which—
(a) falls within subsection (7), and
(b) is grossly offensive, disgusting or otherwise of an obscene character.

(7) An image falls within this subsection if it portrays, in an explicit and realistic way, any of the following—
(a) an act which threatens a person's life,
(b) an act which results, or is likely to result, in serious injury to a person's anus, breasts or genitals,
(c) an act which involves sexual interference with a human corpse, or

(d) a person performing an act of intercourse or oral sex with an animal (whether dead or alive),

and a reasonable person looking at the image would think that any such person or animal was real.
(8) In this section 'image' means—
(a) a moving or still image (produced by any means); or
(b) data (stored by any means) which is capable of conversion into an image within paragraph (a).
(9) In this section references to a part of the body include references to a part surgically constructed (in particular through gender reassignment surgery).
(10) Proceedings for an offence under this section may not be instituted—
(a) in England and Wales, except by or with the consent of the Director of Public Prosecutions; or
(b) …

64. Exclusion of classified films etc. (NYIF)

(1) Section 63 does not apply to excluded images.
(2) An 'excluded image' is an image which forms part of a series of images contained in a recording of the whole or part of a classified work.
(3) But such an image is not an 'excluded image' if—
(a) it is contained in a recording of an extract from a classified work, and
(b) it is of such a nature that it must reasonably be assumed to have been extracted (whether with or without other images) solely or principally for the purpose of sexual arousal.
(4) Where an extracted image is one of a series of images contained in the recording, the question whether the image is of such a nature as is mentioned in subsection (3)(b) is to be determined by reference to—
(a) the image itself, and
(b) (if the series of images is such as to be capable of providing a context for the image) the context in which it occurs in the series of images;

and section 63(5) applies in connection with determining that question as it applies in connection with determining whether an image is pornographic.
(5) In determining for the purposes of this section whether a recording is a recording of the whole or part of a classified work, any alteration attributable to—
(a) a defect caused for technical reasons or by inadvertence on the part of any person, or
(b) the inclusion in the recording of any extraneous material (such as advertisements),

is to be disregarded.
(6) Nothing in this section is to be taken as affecting any duty of a designated authority to have regard to section 63 (along with other enactments creating criminal offences) in determining whether a video work is suitable for a classification certificate to be issued in respect of it.
(7) In this section—

'classified work' means (subject to subsection (8)) a video work in respect of which a classification certificate has been issued by a designated authority (whether before or after the commencement of this section);

'classification certificate' and 'video work' have the same meanings as in the Video Recordings Act 1984;

'designated authority' means an authority which has been designated by the Secretary of State under section 4 of that Act;

'extract' includes an extract consisting of a single image;

'image' and 'pornographic' have the same meanings as in section 63;

'recording' means any disc, tape or other device capable of storing data electronically and from which images may be produced (by any means).
(8) Section 22(3) of the Video Recordings Act 1984 (effect of alterations) applies for the purposes of this section as it applies for the purposes of that Act.

65. Defences: general (NYIF)

(1) Where a person is charged with an offence under section 63, it is a defence for the person to prove any of the matters mentioned in subsection (2).
(2) The matters are—
   (a) that the person had a legitimate reason for being in possession of the image concerned;
   (b) that the person had not seen the image concerned and did not know, nor had any cause to suspect, it to be an extreme pornographic image;
   (c) that the person—
      (i) was sent the image concerned without any prior request having been made by or on behalf of the person, and
      (ii) did not keep it for an unreasonable time.
(3) In this section 'extreme pornographic image' and 'image' have the same meanings as in section 63.

66. Defence: participation in consensual acts (NYIF)

(1) This section applies where—
   (a) a person ('D') is charged with an offence under section 63, and
   (b) the offence relates to an image that portrays an act or acts within paragraphs (a) to (c) (but none within paragraph (d)) of subsection (7) of that section.
(2) It is a defence for D to prove—
   (a) that D directly participated in the act or any of the acts portrayed, and
   (b) that the act or acts did not involve the infliction of any non-consensual harm on any person, and
   (c) if the image portrays an act within section 63(7)(c), that what is portrayed as a human corpse was not in fact a corpse.
(3) For the purposes of this section harm inflicted on a person is 'non-consensual' harm if—
   (a) the harm is of such a nature that the person cannot, in law, consent to it being inflicted on himself or herself; or
   (b) where the person can, in law, consent to it being so inflicted, the person does not in fact consent to it being so inflicted.

67. Penalties etc. for possession of extreme pornographic images (NYIF)

(1) This section has effect where a person is guilty of an offence under section 63.
(2) Except where subsection (3) applies to the offence, the offender is liable—
   (a) on summary conviction, to imprisonment for a term not exceeding the relevant period or a fine not exceeding the statutory maximum or both;
   (b) on conviction on indictment, to imprisonment for a term not exceeding 3 years or a fine or both.
(3) If the offence relates to an image that does not portray any act within section 63(7)(a) or (b), the offender is liable—
   (a) on summary conviction, to imprisonment for a term not exceeding the relevant period or a fine not exceeding the statutory maximum or both;
   (b) on conviction on indictment, to imprisonment for a term not exceeding 2 years or a fine or both.
(4) In subsection (2)(a) or (3)(a) 'the relevant period' means—
   (a) in relation to England and Wales, 12 months;
   ...

76. Reasonable force for purposes of self-defence etc.

(1) This section applies where in proceedings for an offence—
   (a) an issue arises as to whether a person charged with the offence ('D') is entitled to rely on a defence within subsection (2), and
   (b) the question arises whether the degree of force used by D against a person ('V') was reasonable in the circumstances.
(2) The defences are—
   (a) the common law defence of self-defence; and

(b) the defences provided by section 3(1) of the Criminal Law Act 1967 or section 3(1) of the Criminal Law Act (Northern Ireland) 1967 (use of force in prevention of crime or making arrest).
(3) The question whether the degree of force used by D was reasonable in the circumstances is to be decided by reference to the circumstances as D believed them to be, and subsections (4) to (8) also apply in connection with deciding that question.
(4) If D claims to have held a particular belief as regards the existence of any circumstances—
   (a) the reasonableness or otherwise of that belief is relevant to the question whether D genuinely held it; but
   (b) if it is determined that D did genuinely hold it, D is entitled to rely on it for the purposes of subsection (3), whether or not—
      (i) it was mistaken, or
      (ii) (if it was mistaken) the mistake was a reasonable one to have made.
(5) But subsection (4)(b) does not enable D to rely on any mistaken belief attributable to intoxication that was voluntarily induced.
(6) The degree of force used by D is not to be regarded as having been reasonable in the circumstances as D believed them to be if it was disproportionate in those circumstances.
(7) In deciding the question mentioned in subsection (3) the following considerations are to be taken into account (so far as relevant in the circumstances of the case)—
   (a) that a person acting for a legitimate purpose may not be able to weigh to a nicety the exact measure of any necessary action; and
   (b) that evidence of a person's having only done what the person honestly and instinctively thought was necessary for a legitimate purpose constitutes strong evidence that only reasonable action was taken by that person for that purpose.
(8) Subsection (7) is not to be read as preventing other matters from being taken into account where they are relevant to deciding the question mentioned in subsection (3).
(9) This section is intended to clarify the operation of the existing defences mentioned in subsection (2).
(10) In this section—
   (a) 'legitimate purpose' means—
      (i) the purpose of self-defence under the common law, or
      (ii) the prevention of crime or effecting or assisting in the lawful arrest of persons mentioned in the provisions referred to in subsection (2)(b);
   (b) references to self-defence include acting in defence of another person; and
   (c) references to the degree of force used are to the type and amount of force used.

79. Abolition of common law offences of blasphemy and blasphemous libel
(1) The offences of blasphemy and blasphemous libel under the common law of England and Wales are abolished.
   ...

CRIMINAL JUSTICE AND PUBLIC ORDER ACT 1994

51. Intimidation, etc., of witnesses, jurors and others
(1) A person commits an offence if—
   (a) he does an act which intimidates, and is intended to intimidate, another person ('the victim'),
   (b) he does the act knowing or believing that the victim is assisting in the investigation of an offence or is a witness or potential witness or a juror or potential juror in proceedings for an offence, and

(c) he does it intending thereby to cause the investigation or the course of justice to be obstructed, perverted or interfered with.

(2) A person commits an offence if—
   (a) he does an act which harms, and is intended to harm, another person or, intending to cause another person to fear harm, he threatens to do an act which would harm that other person,
   (b) he does or threatens to do the act knowing or believing that the person harmed or threatened to be harmed ('the victim'), or some other person, has assisted in an investigation into an offence or has given evidence or particular evidence in proceedings for an offence, or has acted as a juror or concurred in a particular verdict in proceedings for an offence, and
   (c) he does or threatens to do it because of that knowledge or belief.

(3) For the purposes of subsections (1) and (2) it is immaterial that the act is or would be done, or that the threat is made—
   (a) otherwise than in the presence of the victim, or
   (b) to a person other than the victim.

(4) The harm that may be done or threatened may be financial as well as physical (whether to the person or a person's property) and similarly as respects an intimidatory act which consists of threats.

(5) The intention required by subsection (1)(c) and the motive required by subsection (2)(c) above need not be the only or the predominating intention or motive with which the act is done or, in the case of subsection (2), threatened.

(6) A person guilty of an offence under this section shall be liable—
   (a) on conviction on indictment, to imprisonment for a term not exceeding five years or a fine or both;
   (b) on summary conviction, to imprisonment for a term not exceeding six months or a fine not exceeding the statutory maximum or both.

(7) If, in proceedings against a person for an offence under subsection (1) above, it is proved that he did an act falling within paragraph (a) with the knowledge or belief required by paragraph (b), he shall be presumed, unless the contrary is proved, to have done the act with the intention required by paragraph (c) of that subsection.

(8) If, in proceedings against a person for an offence under subsection (2) above, it is proved that within the relevant period—
   (a) he did an act which harmed, and was intended to harm, another person, or
   (b) intending to cause another person fear of harm, he threatened to do an act which would harm that other person,
   and that he did the act, or (as the case may be) threatened to do the act, with the knowledge or belief required by paragraph (b), he shall be presumed, unless the contrary is proved, to have done the act or (as the case may be) threatened to do the act with the motive required by paragraph (c) of that subsection.

(9) In this section—
   'investigation into an offence' means such an investigation by the police or other person charged with the duty of investigating offences or charging offenders;
   'offence' includes an alleged or suspected offence;
   'potential', in relation to a juror, means a person who has been summoned for jury service at the court at which proceedings for the offence are pending;
   'public prosecutor', 'requisition' and 'written charge' have the same meaning as in section 29 of the Criminal Justice Act 2003;
   'the relevant period'—
   (a) in relation to a witness or juror in any proceedings for an offence, means the period beginning with the institution of the proceedings and ending with the first anniversary of the conclusion of the trial or, if there is an appeal or reference under sections 9 or 11 of the Criminal Appeal Act 1995, of the conclusion of the appeal;
   (b) in relation to a person who has, or is believed by the accused to have, assisted in an investigation into an offence, but was not also a witness in proceedings for an offence, means the period of one year beginning with any act of his, or any act believed by the accused to be an act of his, assisting in the investigation; and

(c) in relation to a person who both has, or is believed by the accused to have, assisted in the investigation into an offence and was a witness in proceedings for the offence, means the period beginning with any act of his, or any act believed by the accused to be an act of his, assisting in the investigation and ending with the anniversary mentioned in paragraph (a) above.

68. Offence of aggravated trespass

(1) A person commits the offence of aggravated trespass if he trespasses on land in the open air and, in relation to any lawful activity which persons are engaging in or are about to engage in on that or adjoining land in the open air, does there anything which is intended by him to have the effect—
   (a) of intimidating those persons or any of them so as to deter them or any of them from engaging in that activity,
   (b) of obstructing that activity, or
   (c) of disrupting that activity.

(1A)…

(2) Activity on any occasion on the part of a person or persons on land is 'lawful' for the purposes of this section if he or they may engage in the activity on the land on that occasion without committing an offence or trespassing on the land.

(3) A person guilty of an offence under this section is liable on summary conviction to imprisonment for a term not exceeding three months or a fine not exceeding level 4 on the standard scale, or both.

(5) In this section 'land' does not include—
   (a) the highways and roads excluded from the application of section 61 by paragraph (b) of the definition of 'land' in subsection (9) of that section; or
   …

69. Powers to remove persons committing or participating in aggravated trespass

(1) If the senior police officer present at the scene reasonably believes—
   (a) that a person is committing, has committed or intends to commit the offence of aggravated trespass on land; or
   (b) that two or more persons are trespassing on land and are present there with the common purpose of intimidating persons so as to deter them from engaging in a lawful activity or of obstructing or disrupting a lawful activity,
   he may direct that person or (as the case may be) those persons (or any of them) to leave the land.

(2) A direction under subsection (1) above, if not communicated to the persons referred to in subsection (1) by the police officer giving the direction, may be communicated to them by any constable at the scene.

(3) If a person knowing that a direction under subsection (1) above has been given which applies to him—
   (a) fails to leave the land as soon as practicable, or
   (b) having left again enters the land as a trespasser within the period of three months beginning with the day on which the direction was given,
   he commits an offence and is liable on summary conviction to imprisonment for a term not exceeding three months or a fine not exceeding level 4 on the standard scale, or both.

(4) In proceedings for an offence under subsection (3) it is a defence for the accused to show—
   (a) that he was not trespassing on the land, or
   (b) that he had a reasonable excuse for failing to leave the land as soon as practicable or, as the case may be, for again entering the land as a trespasser.

(6) In this section 'lawful activity' and 'land' have the same meaning as in section 68.

CRIMINAL LAW ACT 1967

1. Abolition of distinction between felony and misdemeanour
(1) All distinctions between felony and misdemeanour are hereby abolished.
(2) Subject to the provisions of this Act, on all matters on felony and which a distinction has previously been made between felony and misdemeanour, including mode of trial, the law and practice in relation to all offences cognisable under the law of England and Wales (including piracy) shall be the law and practice applicable at the commencement of this Act in relation to misdemeanour.

3. Use of force in making arrest, etc.
(1) A person may use such force as is reasonable in the circumstances in the prevention of crime, or in effecting or assisting in the lawful arrest of offenders or suspected offenders or of persons unlawfully at large.
(2) Subsection (1) above shall replace the rules of the common law on the question when force used for a purpose mentioned in the subsection is justified by that purpose.

4. Penalties for assisting offenders
(1) Where a person has committed a relevant offence, any other person who, knowing or believing him to be guilty of the offence or of some other relevant offence, does without lawful authority or reasonable excuse any act with intent to impede his apprehension or prosecution shall be guilty of an offence.
(1A) In this section and section 5 below, 'relevant offence' means—
   (a) an offence for which the sentence is fixed by law;
   (b) an offence for which a person of 18 years or over (not previously convicted) may be sentenced to imprisonment for a term of five years (or might so be sentenced but for the restrictions imposed by section 33 Magistrates Court Act 1980).
(2) If on the trial of an indictment for a relevant offence the jury are satisfied that the offence charged (or some other offence of which the accused might on that charge be found guilty) was committed, but find the accused not guilty of it, they may find him guilty of any offence under subsection (1) above of which they are satisfied that he is guilty in relation to the offence charged (or that other offence).
(3) A person committing an offence under subsection (1) above with intent to impede another person's apprehension or prosecution shall on conviction on indictment be liable to imprisonment according to the gravity of the other person's offence, as follows—
   (a) if that offence is one for which the sentence is fixed by law, he shall be liable to imprisonment for not more than ten years;
   (b) if it is one for which a person (not previously convicted) may be sentenced to imprisonment for a term of fourteen years, he shall be liable to imprisonment for not more than seven years;
   (c) if it is not one included above but is one for which a person (not previously convicted) may be sentenced to imprisonment for a term of ten years he shall be liable to imprisonment for not more than five years;
   (d) in any other case, he shall be liable to imprisonment for not more than three years.
(4) No proceedings shall be instituted for an offence under subsection (1) above except by or with the consent of the Director of Public Prosecutions.

5. Penalties for concealing or giving false information
(1) Where a person has committed a relevant offence, any other person who knowing or believing that the offence or some other relevant offence has been committed, and that he has information which might be of material assistance in securing the prosecution or conviction of an offender for it accepts or agrees to accept for not disclosing that information any consideration other than the making good of loss or injury caused by the offence, or the making of reasonable compensation for that loss or injury, shall be liable on conviction on indictment to imprisonment for not more than two years.

(2) Where a person causes any wasteful employment of the police by knowingly making to any person a false report tending to show that an offence has been committed, or to give rise to apprehension for the safety of any persons or property, or tending to show that he has information material to any police inquiry, he shall be liable on summary conviction to imprisonment for not more than six months or to a fine of not more than level 4 on the standard scale or to both.

(3) No proceedings shall be instituted for an offence under this section except by or with the consent of the Director of Public Prosecutions.

(5) The compounding of an offence other than treason shall not be an offence otherwise than under this section.

6. Trial of offences

(1) Where a person is arraigned on an indictment—
   (a) he shall in all cases be entitled to make a plea of not guilty in addition to any demurrer or special plea;
   (b) he may plead not guilty of the offence specifically charged in the indictment but guilty of another offence of which he might be found guilty on that indictment;
   (c) if he stands mute of malice or will not answer directly to the indictment, the court may order a plea of not guilty to be entered on his behalf, and he shall then be treated as having pleaded not guilty.

(2) On an indictment for murder a person found not guilty of murder may be found guilty—
   (a) of manslaughter, or of causing grievous bodily harm with intent to do so; or
   (b) of any offence of which he may be found guilty under an enactment specifically so providing, or under section 4(2) of this Act; or
   (c) of an attempt to commit murder, or of an attempt to commit any other offence of which he might be found guilty;
   but may not be found guilty of any offence not included above.

(3) Where, on a person's trial on indictment for any offence except treason or murder, the jury find him not guilty of the offence specifically charged in the indictment, but the allegations in the indictment amount to or include (expressly or by implication) an allegation of another offence falling within the jurisdiction of the court of trial, the jury may find him guilty of that other offence or of an offence of which he could be found guilty on an indictment specifically charging that other offence.

(3A) For the purposes of subsection (3) above an offence falls within the jurisdiction of the court of trial if it is an offence to which section 40 of the Criminal Justice Act 1988 applies (power to join in indictment count for common assault etc), even if a count charging the offence is not included in the indictment.

(3B) A person convicted of an offence by virtue of subsection (3A) may only be dealt with for it in a manner in which a magistrates' court could have dealt with him.

(4) For purposes of subsection (3) above any allegation of an offence shall be taken as including an allegation of attempting to commit that offence; and where a person is charged on indictment with attempting to commit an offence or with any assault or other act preliminary to an offence, but not with the completed offence, then (subject to the discretion of the court to discharge the jury or otherwise act with a view to the preferment of an indictment for the completed offence) he may be convicted of the offence charged notwithstanding that he is shown to be guilty of the completed offence.

(5) Where a person arraigned on an indictment pleads not guilty of an offence charged in the indictment but guilty of some other offence of which he might be found guilty on that charge, and he is convicted on that plea of guilty without trial for the offence of which he has pleaded not guilty, then (whether or not the two offences are separately charged in distinct counts) his conviction of the one offence shall be an acquittal of the other.

(6) Any power to bring proceedings for an offence by criminal information in the High Court is hereby abolished.

(7) Subsections (1) to (3) above shall apply to an indictment containing more than one count as if each count were a separate indictment.

CRIMINAL LAW ACT 1977

1. The offence of conspiracy

(1) Subject to the following provisions of this Part of this Act, if a person agrees with any other person or persons that a course of conduct shall be pursued, if the agreement is carried out in accordance with their intentions, either—
   (a) will necessarily amount to or involve the commission of any offence or offences by one or more of the parties to the agreement, or
   (b) would do so but for the existence of facts which render the commission of the offence or any offences impossible, he is guilty of conspiracy to commit the offence or offences in question.

(2) Where liability for any offence may be incurred without knowledge on the part of the person committing it of any particular fact or circumstance necessary for the commission of the offence, a person shall nevertheless not be guilty of conspiracy to commit that offence by virtue of subsection (1) above unless he and at least one other party to the agreement intend or know that that fact or circumstance shall or will exist at the time when the conduct constituting the offence is to take place.

(4) In this Part of this Act 'offence' means an offence triable in England and Wales.

1A. Conspiracy to commit offences outside of the United Kingdom

(1) Where each of the following conditions is satisfied in the case of an agreement, this Part of this Act has effect in relation to the agreement as it has effect in relation to an agreement falling within section 1(1) above.

(2) The first condition is that the pursuit of the agreed course of conduct would at some stage involve—
   (a) an act by one or more of the parties, or
   (b) the happening of some other event, intended to take place in a country or territory outside the United Kingdom.

(3) The second condition is that that act or other event constitutes an offence under the law in force in that country or territory.

(4) The third condition is that the agreement would fall within section 1(1) above as an agreement relating to the commission of an offence but for the fact that the offence would not be an offence triable in England and Wales if committed in accordance with the parties' intentions.

(5) The fourth condition is that—
   (a) a party to the agreement, or a party's agent, did anything in England and Wales in relation to the agreement before its formation, or
   (b) a party to the agreement became a party in England and Wales (by joining it either in person or through an agent), or
   (c) a party to the agreement, or a party's agent, did or omitted anything in England and Wales in pursuance of the agreement.

(6) In the application of this Part of this Act to an agreement in the case of which each of the above conditions is satisfied, a reference to an offence is to be read as a reference to what would be the offence in question but for the fact that it is not an offence triable in England and Wales.

(7) Conduct punishable under the law in force in any country or territory is an offence under that law for the purposes of this section, however it is described in that law.

(8) Subject to subsection (9) below, the second condition is to be taken to be satisfied unless, not later than rules of court may provide, the defence serve on the prosecution a notice—
   (a) stating that, on the facts as alleged with respect to the agreed course of conduct, the condition is not in their opinion satisfied,
   (b) showing their grounds for that opinion, and
   (c) requiring the prosecution to show that it is satisfied.

(9) The court may permit the defence to require the prosecution to show that the second condition is satisfied without the prior service of a notice under subsection (8) above.

(10) In the Crown Court the question whether the second condition is satisfied shall be decided by the judge alone, and shall be treated as a question of law for the purposes of—
   (a) section 9(3) of the Criminal Justice Act 1987 (preparatory hearing in fraud cases), and
   (b) section 31(3) of the Criminal Procedure and Investigations Act 1996 (preparatory hearing in other cases).
(11) Any act done by means of a message (however communicated) is to be treated for the purposes of the fourth condition as done in England and Wales if the message is sent or received in England and Wales.
(12) In any proceedings in respect of an offence triable by virtue of this section, it is immaterial to guilt whether or not the accused was a British citizen at the time of any act or other event proof of which is required for conviction of the offence.
(13) References in any enactment, instrument or document (except those in this Part of this Act) to an offence of conspiracy to commit an offence include an offence triable in England and Wales as such a conspiracy by virtue of this section (without prejudice to subsection (6) above).
(14) Nothing in this section—
   (a) applies to an agreement entered into before the day on which the Criminal Justice (Terrorism and Conspiracy) Act 1998 was passed, or
   (b) imposes criminal liability on any person acting on behalf of, or holding office under, the Crown.

2. Exemptions from liability for conspiracy

(1) A person shall not by virtue of section 1 above be guilty of conspiracy to commit any offence if he is an intended victim of that offence.
(2) A person shall not by virtue of section 1 above be guilty of conspiracy to commit any offence or offences if the only other person or persons with whom he agrees are (both initially and at all times during the currency of the agreement) persons of any one or more of the following descriptions, that is to say—
   (a) his spouse or civil partner;
   (b) a person under the age of criminal responsibility; and
   (c) an intended victim of that offence or of each of those offences.
(3) A person is under the age of criminal responsibility for the purposes of subsection (2)(b) above so long as it is conclusively presumed, by virtue of section 50 of the Children and Young Persons Act 1933, that he cannot be guilty of any offence.

3. Penalties for conspiracy

(1) A person guilty by virtue of section 1 above of conspiracy to commit any offence or offences shall be liable on conviction on indictment—
   (a) in a case falling within subsection (2) or (3) below, to imprisonment for a term related in accordance with that subsection to the gravity of the offence or offences in question (referred to below in this section as the relevant offence or offences); and
   (b) in any other case, to a fine.
   Paragraph (b) above shall not be taken as prejudicing the application of section 163 of the Criminal Justice Act 2003 (general power of court to fine offender convicted on indictment) in a case falling within subsection (2) or (3) below.
(2) Where the relevant offence or any of the relevant offences is an offence of any of the following descriptions, that is to say—
   (a) murder, or any other offence the sentence for which is fixed by law;
   (b) an offence for which a sentence extending to imprisonment for life is provided; or
   (c) an indictable offence punishable with imprisonment for which no maximum term of imprisonment is provided,
   the person convicted shall be liable to imprisonment for life.
(3) Where in a case other than one to which subsection (2) above applies the relevant offence or any of the relevant offences is punishable with imprisonment, the person convicted shall be liable to imprisonment for a term not exceeding the maximum term provided for that offence or (where more than one such offence is in question) for any one of those offences (taking the longer or the longest term as the limit for the purposes of this section where the terms provided differ).

In the case of an offence triable either way the references above in this subsection to the maximum term provided for that offence are references to the maximum term so provided on conviction on indictment.

CRIMINAL PROCEDURE (INSANITY) ACT 1964

5. Powers to deal with persons not guilty by reason of insanity or unfit to plead etc.
(1) This section applies where—
   (a) a special verdict is returned that the accused is not guilty by reason of insanity; or
   (b) findings are recorded that the accused is under a disability and that he did the act or made the omission charged against him.
(2) The court shall make in respect of the accused—
   (a) a hospital order (with or without a restriction order); or
   (b) a supervision order; or
   (c) an order for his absolute discharge.
(3) Where—
   (a) the offence to which the special verdict or findings relate is an offence the sentence for which is fixed by law, and
   (b) the court have the power to make a hospital order,
   the court shall make a hospital order with a restriction order (whether or not they would have the power to make a restriction order apart from this subsection).
(4) In this section—
   'hospital order' has the meaning given to it in section 37 of the Mental Health Act 1983;
   'restriction order' has the meaning given to it in by section 41 of that Act;
   'supervision order' has the meaning given in Part 1 of Schedule 1A to this Act.

CRIMINAL PROCEDURE (INSANITY AND UNFITNESS TO PLEAD) ACT 1991

1. Acquittals on grounds of insanity
(1) A jury shall not return a special verdict under section 2 of the Trial of Lunatics Act 1883 (acquittal on ground of insanity) except on the written or oral evidence of two or more registered medical practitioners at least one of whom is duly approved.
(2) Subsections (2) and (3) of section 54 of the Mental Health Act 1983 ('the 1983 Act') shall have effect with respect to proof of the accused's mental condition for the purposes of the said section 2 as they have effect with respect to proof of an offender's mental condition for the purposes of section 37(2)(a) of that Act.

6. Interpretation etc.
(1) In this Act—
   'duly approved', in relation to a registered medical practitioner, means approved for the purposes of section 12 of the 1983 Act by the Secretary of State as having special experience in the diagnosis or treatment of mental disorder.

DANGEROUS DOGS ACT 1991

1. Dogs bred for fighting
(1) This section applies to—
   (a) any dog of the type known as the pit bull terrier;
   (b) any dog of the type known as the Japanese tosa; and
   (c) any dog of any type designated for the purposes of this section by an order of the Secretary of State, being a type appearing to him to be bred for fighting or to have the characteristics of a type bred for that purpose.
(2) No person shall—
   (a) breed, or breed from, a dog to which this section applies;
   (b) sell or exchange such a dog or offer, advertise or expose such a dog for sale or exchange;
   (c) make or offer to make a gift of such a dog or advertise or expose such a dog as a gift;
   (d) allow such a dog of which he is the owner or of which he is for the time being in charge to be in a public place without being muzzled and kept on a lead; or
   (e) abandon such a dog of which he is the owner or, being the owner or for the time being in charge of such a dog, allow it to stray.
   …
(7) Any person who contravenes this section is guilty of an offence and liable on summary conviction to imprisonment for a term not exceeding six months or a fine not exceeding level 5 on the standard scale or both except that a person who publishes an advertisement in contravention of subsection (2)(b) or (c)—
   (a) shall not on being convicted be liable to imprisonment if he shows that he published the advertisement to the order of someone else and did not himself devise it; and
   (b) shall not be convicted if, in addition, he shows that he did not know and had no reasonable cause to suspect that it related to a dog to which this section applies.

2. Other specially dangerous dogs
(1) If it appears to the Secretary of State that dogs of any type to which section 1 above does not apply present a serious danger to the public he may by order impose in relation to dogs of that type restrictions corresponding, with such modifications, if any, as he thinks appropriate, to all or any of those in subsection (2)(d) and (e) of that section.
(2) An order under this section may provide for exceptions from any restriction imposed by the order in such cases and subject to compliance with such conditions as are specified in the order.
(3) An order under this section may contain such supplementary or transitional provisions as the Secretary of State thinks necessary or expedient and may create offences punishable on summary conviction with imprisonment for a term not exceeding six months or a fine not exceeding level 5 on the standard scale or both.
(4) In determining whether to make an order under this section in relation to dogs of any type and, if so, what the provisions of the order should be, the Secretary of State shall consult with such persons or bodies as appear to him to have relevant knowledge or experience, including a body concerned with animal welfare, a body concerned with veterinary science and practice and a body concerned with breeds of dogs.

3. Keeping dogs under proper control
(1) If a dog is dangerously out of control in a public place—
   (a) the owner; and
   (b) if different, the person for the time being in charge of the dog,
   is guilty of an offence, or, if the dog while so out of control injures any person, an aggravated offence, under this subsection.
(2) In proceedings for an offence under subsection (1) above against a person who is the owner of a dog but was not at the material time in charge of it, it shall be a defence for the accused to prove that the dog was at the material time in the charge of a person whom he reasonably believed to be a fit and proper person to be in charge of it.

(3) If the owner or, if different, the person for the time being in charge of a dog allows it to enter a place which is not a public place but where it is not permitted to be and while it is there—
   (a) it injures any person; or
   (b) there are grounds for reasonable apprehension that it will do so,
   he is guilty of an offence, or, if the dog injures any person, an aggravated offence, under this subsection.
(4) A person guilty of an offence under subsection (1) or (3) above other than an aggravated offence is liable on summary conviction to imprisonment for a term not exceeding six months or a fine not exceeding level 5 on the standard scale or both; and a person guilty of an aggravated offence under either of those subsections is liable—
   (a) on summary conviction, to imprisonment for a term not exceeding six months or a fine not exceeding the statutory maximum or both;
   (b) on conviction on indictment, to imprisonment for a term not exceeding two years or a fine or both.
(5) It is hereby declared for the avoidance of doubt that an order under section 2 of the Dogs Act 1871 (order on complaint that dog is dangerous and not kept under proper control)—
   (a) may be made whether or not the dog is shown to have injured any person; and
   (b) may specify the measures to be taken for keeping the dog under proper control, whether by muzzling, keeping on a lead, excluding it from specified places or otherwise.
(6) If it appears to a court on a complaint under section 2 of the said Act of 1871 that the dog to which the complaint relates is a male and would be less dangerous if neutered the court may under that section make an order requiring it to be neutered.
(7) The reference in section 1(3) of the Dangerous Dogs Act 1989 (penalties) to failing to comply with an order under section 2 of the said Act of 1871 to keep a dog under proper control shall include a reference to failing to comply with any other order made under that section; but no order shall be made under that section by virtue of subsection (6) above where the matters complained of arose before the coming into force of that subsection.

4. Destruction and disqualification orders

(1) Where a person is convicted of an offence under section 1 or 3(1) or (3) above or of an offence under an order made under section 2 above the court—
   (a) may order the destruction of any dog in respect of which the offence was committed and, subject to subsection (1A) below, shall do so in the case of an offence under section 1 or an aggravated offence under section 3(1) or (3) above; and
   (b) may order the offender to be disqualified, for such period as the court thinks fit, for having custody of a dog.
(1A) Nothing in subsection (1)(a) above shall require the court to order the destruction of a dog if the court is satisfied—
   (a) that the dog would not constitute a danger to public safety; and
   (b) where the dog was born before 30th November 1991 and is subject to the prohibition in section 1(3) above, that there is a good reason why the dog has not been exempted from that prohibition.
(2) Where a court makes an order under subsection (1)(a) above for the destruction of a dog owned by a person other than the offender ..., the owner may appeal to the Crown Court against the order.
(3) A dog shall not be destroyed pursuant to an order under subsection (1)(a) above—
   (a) until the end of the period for giving notice of appeal against the conviction or against the order; and
   (b) if notice of appeal is given within that period, until the appeal is determined or withdrawn,
   unless the offender and, in a case to which subsection (2) above applies, the owner of the dog give notice to the court that made the order that there is to be no appeal.
(4) Where a court makes an order under subsection (1)(a) above it may—
   (a) appoint a person to undertake the destruction of the dog and require any person having custody of it to deliver it up for that purpose; and
   (b) order the offender to pay such sum as the court may determine to be the reasonable expenses of destroying the dog and of keeping it pending its destruction.

(5) Any sum ordered to be paid under subsection (4)(b) above shall be treated for the purposes of enforcement as if it were a fine imposed on conviction.

(6) Any person who is disqualified for having custody of a dog by virtue of an order under subsection (1)(b) above may, at any time after the end of the period of one year beginning with the date of the order, apply to the court that made it (or a magistrates' court acting in the same local justice area as that court) for a direction terminating the disqualification.

(7) On an application under subsection (6) above the court may—
   (a) having regard to the applicant's character, his conduct since the disqualification was imposed and any other circumstances of the case, grant or refuse the application; and
   (b) order the applicant to pay all or any part of the costs of the application;
   and where an application in respect of an order is refused no further application in respect of that order shall be entertained if made before the end of the period of one year beginning with the date of the refusal.

(8) Any person who—
   (a) has custody of a dog in contravention of an order under subsection (1)(b) above; or
   (b) fails to comply with a requirement imposed on him under subsection (4)(a) above,
   is guilty of an offence and liable on summary conviction to a fine not exceeding level 5 on the standard scale.

5. Seizure, entry of premises and evidence

...

(5) If in any proceedings it is alleged by the prosecution that a dog is one to which section 1 or an order under section 2 above applies it shall be presumed that it is such a dog unless the contrary is shown by the accused by such evidence as the court considers sufficient; and the accused shall not be permitted to adduce such evidence unless he has given the prosecution notice of his intention to do so not later than the fourteenth day before that on which the evidence is to be adduced.

7. Muzzling and leads

(1) In this Act—
   (a) references to a dog being muzzled are to its being securely fitted with a muzzle sufficient to prevent it biting any person; and
   (b) references to its being kept on a lead are to its being securely held on a lead by a person who is not less than sixteen years old.
   ...

10. Short title, interpretation, commencement and extent

...

(2) In this Act—
   'advertisement' includes any means of bringing a matter to the attention of the public and 'advertise' shall be construed accordingly;
   'public place' means any street, road or other place (whether or not enclosed) to which the public have or are permitted to have access whether for payment or otherwise and includes the common parts of a building containing two or more separate dwellings.

(3) For the purposes of this Act a dog shall be regarded as dangerously out of control on any occasion on which there are grounds for reasonable apprehension that it will injure any person, whether or not it actually does so, but references to a dog injuring a person or there being grounds for reasonable apprehension that it will do so do not include references to any case in which the dog is being used for a lawful purpose by a constable or a person in the service of the Crown.

DEALING IN CULTURAL OBJECTS ACT 2003

1. Offence of dealing in tainted cultural objects
(1) A person is guilty of an offence if he dishonestly deals in a cultural object that is tainted, knowing or believing that the object is tainted.
(2) It is immaterial whether he knows or believes that the object is a cultural object.
(3) A person guilty of the offence is liable—
   (a) on conviction on indictment, to imprisonment for a term not exceeding seven years or a fine (or both),
   (b) on summary conviction, to imprisonment for a term not exceeding six months or a fine not exceeding the statutory maximum (or both).

2. Meaning of 'tainted cultural object'
(1) 'Cultural object' means an object of historical, architectural or archaeological interest.
(2) A cultural object is tainted if, after the commencement of this Act—
   (a) a person removes the object in a case falling within subsection (4) or he excavates the object, and
   (b) the removal or excavation constitutes an offence.
(3) It is immaterial whether—
   (a) the removal or excavation was done in the United Kingdom or elsewhere,
   (b) the offence is committed under the law of a part of the United Kingdom or under the law of any other country or territory.
(4) An object is removed in a case falling within this subsection if—
   (a) it is removed from a building or structure of historical, architectural or archaeological interest where the object has at any time formed part of the building or structure, or
   (b) it is removed from a monument of such interest.
(5) 'Monument' means—
   (a) any work, cave or excavation,
   (b) any site comprising the remains of any building or structure or of any work, cave or excavation,
   (c) any site comprising, or comprising the remains of, any vehicle, vessel, aircraft or other movable structure, or part of any such thing.
(6) 'Remains' includes any trace or sign of the previous existence of the thing in question.
(7) It is immaterial whether—
   (a) a building, structure or work is above or below the surface of the land,
   (b) a site is above or below water.
(8) This section has effect for the purposes of section 1.

3. Meaning of 'deals in'
(1) A person deals in an object if (and only if) he—
   (a) acquires, disposes of, imports or exports it,
   (b) agrees with another to do an act mentioned in paragraph (a), or
   (c) makes arrangements under which another person does such an act or under which another person agrees with a third person to do such an act.
(2) 'Acquires' means buys, hires, borrows or accepts.
(3) 'Disposes of' means sells, lets on hire, lends or gives.
(4) In relation to agreeing or arranging to do an act, it is immaterial whether the act is agreed or arranged to take place in the United Kingdom or elsewhere.
(5) This section has effect for the purposes of section 1.

5. Offences by bodies corporate
(1) If an offence under section 1 committed by a body corporate is proved—
   (a) to have been committed with the consent or connivance of an officer, or

(b) to be attributable to any neglect on his part,
he (as well as the body corporate) is guilty of the offence and liable to be proceeded against and punished accordingly.
(2) 'Officer', in relation to a body corporate, means—
   (a) a director, manager, secretary or other similar officer of the body,
   (b) a person purporting to act in any such capacity.
(3) If the affairs of a body corporate are managed by its members, subsection (1) applies in relation to the acts and defaults of a member in connection with his functions of management as if he were a director of the body.

DOGS ACT 1871

2. Dangerous dogs may be destroyed
Any court of summary jurisdiction may take cognizance of a complaint that a dog is dangerous, and not kept under proper control, and if it appears to the court having cognizance of such complaint that such dog is dangerous, the court may make an order in a summary way directing the dog to be kept by the owner under proper control or destroyed, …

DOMESTIC VIOLENCE, CRIME AND VICTIMS ACT 2004

5. The offence
(1) A person ('D') is guilty of an offence if—
   (a) a child or vulnerable adult ('V') dies as a result of the unlawful act of a person who—
      (i) was a member of the same household as V, and
      (ii) had frequent contact with him,
   (b) D was such a person at the time of that act,
   (c) at that time there was a significant risk of serious physical harm being caused to V by the unlawful act of such a person, and
   (d) either D was the person whose act caused V's death or—
      (i) D was, or ought to have been, aware of the risk mentioned in paragraph (c),
      (ii) D failed to take such steps as he could reasonably have been expected to take to protect V from the risk, and
      (iii) the act occurred in circumstances of the kind that D foresaw or ought to have foreseen.
(2) The prosecution does not have to prove whether it is the first alternative in subsection (1)(d) or the second (sub-paragraphs (i) to (iii)) that applies.
(3) If D was not the mother or father of V—
   (a) D may not be charged with an offence under this section if he was under the age of 16 at the time of the act that caused V's death;
   (b) for the purposes of subsection (1)(d)(ii) D could not have been expected to take any such step as is referred to there before attaining that age.
(4) For the purposes of this section—
   (a) a person is to be regarded as a 'member' of a particular household, even if he does not live in that household, if he visits it so often and for such periods of time that it is reasonable to regard him as a member of it;
   (b) where V lived in different households at different times, 'the same household as V' refers to the household in which V was living at the time of the act that caused V's death.
(5) For the purposes of this section an 'unlawful' act is one that—
   (a) constitutes an offence, or

(b) would constitute an offence but for being the act of—
   (i) a person under the age of ten, or
   (ii) a person entitled to rely on a defence of insanity.
Paragraph (b) does not apply to an act of D.
(6) In this section—
'act' includes a course of conduct and also includes omission;
'child' means a person under the age of 16;
'serious' harm means harm that amounts to grievous bodily harm for the purposes of the Offences against the Person Act 1861;
'vulnerable adult' means a person aged 16 or over whose ability to protect himself from violence, abuse or neglect is significantly impaired through physical or mental disability or illness, through old age or otherwise.
(7) A person guilty of an offence under this section is liable on conviction on indictment to imprisonment for a term not exceeding 14 years or to a fine, or to both.

EDUCATION ACT 1996

4 Schools: general
(1) In this Act 'school' means an educational institution which is outside the further education sector and the higher education sector and is an institution for providing any one or more of the following—
   (a) primary education,
   (b) education which is secondary education by virtue of section 2(2)(a), or
   (c) full-time education suitable to the requirements of persons who are over compulsory school age but under the age of 19,
   whether or not the institution also provides part-time education suitable to the requirements of junior pupils, further education or secondary education not within paragraph (b).
(2) For the purposes of this Act an educational institution that would fall within subsection (1) but for the fact that it provides part-time rather than full-time education shall nevertheless be treated as a school if that part-time education is provided under arrangements made under section 19(1) (pupil referral units).
(3) For the purposes of this Act an institution is outside the further education sector if it is not—
   (a) an institution conducted by a further education corporation established under section 15 or 16 of the Further and Higher Education Act 1992, or
   (b) a designated institution for the purposes of Part I of that Act (defined in section 28(4) of that Act);
   and references to institutions within that sector shall be construed accordingly.
(4) For the purposes of this Act an institution is outside the higher education sector if it is not—
   (a) a university receiving financial support under section 65 of that Act,
   (b) an institution conducted by a higher education corporation within the meaning of that Act, or
   (c) a designated institution for the purposes of Part II of that Act (defined in section 72(3) of that Act);
   and references to institutions within that sector shall be construed accordingly.

EXPLOSIVES ACT 1875

3. Substances to which this Act applies
This Act shall apply to gunpowder and other explosives as defined by this section.

The term 'explosive' in this Act—
(1) Means gunpowder, nitro-glycerine, dynamite, gun-cotton, blasting powders, fulminate of mercury or of other metals, coloured fires, and every other substance, whether similar to those above-mentioned or not, used or manufactured with a view to produce a practical effect by explosion or a pyrotechnical effect; and
(2) Includes fog-lights, fireworks, fuzes, percussion caps, detonators, cartridges, ammunition of all descriptions, and every adaptation or preparation of an explosive as above defined.

EXPLOSIVE SUBSTANCES ACT 1883

2. Causing explosion likely to endanger life or property
A person who in the United Kingdom or (being a citizen of the United Kingdom and Colonies) in the Republic of Ireland unlawfully and maliciously causes by any explosive substance an explosion of a nature likely to endanger life or to cause serious injury to property shall, whether any injury to person or property has been actually caused or not, be guilty of an offence and on conviction on indictment shall be liable to imprisonment for life.

3. Attempt to cause explosion, or making or keeping explosive with intent to endanger life or property
(1) A person who in the United Kingdom or a dependency or (being a citizen of the United Kingdom and Colonies) elsewhere unlawfully and maliciously—
   (a) does any act with intent to cause, or conspires to cause, by an explosive substance an explosion of a nature likely to endanger life, or cause serious injury to property, whether in the United Kingdom or elsewhere, or
   (b) makes or has in his possession or under his control an explosive substance with intent by means thereof to endanger life, or cause serious injury to property, whether in the United Kingdom or elsewhere, or to enable any other person so to do,
   shall, whether any explosion does or does not take place, and whether any injury to person or property is actually caused or not, be guilty of an offence and on conviction on indictment shall be liable to imprisonment for life, and the explosive substance shall be forfeited.
(2) In this section 'dependency' means the Channel Islands, the Isle of Man and any colony, other than a colony for whose external relations a country other than the United Kingdom is responsible.

4. Punishment for making or possession of explosive under suspicious circumstances
(1) Any person who makes or knowingly has in his possession or under his control any explosive substance, under such circumstances as to give rise to a reasonable suspicion that he is not making it or does not have it in his possession or under his control for a lawful object, shall, unless he can show that he made it or had it in his possession or under his control for a lawful object, be guilty of felony, and, on conviction, shall be liable to penal servitude for a term not exceeding fourteen years, or to imprisonment for a term not exceeding two years, and the explosive substance shall be forfeited.
(2) In any proceeding against any person for a crime under this section, such person and his wife, or husband, as the case may be, may, if such person thinks fit, be called, sworn, examined, and cross-examined as an ordinary witness in the case.

5. Punishment of accessories

Any person who within or (being a subject of Her Majesty) without Her Majesty's dominions by the supply of or solicitation for money, the providing of premises, the supply of materials, or in any manner whatsoever, procures, counsels, aids, abets, or is accessory to, the commission of any crime under this Act, shall be guilty of felony, and shall be liable to be tried and punished for that crime, as if he had been guilty as a principal.

9. Definitions

(1) In this Act, unless the context otherwise requires—

the expression 'explosive substance' shall be deemed to include any materials for making any explosive substance; also any apparatus, machine, implement, or materials used, or intended to be used, or adapted for causing, or aiding in causing, any explosion in or with any explosive substance; also any part of any such apparatus, machine, or implement.

The expression 'Attorney General' means Her Majesty's Attorney General for England or Ireland, as the case may be ...

FEMALE GENITAL MUTILATION ACT 2003

1. Offence of female genital mutilation

(1) A person is guilty of an offence if he excises, infibulates or otherwise mutilates the whole or any part of a girl's labia majora, labia minora or clitoris.
(2) But no offence is committed by an approved person who performs—
    (a) a surgical operation on a girl which is necessary for her physical or mental health, or
    (b) a surgical operation on a girl who is in any stage of labour, or has just given birth, for purposes connected with the labour or birth.
(3) The following are approved persons—
    (a) in relation to an operation falling within subsection (2)(a), a registered medical practitioner,
    (b) in relation to an operation falling within subsection (2)(b), a registered medical practitioner, a registered midwife or a person undergoing a course of training with a view to becoming such a practitioner or midwife.
(4) There is also no offence committed by a person who—
    (a) performs a surgical operation falling within subsection (2)(a) or (b) outside the United Kingdom, and
    (b) in relation to such an operation exercises functions corresponding to those of an approved person.
(5) For the purpose of determining whether an operation is necessary for the mental health of a girl it is immaterial whether she or any other person believes that the operation is required as a matter of custom or ritual.

2. Offence of assisting a girl to mutilate her own genitalia

A person is guilty of an offence if he aids, abets, counsels or procures a girl to excise, infibulate or otherwise mutilate the whole or any part of her own labia majora, labia minora or clitoris.

3. Offence of assisting a non-UK person to mutilate overseas a girl's genitalia

(1) A person is guilty of an offence if he aids, abets, counsels or procures a person who is not a United Kingdom national or permanent United Kingdom resident to do a relevant act of female genital mutilation outside the United Kingdom.
(2) An act is a relevant act of female genital mutilation if—
    (a) it is done in relation to a United Kingdom national or permanent United Kingdom resident, and
    (b) it would, if done by such a person, constitute an offence under section 1.
(3) But no offence is committed if the relevant act of female genital mutilation—
    (a) is a surgical operation falling within section 1(2)(a) or (b), and

(b) is performed by a person who, in relation to such an operation, is an approved person or exercises functions corresponding to those of an approved person.

4. Extension of sections 1 to 3 to extra-territorial acts
(1) Sections 1 to 3 extend to any act done outside the United Kingdom by a United Kingdom national or permanent United Kingdom resident.
(2) If an offence under this Act is committed outside the United Kingdom—
   (a) proceedings may be taken, and
   (b) the offence may for incidental purposes be treated as having been committed, in any place in England and Wales or Northern Ireland.

5. Penalties for offences
A person guilty of an offence under this Act is liable—
(a) on conviction on indictment, to imprisonment for a term not exceeding 14 years or a fine (or both),
(b) on summary conviction, to imprisonment for a term not exceeding six months or a fine not exceeding the statutory maximum (or both).

6. Definitions
(1) 'Girl' includes woman.
(2) A United Kingdom national is an individual who is—
   (a) a British citizen, a British overseas territories citizen, a British National (Overseas) or a British Overseas citizen,
   (b) a person who under the British Nationality Act 1981 is a British subject, or
   (c) a British protected person within the meaning of that Act.
(3) A permanent United Kingdom resident is an individual who is settled in the United Kingdom (within the meaning of the Immigration Act 1971).
(4) This section has effect for the purposes of this Act.

FINANCE ACT 2000

144. Offence of fraudulent evasion of income tax
(1) A person commits an offence if he is knowingly concerned in the fraudulent evasion of income tax by him or any other person.
(2) A person guilty of an offence under this section is liable—
   (a) on summary conviction, to imprisonment for a term not exceeding six months or a fine not exceeding the statutory maximum, or both;
   (b) on conviction on indictment, to imprisonment for a term not exceeding seven years or a fine, or both.
(3) This section applies to things done or omitted on or after 1st January 2001.

FIREARMS ACT 1968

1. Requirement of firearm certificate
(1) Subject to any exemption under this Act, it is an offence for a person—
   (a) to have in his possession, or to purchase or acquire, a firearm to which this section applies without holding a firearm certificate in force at the time, or otherwise than as authorised by such a certificate;
   (b) to have in his possession, or to purchase or acquire, any ammunition to which this section applies without holding a firearm certificate in force at the time, or otherwise than as

authorised by such a certificate, or in quantities in excess of those so authorised.
(2) It is an offence for a person to fail to comply with a condition subject to which a firearm certificate is held by him.
(3) This section applies to every firearm except—
    (a) a shot gun within the meaning of this Act, that is to say a smooth-bore gun (not being an air gun) which—
        (i) has a barrel not less than 24 inches in length and does not have any barrel with a bore exceeding 2 inches in diameter;
        (ii) either has no magazine or has a non-detachable magazine incapable of holding more than two cartridges; and
        (iii) is not a revolver gun; and
    (b) an air weapon (that is to say, an air rifle, air gun or air pistol which does not fall within section 5(1) and which is not of a type declared by rules made by the Secretary of State under section 53 of this Act to be specially dangerous).
(3A) A gun which has been adapted to have such a magazine as is mentioned in subsection (3)(a)(ii) above shall not be regarded as falling within that provision unless the magazine bears a mark approved by the Secretary of State for denoting that fact and that mark has been made, and the adaptation has been certified in writing as having been carried out in a manner approved by him, either by one of the two companies mentioned in section 58(1) of this Act or by such other person as may be approved by him for that purpose.
(4) This section applies to any ammunition for a firearm, except the following articles, namely—
    (a) cartridges containing five or more shot, none of which exceeds ·36 inch in diameter;
    (b) ammunition for an air gun, air rifle or air pistol; and
    (c) blank cartridges not more than one inch in diameter measured immediately in front of the rim or cannelure of the base of the cartridge.

2. Requirement of certificate for possession of shot guns

(1) Subject to any exemption under this Act, it is an offence for a person to have in his possession, or to purchase or acquire, a shot gun without holding a certificate under this Act authorising him to possess shot guns.
(2) It is an offence for a person to fail to comply with a condition subject to which a shot gun certificate is held by him.

3. Business and other transactions with firearms and ammunition

(1) A person commits an offence if, by way of trade or business, he—
    (a) manufactures, sells, transfers, repairs, tests or proves any firearm or ammunition to which section 1 of this Act applies, or a shot gun; or
    (b) exposes for sale or transfer, or has in his possession for sale, transfer, repair, test or proof any such firearm or ammunition, or a shot gun,
    without being registered under this Act as a firearms dealer.
(2) It is an offence for a person to sell or transfer to any other person in the United Kingdom, other than a registered firearms dealer, any firearm or ammunition to which section 1 of this Act applies, or a shot gun, unless that other produces a firearm certificate authorising him to purchase or acquire it or, as the case may be, his shot gun certificate, or shows that he is by virtue of this Act entitled to purchase or acquire it without holding a certificate.
(3) It is an offence for a person to undertake the repair, test or proof of a firearm or ammunition to which section 1 of this Act applies, or of a shot gun, for any other person in the United Kingdom other than a registered firearms dealer as such, unless that other produces or causes to be produced a firearm certificate authorising him to have possession of the firearm or ammunition or, as the case may be, his shot gun certificate, or shows that he is by virtue of this Act entitled to have possession of it without holding a certificate.
(4) Subsections (1) to (3) above have effect subject to any exemption under subsequent provisions of this Part of this Act.
(5) A person commits an offence if, with a view to purchasing or acquiring, or procuring the repair, test or proof of, any firearm or ammunition to which section 1 of this Act applies, or a shot gun, he produces a false certificate or a certificate in which any false entry has been made, or

personates a person to whom a certificate has been granted, or knowingly or recklessly makes a statement false in any material particular.
(6) It is an offence for a pawnbroker to take in pawn any firearm or ammunition to which section 1 of this Act applies, or a shot gun.

4. Conversion of weapons

(1) Subject to this section, it is an offence to shorten the barrel of a shot gun to a length less than 24 inches.
(2) It is not an offence under subsection (1) above for a registered firearms dealer to shorten the barrel of a shot gun for the sole purpose of replacing a defective part of the barrel so as to produce a barrel not less than 24 inches in length.
(3) It is an offence for a person other than a registered firearms dealer to convert into a firearm anything which, though having the appearance of being a firearm, is so constructed as to be incapable of discharging any missile through its barrel.
(4) A person who commits an offence under section 1 of this Act by having in his possession, or purchasing or acquiring, a shotgun which has been shortened contrary to subsection (1) above or a firearm which has been converted as mentioned in subsection (3) above (whether by a registered firearms dealer or not), without holding a firearm certificate authorising him to have it in his possession, or to purchase or acquire it, shall be treated for the purposes of provisions of this Act relating to the punishment of offences as committing that offence in an aggravated form.

5. Weapons subject to general prohibition

(1) A person commits an offence if, without the authority of the Defence Council ... he has in his possession, or purchases or acquires, or manufactures, sells or transfers—
   (a) any firearm which is so designed or adapted that two or more missiles can be successively discharged without repeated pressure on the trigger;
   (ab) any self-loading or pump-action rifled gun other than one which is chambered for .22 rim-fire cartridges;
   (aba) any firearm which either has a barrel less than 30 centimetres in length or is less than 60 centimetres in length overall, other than an air weapon, ... a muzzle-loading gun or a firearm designed as signalling apparatus;
   (ac) any self-loading or pump-action smooth-bore gun which is not an air weapon or chambered for .22 rim-fire cartridges and either has a barrel less than 24 inches in length or ... is less than 40 inches in length overall;
   (ad) any smooth-bore revolver gun other than one which is chambered for 9mm rim-fire cartridges or a muzzle-loading gun;
   (ae) any rocket launcher, or any mortar, for projecting a stabilised missile, other than a launcher or mortar designed for line-throwing or pyrotechnic purposes or as signalling apparatus;
   (af) any air rifle, air gun or air pistol which uses, or is designed or adapted for use with, a self-contained gas cartridge system;
   (b) any weapon of whatever description designed or adapted for the discharge of any noxious liquid, gas or other thing; and
   (c) any cartridge with a bullet designed to explode on or immediately before impact, any ammunition containing or designed or adapted to contain any such noxious thing as is mentioned in paragraph (b) above and, if capable of being used with a firearm of any description, any grenade, bomb (or other like missile), or rocket or shell designed to explode as aforesaid.
(1A) Subject to section 5A of this Act, a person commits an offence if, without the authority of the Secretary of State he has in his possession, or purchases or acquires, or sells or transfers—
   (a) any firearm which is disguised as another object;
   (b) any rocket or ammunition not falling within paragraph (c) of subsection (1) of this section which consists in or incorporates a missile designed to explode on or immediately before impact and is for military use;
   (c) any launcher or other projecting apparatus not falling within paragraph (ae) of that subsection which is designed to be used with any rocket or ammunition falling within

paragraph (b) above or with ammunition which would fall within that paragraph but for its being ammunition falling within paragraph (c) of that subsection;
(d) any ammunition for military use which consists in or incorporates a missile designed so that a substance contained in the missile will ignite on or immediately before impact;
(e) any ammunition for military use which consists in or incorporates a missile designed, on account of its having a jacket and hard-core, to penetrate armour plating, armour screening or body armour;
(f) any ammunition which incorporates a missile designed or adapted to expand on impact;
(g) anything which is designed to be projected as a missile from any weapon and is designed to be, or has been, incorporated in—
   (i) any ammunition falling within any of the preceding paragraphs; or
   (ii) any ammunition which would fall within any of those paragraphs but for its being specified in subsection (1) of this section.
(2) The weapons and ammunition specified in subsections (1) and (1A) of this section (including, in the case of ammunition, any missiles falling within subsection (1A)(g) of this section) are referred to in this Act as 'prohibited weapons' and 'prohibited ammunition' respectively.
(3) An authority given to a person by the Secretary of State … under this section shall be in writing and be subject to conditions specified therein.
…
(5) It is an offence for a person to whom an authority is given under this section to fail to comply with any condition of the authority.
…
(7) For the purposes of this section and section 5A of this Act—
(a) any rocket or ammunition which is designed to be capable of being used with a military weapon shall be taken to be for military use;
(b) references to a missile designed so that a substance contained in the missile will ignite on or immediately before impact include references to any missile containing a substance that ignites on exposure to air; and
(c) references to a missile's expanding on impact include references to its deforming in any predictable manner on or immediately after impact.
(8) For the purposes of subsection (1)(aba) and (ac) above, any detachable, folding, retractable or other movable butt-stock shall be disregarded in measuring the length of any firearm.
(9) Any reference in this section to a muzzle-loading gun is a reference to a gun which is designed to be loaded at the muzzle end of the barrel or chamber with a loose charge and a separate ball (or other missile).

5A. Exemptions from requirement of authority under section 5

(1) Subject to subsection (2) below, the authority of the Secretary of State … shall not be required by virtue of subsection (1A) of section 5 of this Act for any person to have in his possession, or to purchase, acquire, sell or transfer, any prohibited weapon or ammunition if he is authorised by a certificate under this Act to possess, purchase or acquire that weapon or ammunition subject to a condition that he does so only for the purpose of its being kept or exhibited as part of a collection.
(2) No sale or transfer may be made under subsection (1) above except to a person who—
(a) produces the authority of the Secretary of State … under section 5 of this Act for his purchase or acquisition; or
(b) shows that he is, under this section or a licence under the Schedule to the Firearms (Amendment) Act 1988 (museums etc.), entitled to make the purchase or acquisition without the authority of the Secretary of State.
(3) The authority of the Secretary of State … shall not be required by virtue of subsection (1A) of section 5 of this Act for any person to have in his possession, or to purchase or acquire, any prohibited weapon or ammunition if his possession, purchase or acquisition is exclusively in connection with the carrying on of activities in respect of which—
(a) that person; or
(b) the person on whose behalf he has possession, or makes the purchase or acquisition,

is recognised, for the purposes of the law of another member State relating to firearms, as a collector of firearms or a body concerned in the cultural or historical aspects of weapons.
(4) The authority of the Secretary of State ... shall not be required by virtue of subsection (1A) of section 5 of this Act for any person to have in his possession, or to purchase or acquire, or to sell or transfer, any expanding ammunition or the missile for any such ammunition if—
　(a) he is authorised by a firearm certificate or visitor's firearm permit to possess, or purchase or acquire, any expanding ammunition; and
　(b) the certificate or permit is subject to a condition restricting the use of any expanding ammunition to use in connection with any one or more of the following, namely—
　　(i) the lawful shooting of deer;
　　(ii) the shooting of vermin or, in the course of carrying on activities in connection with the management of any estate, other wildlife;
　　(iii) the humane killing of animals;
　　(iv) the shooting of animals for the protection of other animals or humans.
(5) The authority of the Secretary of State ... shall not be required by virtue of subsection (1A) of section 5 of this Act for any person to have in his possession any expanding ammunition or the missile for any such ammunition if—
　(a) he is entitled, under section 10 of this Act, to have a slaughtering instrument and the ammunition for it in his possession; and
　(b) the ammunition or missile in question is designed to be capable o being used with a slaughtering instrument.
(6) The authority of the Secretary of State ... shall not be required by virtue of subsection (1A) of section 5 of this Act for the sale or transfer of any expanding ammunition or the missile for any such ammunition to any person who produces a certificate by virtue of which he is authorised under subsection (4) above to purchase or acquire it without the authority of the Secretary of State.
(7) The authority of the Secretary of State ... shall not be required by virtue of subsection (1A) of section 5 of this Act for a person carrying on the business of a firearms dealer, or any servant of his, to have in his possession, or to purchase, acquire, sell or transfer, any expanding ammunition or the missile for any such ammunition in the ordinary course of that business.
(8) In this section—
　(a) references to expanding ammunition are references to any ammunition which ... incorporates a missile which is designed to expand on impact; and
　(b) references to the missile for any such ammunition are references to anything which, in relation to any such ammunition, falls within section 5(1A)(g) of this Act.

7. Police permit
(1) A person who has obtained from the chief officer of police for the area in which he resides a permit for the purpose in the prescribed form may, without holding a certificate under this Act, have in his possession a firearm and ammunition in accordance with the terms of the permit.
(2) It is an offence for a person knowingly or recklessly to make a statement false in any material particular for the purpose of procuring, whether for himself or for another person, the grant of a permit under this section.

16. Possession of firearm with intent to injure
It is an offence for a person to have in his possession any firearm or ammunition with intent by means thereof to endanger life or cause serious injury to property, or to enable another person by means thereof to endanger life or cause serious injury to property, whether any injury to person or property has been caused or not.

16A. Possession of firearm with intent to cause fear of violence
It is an offence for a person to have in his possession any firearm or imitation firearm with intent—
　(a) by means thereof to cause, or
　(b) to enable another person by means thereof to cause,
any person to believe that unlawful violence will be used against him or another person.

17. Use of firearm to resist arrest

(1) It is an offence for a person to make or attempt to make any use whatsoever of a firearm or imitation firearm with intent to resist or prevent the lawful arrest or detention of himself or another person.
(2) If a person, at the time of his committing or being arrested for an offence specified in Schedule 1 to this Act, has in his possession a firearm or imitation firearm, he shall be guilty of an offence under this subsection unless he shows that he had it in his possession for a lawful object.
(4) For purposes of this section, the definition of 'firearm' in section 57(1) of this Act shall apply without paragraphs (b) and (c) of that subsection, and 'imitation firearm' shall be construed accordingly.

18. Carrying firearm with criminal intent

(1) It is an offence for a person to have with him a firearm or imitation firearm with intent to commit an indictable offence, or to resist arrest or prevent the arrest of another, in either case while he has the firearm or imitation firearm with him.
(2) In proceedings for an offence under this section proof that the accused had a firearm or imitation firearm with him and intended to commit an offence, or to resist or prevent arrest, is evidence that he intended to have it with him while doing so.
...

19. Carrying firearm in a public place

A person commits an offence if, without lawful authority or reasonable excuse (the proof whereof lies on him) he has with him in a public place
    (a) a loaded shot gun,
    (b) an air weapon (whether loaded or not),
    (c) any other firearm (whether loaded or not) together with ammunition suitable for use in that firearm, or
    (d) an imitation firearm.

20. Trespassing with firearm

(1) A person commits an offence if, while he has a firearm or imitation firearm with him, he enters or is in any building or part of a building as a trespasser and without reasonable excuse (the proof whereof lies on him).
(2) A person commits an offence if, while he has a firearm or imitation firearm with him, he enters or is on any land as a trespasser and without reasonable excuse (the proof whereof lies on him).
(3) In subsection (2) of this section the expression 'land' includes land covered with water.

21. Possession of firearms by persons previously convicted of crime

(1) A person who has been sentenced to custody for life or to preventive detention, or to imprisonment or to corrective training for a term of three years or more or to youth custody or detention in a young offender institution for such a term, or who has been sentenced be detained for such a term in a young offenders institution in Scotland, shall not at any time have a firearm or ammunition in his possession.
(2) A person who has been sentenced to imprisonment for a term of three months or more but less than three years or to youth custody or detention in a young offender institution for such a term, or who has been sentenced to be detained for such a term in a detention centre or in a young offenders institution in Scotland or who has been subject to a secure training order or a detention and training order, shall not at any time before the expiration of the period of five years from the date of his release have a firearm or ammunition in his possession.
(2A) For the purposes of subsection (2) above, 'the date of his release' means—
    (a) in the case of a person sentenced to imprisonment with an order under section 47(1) of the Criminal Law Act 1977 (prison sentence partly served and partly suspended), the date on which he completes service of so much of the sentence as was by that order required to be served in prison;
    (b) in the case of a person who has been subject to a secure training order—
        (i) the date on which he is released from detention under the order;

(ii) the date on which he is released from detention ordered under section 4 of the Criminal Justice and Public Order Act 1994; or
   (iii) the date halfway through the total period specified by the court in making the order, whichever is the later.
  (c) in the case of a person who has been subject to a detention and training order—
   (i) the date on which he is released from detention under the order;
   (ii) the date on which he is released from detention ordered under section 104 of the Powers of Criminal Courts (Sentencing) Act 2000; or
   (iii) the date of the half-way point of the term of the order, whichever is the later.
  (d) in the case of a person who has been subject to a sentence of imprisonment to which an intermittent custody order under section 183(1)(b) of the Criminal Justice Act 2003 relates, the date of his final release.
(2B) A person who is serving a sentence of imprisonment to which an intermittent custody order under section 183 of the Criminal Justice Act 2003 relates shall not during any licence period specified for the purposes of subsection (1)(b)(i) of that section have a firearm or ammunition in his possession.
(3) A person who—
  (a) is the holder of a licence issued under section 53 of the Children and Young Persons Act 1933 ... (which sections provide for the detention of children and young persons convicted of serious crime, but enable them to be discharged on licence by the Secretary of State); or
  (b) is subject to a recognizance to keep the peace or to be of good behaviour, a condition of which is that he shall not possess, use or carry a firearm, or is subject to a community order containing a requirement that he shall not possess, use or carry a firearm; or
  ...
  shall not, at any time during which he holds the licence or is so subject or has been so ordained, have a firearm or ammunition in his possession.
(4) It is an offence for a person to contravene any of the foregoing provisions of this section.
(5) It is an offence for a person to sell or transfer a firearm or ammunition to, or to repair, test or prove a firearm or ammunition for, a person whom he knows or has reasonable ground for believing to be prohibited by this section from having a firearm or ammunition in his possession.

22. Acquisition and possession of firearms by minors

(1) It is an offence for a person under the age of seventeen to purchase or hire any firearm or ammunition.
(1A) Where a person under the age of eighteen is entitled, as the holder of a certificate under this Act, to have a firearm in his possession, it is an offence for that person to use that firearm for a purpose not authorised by the European weapons directive.
(2) It is an offence for a person under the age of fourteen to have in his possession any firearm or ammunition to which section 1 of this Act or section 15 of the Firearms (Amendment) Act 1988 applies, except in circumstances where under section 11(1), (3) or (4) of this Act he is entitled to have possession of it without holding a firearm certificate.
(3) It is an offence for a person under the age of fifteen to have with him an assembled shot gun except while under the supervision of a person of or over the age of twenty-one, or while the shot gun is so covered with a securely fastened gun cover that it cannot be fired.
(4) Subject to section 23 below, it is an offence for a person under the age of seventeen to have with him an air weapon or ammunition for an air weapon.

23. Exceptions from section 22(4)

(1) It is not an offence under section 22(4) of this Act for a person to have with him an air weapon or ammunition while he is under the supervision of a person of or over the age of twenty-one; but where a person has with him an air weapon on any premises in circumstances where he would be prohibited from having it with him but for this subsection, it is an offence—
  (a) for him to use it for firing any missile beyond those premises; or
  (b) for the person under whose supervision he is to allow him so to use it.

(2) It is not an offence under section 22(4) of this Act for a person to have with him an air weapon or ammunition at a time when—
   (a) being a member of a rifle club or miniature rifle club for the time being approved by the Secretary of State for the purposes of this section or section 15 of the Firearms (Amendment) Act 1988, he is engaged as such a member in connection with target shooting; or
   (b) he is using the weapon or ammunition at a shooting gallery where the only firearms used are either air weapons or miniature rifles not exceeding ·23 inch calibre.
(3) It is not an offence under section 22(4) of this Act for a person of or over the age of fourteen to have with him an air weapon or ammunition on private premises with the consent of the occupier.
(4) But where a person has with him an air weapon on premises in circumstances where he would be prohibited from having it with him but for subsection (3), it is an offence for him to use it for firing any missile beyond those premises.

24. Supplying firearms to minors

(1) It is an offence to sell or let on hire any firearm or ammunition to a person under the age of seventeen.
(2) It is an offence—
   (a) to make a gift of or lend any firearm or ammunition to which section 1 of this Act applies to a person under the age of fourteen; or
   (b) to part with the possession of any such firearm or ammunition to a person under that age, except in circumstances where that person is entitled under section 11(1), (3) or (4) of this Act or section 15 of the Firearms (Amendment) Act 1988 to have possession thereof without holding a firearm certificate.
(3) It is an offence to make a gift of a shot gun or ammunition for a shot gun to a person under the age of fifteen.
(4) It is an offence—
   (a) to make a gift of an air weapon or ammunition for an air weapon to a person under the age of seventeen; or
   (b) to part with the possession of an air weapon or ammunition for an air weapon to a person under the age of seventeen except where by virtue of section 23 of this Act the person is not prohibited from having it with him.
(5) In proceedings for an offence under any provision of this section it is a defence to prove that the person charged with the offence believed the other person to be of or over the age mentioned in that provision and had reasonable ground for the belief.

25. Supplying firearm to person drunk or insane

It is an offence for a person to sell or transfer any firearm or ammunition to, or to repair, prove or test any firearm or ammunition for, another person whom he knows or has reasonable cause for believing to be drunk or of unsound mind.

57. Interpretation

(1) In this Act, the expression 'firearm' means a lethal barrelled weapon of any description from which any shot, bullet or other missile can be discharged and includes—
   (a) any prohibited weapon, whether it is such a lethal weapon as aforesaid or not; and
   (b) any component part of such a lethal or prohibited weapon; and
   (c) any accessory to any such weapon designed or adapted to diminish the noise or flash caused by firing the weapon;
   and so much of section 1 of this Act as excludes any description of firearm from the category of firearms to which that section applies shall be construed as also excluding component parts of, and accessories to, firearms of that description.
(2) In this Act, the expression 'ammunition' means ammunition for any firearm and includes grenades, bombs and other like missiles, whether capable of use with a firearm or not, and also includes prohibited ammunition.
(2A) In this Act 'self-loading' and 'pump-action' in relation to any weapon mean respectively that it is designed or adapted (otherwise than as mentioned in section 5(1)(a)) so that it is automatically

re-loaded or that it is so designed or adapted that it is re-loaded by the manual operation of the fore-end or forestock of the weapon.

(2B) In this Act 'revolver', in relation to a smooth-bore gun, means a gun containing a series of chambers which revolve when the gun is fired.

(3) For purposes of sections 45, 46, 50, 51(4) and 52 of this Act, the offences under this Act relating specifically to air weapons are those under sections 22(4), 22(5), 23(1) and 24(4).

(4) In this Act—

'acquire' means hire, accept as a gift or borrow and 'acquisition' shall be construed accordingly;

'air weapon' has the meaning assigned to it by section 1(3)(b) of this Act;

'another member State' means a member State other than the United Kingdom, and 'other member States' shall be construed accordingly;

'area' means a police area;

'Article 7 authority' means a document issued by virtue of section 32A(1)(b) or (2) of this Act;

'British Transport Police Force' means the constables appointed under section 53 of the British Transport Commission Act 1949;

'certificate' (except in a context relating to the registration of firearms dealers) and 'certificate under this Act' mean a firearm certificate or a shot gun certificate and—

(a) 'firearm certificate' means a certificate granted by a chief officer of police under this Act in respect of any firearm or ammunition to which section 1 of this Act applies and includes a certificate granted in Northern Ireland under section 1 of the Firearms Act 1920 or under an enactment of the Parliament of Northern Ireland amending or substituted for that section; and

(b) 'shot gun certificate' means a certificate granted by a chief officer of police under this Act and authorising a person to possess shot guns;

'civilian officer' means—

(a) a person employed by a police authority or the Corporation of the City of London who is under the direction and control of a chief officer of police;

...

'European firearms pass' means a document to which the holder of a certificate under this Act is entitled by virtue of section 32A(1)(a) of this Act;

'European weapons directive' means the directive of the Council of the European Communities No. 91/477/EEC (directive on the control of the acquisition and possession of weapons);

'firearms dealer' means a person who, by way of trade or business, manufactures, sells, transfers, repairs, tests or proves firearms or ammunition to which section 1 of this Act applies, or shot guns;

'imitation firearm' means anything which has the appearance of being a firearm (other than such a weapon as is mentioned in section 5(1)(b) of this Act) whether or not it is capable of discharging any shot, bullet or other missile;

'premises' includes any land;

'prescribed' means prescribed by rules made by the Secretary of State under section 53 of this Act;

'prohibited weapon' and 'prohibited ammunition' have the meanings assigned to them by section 5(2) of this Act;

'public place' includes any highway and other premises or place to which at the material time the public have or are permitted to have access, whether on payment or otherwise;

'registered', in relation to a firearms dealer, means registered either—

(a) in Great Britain, under section 33 of this Act, or

...

and references to 'the register', 'registration' and a 'certificate of registration' shall be construed accordingly, except in section 40;

'rifle' includes carbine;

'shot gun' has the meaning assigned to it by section 1(3)(a) of this Act and, in sections 3(1) and 45(2) of this Act and in the definition of 'firearms dealer', includes any component part of a shot gun and any accessory to a shot gun designed or adapted to diminish the noise or flash caused by firing the gun;

'slaughtering instrument' means a firearm which is specially designed or adapted for the instantaneous slaughter of animals or for the instantaneous stunning of animals with a view to slaughtering them; and

'transfer' includes let on hire, give, lend and part with possession, and 'transferee' and 'transferor' shall be construed accordingly.

(4A) For the purposes of any reference in this Act to the use of any firearm or ammunition for a purpose not authorised by the European weapons directive, the directive shall be taken to authorise the use of a firearm or ammunition as or with a slaughtering instrument and the use of a firearm and ammunition—
   (a) for sporting purposes;
   (b) for the shooting of vermin, or, in the course of carrying on activities in connection with the management of any estate, of other wildlife; and
   (c) for competition purposes and target shooting outside competitions.

(5) The definitions in subsections (1) to (3) above apply to the provisions of this Act except where the context otherwise requires.

(6) For purposes of this Act—
   (a) the length of the barrel of a firearm shall be measured from the muzzle to the point at which the charge is exploded on firing; and
   (b) a shot gun or an air weapon shall be deemed to be loaded if there is ammunition in the chamber or barrel or in any magazine or other device which is in such a position that the ammunition can be fed into the chamber or barrel by the manual or automatic operation of some part of the gun or weapon.

58. Particular savings

...

(2) Nothing in this Act relating to firearms shall apply to an antique firearm which is sold, transferred, purchased, acquired or possessed as a curiosity or ornament.

(3) The provisions of this Act relating to ammunition shall be in addition to and not in derogation of any enactment relating to the keeping and sale of explosives.

SCHEDULE 1 | OFFENCES TO WHICH SECTION 17(2) APPLIES

1. Offences under section 1 of the Criminal Damage Act 1971.
2. Offences under any of the following provisions of the Offences Against the Person Act 1861—
   sections 20 to 22 (inflicting bodily injury; garrotting; criminal use of stupefying drugs);
   section 30 (laying explosive to building etc.);
   section 32 (endangering railway passengers by tampering with track);
   section 38 (assault with intent to commit felony or resist arrest);
   section 47 (criminal assaults);
2A Offences under Part I of the Child Abduction Act 1984 (abduction of children).
3 Offences under such of the provisions of section 4 of the Vagrancy Act 1824 as are referred to in and amended by section 15 of the Prevention of Crimes Act 1871 and section 7 of the Penal Servitude Act 1891 (suspected persons and reputed thieves being abroad with criminal intent).
4 Theft, robbery, burglary, blackmail and any offence under section 12(1) (taking of motor vehicle or other conveyance without owner's consent) of the Theft Act 1968.
5 Offences under section 89(1) of the Police Act 1996 or section 41 of the Police (Scotland) Act 1967 (assaulting constable in execution of his duty).
5A An offence under section 90(1) of the Criminal Justice Act 1991 (assaulting prisoner custody officer).
5B An offence under section 13(1) of the Criminal Justice and Public Order Act 1994 (assaulting secure training centre custody officer).
6 Offences under any of the following provisions of the Sexual Offences Act 2003—
   (a) section 1 (rape);
   (b) section 2 (assault by penetration);

(c) section 4 (causing a person to engage in sexual activity without consent), where the activity caused involved penetration within subsection (4)(a) to (d) of that section;
(d) section 5 (rape of a child under 13);
(e) section 6 (assault of a child under 13 by penetration);
(f) section 8 (causing or inciting a child under 13 to engage in sexual activity), where an activity involving penetration within subsection (3)(a) to (d) of that section was caused;
(g) section 30 (sexual activity with a person with a mental disorder impeding choice), where the touching involved penetration within subsection (3)(a) to (d) of that section;
(h) section 31 (causing or inciting a person, with a mental disorder impeding choice, to engage in sexual activity), where an activity involving penetration within subsection (3)(a) to (d) of that section was caused.

8 Aiding or abetting the commission of any offence specified in paragraphs 1 to 6 of this Schedule.

9 Attempting to commit any offence so specified.

FIREARMS (AMENDMENT) ACT 1988

5. Restriction on sale of ammunition for smooth-bore guns

(1) This section applies to ammunition to which section 1 of the principal Act does not apply and which is capable of being used in a shot gun or in a smooth-bore gun to which that section applies.

(2) It is an offence for a person to sell any such ammunition to another person in the United Kingdom who is neither a registered firearms dealer nor a person who sells such ammunition by way of trade or business unless that other person—
   (a) produces a certificate authorising him to possess a gun of a kind mentioned in subsection (1) above; or
   (b) shows that he is by virtue of that Act or this Act entitled to have possession of such a gun without holding a certificate; or
   (c) produces a certificate authorising another person to possess such a gun, together with that person's written authority to purchase the ammunition on his behalf.

(3) An offence under this section shall be punishable on summary conviction with imprisonment for a term not exceeding six months or a fine not exceeding level 5 on the standard scale or both.

6. Shortening of barrels

(1) Subject to subsection (2) below, it is an offence to shorten to a length less than 24 inches the barrel of any smooth-bore gun to which section 1 of the principal Act applies other than one which has a barrel with a bore exceeding 2 inches in diameter; and that offence shall be punishable—
   (a) on summary conviction, with imprisonment for a term not exceeding six months or a fine not exceeding the statutory maximum or both;
   (b) on indictment, with imprisonment for a term not exceeding five years or a fine or both.

(2) It is not an offence under this section for a registered firearms dealer to shorten the barrel of a gun for the sole purpose of replacing a defective part of the barrel so as to produce a barrel not less than 24 inches in length.

7. Conversion not to affect classification

(1) Any weapon which—
   (a) has at any time (whether before or after the passing of the Firearms (Amendment) Act 1997) been a weapon of a kind described in section 5(1) or (1A) of the principal Act (including any amendments to section 5(1) made under section 1(4) of this Act);
   (b) is not a self-loading or pump-action smooth-bore gun which has at any such time been such a weapon by reason only of having had a barrel less than 24 inches in length,

shall be treated as a prohibited weapon notwithstanding anything done for the purpose of converting it into a weapon of a different kind.
(2) Any weapon which—
   (a) has at any time since the coming into force of section 2 above been a weapon to which section 1 of the principal Act applies; or
   (b) would at any previous time have been such a weapon if those sections had then been in force,

   shall, if it has, or at any time has had, a rifled barrel less than 24 inches in length, be treated as a weapon to which section 1 of the principal Act applies notwithstanding anything done for the purpose of converting it into a shot gun or an air weapon.
(3) For the purposes of subsection (2) above there shall be disregarded the shortening of a barrel by a registered firearms dealer for the sole purpose of replacing part of it so as to produce a barrel not less than 24 inches in length.

8. De-activated weapons

For the purposes of the principal Act and this Act it shall be presumed, unless the contrary is shown, that a firearm has been rendered incapable of discharging any shot, bullet or other missile, and has consequently ceased to be a firearm within the meaning of those Acts, if—
   (a) it bears a mark which has been approved by the Secretary of State for denoting that fact and which has been made either by one of the two companies mentioned in section 58(1) of the principal Act or by such other person as may be approved by the Secretary of State for the purposes of this section; and
   (b) that company or person has certified in writing that work has been carried out on the firearm in a manner approved by the Secretary of State for rendering it incapable of discharging any shot, bullet or other missile.

▎FIREARMS (AMENDMENT) ACT 1997

2. Slaughtering instruments

The authority of the Secretary of State is not required by virtue of subsection (1)(aba) of section 5 of the [Firearms Act] 1968—
   (a) for a person to have in his possession, or to purchase or acquire, or to sell or transfer, a slaughtering instrument if he is authorised by a firearm certificate to have the instrument in his possession, or to purchase or acquire it;
   (b) for a person to have a slaughtering instrument in his possession if he is entitled, under section 10 of the 1968 Act, to have it in his possession without a firearm certificate.

3. Firearms used for humane killing of animals

The authority of the Secretary of State is not required by virtue of subsection (1)(aba) of section 5 of the 1968 Act for a person to have in his possession, or to purchase or acquire, or to sell or transfer, a firearm if he is authorised by a firearm certificate to have the firearm in his possession, or to purchase or acquire it, subject to a condition that it is only for use in connection with the humane killing of animals.

4. Shot pistols used for shooting vermin

(1) The authority of the Secretary of State is not required by virtue of subsection (1)(aba) of section 5 of the 1968 Act for a person to have in his possession, or to purchase or acquire, or to sell or transfer, a shot pistol if he is authorised by a firearm certificate to have the shot pistol in his possession, or to purchase or acquire it, subject to a condition that it is only for use in connection with the shooting of vermin.
(2) For the purposes of this section, 'shot pistol' means a smooth-bored gun which is chambered for .410 cartridges or 9mm rim-fire cartridges.

5. Races at athletic meetings

The authority of the Secretary of State is not required by virtue of subsection (1)(aba) of section 5 of the 1968 Act—
- (a) for a person to have a firearm in his possession at an athletic meeting for the purpose of starting races at that meeting; or
- (b) for a person to have in his possession, or to purchase or acquire, or to sell or transfer, a firearm if he is authorised by a firearm certificate to have the firearm in his possession, or to purchase or acquire it, subject to a condition that it is only for use in connection with starting races at athletic meetings.

6. Trophies of war

The authority of the Secretary of State is not required by virtue of subsection (1)(aba) of section 5 of the 1968 Act for a person to have in his possession a firearm which was acquired as a trophy of war before 1st January 1946 if he is authorised by a firearm certificate to have it in his possession.

7. Firearms of historic interest

(1) The authority of the Secretary of State is not required by virtue of subsection (1)(aba) of section 5 of the 1968 Act for a person to have in his possession, or to purchase or acquire, or to sell or transfer, a firearm which—
- (a) was manufactured before 1st January 1919; and
- (b) is of a description specified under subsection (2) below,

if he is authorised by a firearm certificate to have the firearm in his possession, or to purchase or acquire it, subject to a condition that he does so only for the purpose of its being kept or exhibited as part of a collection.

(2) The Secretary of State may by order made by statutory instrument specify a description of firearm for the purposes of subsection (1) above if it appears to him that—
- (a) firearms of that description were manufactured before 1st January 1919; and
- (b) ammunition for firearms of that type is not readily available.

(3) The authority of the Secretary of State is not required by virtue of subsection (1)(aba) of section 5 of the 1968 Act for a person to have in his possession, or to purchase or acquire, or to sell or transfer, a firearm which—
- (a) is of particular rarity, aesthetic quality or technical interest, or
- (b) is of historical importance,

if he is authorised by a firearm certificate to have the firearm in his possession subject to a condition requiring it to be kept and used only at a place designated for the purposes of this subsection by the Secretary of State.

(4) This section has effect without prejudice to section 58(2) of the 1968 Act (antique firearms).

8. Weapons and ammunition used for treating animals

The authority of the Secretary of State is not required by virtue of subsection (1)(aba), (b) or (c) of section 5 of the 1968 Act for a person to have in his possession, or to purchase or acquire, or to sell or transfer, any firearm, weapon or ammunition designed or adapted for the purpose of tranquillising or otherwise treating any animal, if he is authorised by a firearm certificate to possess, or to purchase or acquire, the firearm, weapon or ammunition subject to a condition restricting its use to use in connection with the treatment of animals.

FOOTBALL OFFENCES ACT 1991

1. Designated football matches

(1) In this Act a 'designated football match' means an association football match designated, or of a description designated, for the purposes of this Act by order of the Secretary of State.

Any such order shall be made by statutory instrument which shall be subject to annulment in pursuance of a resolution of either House of Parliament.

(2) References in this Act to things done at a designated football match include anything done at the ground—
   (a) within the period beginning two hours before the start of the match or (if earlier) two hours before the time at which it is advertised to start and ending one hour after the end of the match; or
   (b) where the match is advertised to start at a particular time on a particular day but does not take place on that day, within the period beginning two hours before and ending one hour after the advertised starting time.

2. Throwing of missiles
It is an offence for a person at a designated football match to throw anything at or towards—
   (a) the playing area, or any area adjacent to the playing area to which spectators are not generally admitted, or
   (b) any area in which spectators or other persons are or may be present,
without lawful authority or lawful excuse (which shall be for him to prove).

3. Indecent or racialist chanting
(1) It is an offence to engage or take part in chanting of an indecent or racialist nature at a designated football match.
(2) For this purpose—
   (a) 'chanting' means the repeated uttering of any words or sounds whether alone or in concert with one more others; and
   (b) 'of a racialist nature' means consisting of or including matter which is threatening, abusive or insulting to a person by reason of his colour, race, nationality (including citizenship) or ethnic or national origins.

4. Going onto the playing area
It is an offence for a person at a designated football match to go onto the playing area, or any area adjacent to the playing area to which spectators are not generally admitted, without lawful authority or lawful excuse (which shall be for him to prove).

FORGERY AND COUNTERFEITING ACT 1981

1. The offence of forgery
A person is guilty of forgery if he makes a false instrument, with the intention that he or another shall use it to induce somebody to accept it as genuine, and by reason of so accepting it to do or not to do some act to his own or any other person's prejudice.

2. The offence of copying a false instrument
It is an offence for a person to make a copy of an instrument which is, and which he knows or believes to be, a false instrument, with the intention that he or another shall use it to induce somebody to accept it as a copy of a genuine instrument, and by reason of so accepting it to do or not to do some act to his own or any other person's prejudice.

3. The offence of using a false instrument
It is an offence for a person to use an instrument which is, and which he knows or believes to be, false, with the intention of inducing somebody to accept it as genuine, and by reason of so accepting it to do or not to do some act to his own or any other person's prejudice.

4. The offence of using a copy of a false instrument
It is an offence for a person to use a copy of an instrument which is, and which he knows or believes to be, a false instrument, with the intention of inducing somebody to accept it as a copy of a genuine instrument, and by reason of so accepting it to do or not to do some act to his own or any other person's prejudice.

5. Offences relating to money orders, share certificates, passports, etc.

(1) It is an offence for a person to have in his custody or under his control an instrument to which this section applies which is, and which he knows or believes to be, false, with the intention that he or another shall use it to induce somebody to accept it as genuine, and by reason of so accepting it to do or not to do some act to his own or any other person's prejudice.

(2) It is an offence for a person to have in his custody or under his control, without lawful authority or excuse, an instrument to which this section applies which is, and which he knows or believes to be, false.

(3) It is an offence for a person to make or to have in his custody or under his control a machine or implement, or paper or any other material, which to his knowledge is or has been specially designed or adapted for the making of an instrument to which this section applies, with the intention that he or another shall make an instrument to which this section applies which is false and that he or another shall use the instrument to induce somebody to accept it as genuine, and by reason of so accepting it to do or not to do some act to his own or any other person's prejudice.

(4) It is an offence for a person to make or to have in his custody or under his control any such machine, implement, paper or material, without lawful authority or excuse.

(5) The instruments to which this section applies are—
   (a) money orders;
   (b) postal orders;
   (c) United Kingdom postage stamps;
   (d) Inland Revenue stamps;
   (e) share certificates;
   (g) cheques and other bills of exchange;
   (h) travellers' cheques;
   (ha) bankers' drafts
   (hb) promissory notes;
   (j) cheque cards;
   (ja) debit cards;
   (k) credit cards;
   (l) certified copies relating to an entry in a register of births, adoptions, marriages, civil partnerships or deaths and issued by the Registrar General, the Registrar General for Northern Ireland, a registration officer or a person lawfully authorised to issue certified copies relating to such entries and
   (m) certificates relating to entries in such registers.

(6) In subsection (5)(e) above 'share certificate' means an instrument entitling or evidencing the title of a person to a share or interest—
   (a) in any public stock, annuity, fund or debt of any government or state, including a state which forms part of another state; or
   (b) in any stock, fund or debt of a body (whether corporate or unincorporated) established in the United Kingdom or elsewhere.

(7) An instrument is also an instrument to which this section applies if it is a monetary instrument specified for the purposes of this section by an order made by the Secretary of State.

(8) The power under subsection (7) above is exercisable by statutory instrument subject to annulment in pursuance of a resolution of either House of Parliament.

8. Meaning of 'instrument'

(1) Subject to subsection (2) below, in this Part of this Act 'instrument' means—
   (a) any document, whether of a formal or informal character;
   (b) any stamp issued or sold by a postal operator;
   (c) any Inland Revenue stamp; and
   (d) any disc, tape, sound track or other device on or in which information is recorded or stored by mechanical, electronic or other means.

(2) A currency note within the meaning of Part II of this Act is not an instrument for the purposes of this Part of this Act.

(3) A mark denoting payment of postage which a postal operator authorises to be used instead of an adhesive stamp is to be treated for the purposes of this Part of this Act as if it were a stamp issued by the postal operator concerned.

(3A) In this section 'postal operator' has the same meaning as in the Postal Services Act 2000.

(4) In this Part of this Act 'Inland Revenue stamp' means a stamp as defined in section 27 of the Stamp Duties Management Act 1891.

9. Meaning of 'false' and 'making'

(1) An instrument is false for the purposes of this Part of this Act—
   (a) if it purports to have been made in the form in which it is made by a person who did not in fact make it in that form; or
   (b) if it purports to have been made in the form in which it is made on the authority of a person who did not in fact authorise its making in that form; or
   (c) if it purports to have been made in the terms in which it is made by a person who did not in fact make it in those terms; or
   (d) if it purports to have been made in the terms in which it is made on the authority of a person who did not in fact authorise its making in those terms; or
   (e) if it purports to have been altered in any respect by a person who did not in fact alter it in that respect; or
   (f) if it purports to have been altered in any respect on the authority of a person who did not in fact authorise the alteration in that respect; or
   (g) if it purports to have been made or altered on a date on which, or at a place at which, or otherwise in circumstances in which, it was not in fact made or altered; or
   (h) if it purports to have been made or altered by an existing person but he did not in fact exist.

(2) A person is to be treated for the purposes of this Part of this Act as making a false instrument if he alters an instrument so as to make it false in any respect (whether or not it is false in some other respect apart from that alteration).

10. Meaning of 'prejudice' and 'induce'

(1) Subject to subsections (2) and (4) below, for the purposes of this Part of this Act an act or omission intended to be induced is to a person's prejudice if, and only if, it is one which, if it occurs—
   (a) will result—
      (i) in his temporary or permanent loss of property; or
      (ii) in his being deprived of an opportunity to earn remuneration or greater remuneration; or
      (iii) in his being deprived of an opportunity to gain a financial advantage otherwise than by way of remuneration; or
   (b) will result in somebody being given an opportunity—
      (i) to earn remuneration or greater remuneration from him; or
      (ii) to gain a financial advantage from him otherwise than by way of remuneration; or
   (c) will be the result of his having accepted a false instrument as genuine, or a copy of a false instrument as a copy of a genuine one, in connection with his performance of any duty.

(2) An act which a person has an enforceable duty to do and an omission to do an act which a person is not entitled to do shall be disregarded for the purposes of this Part of this Act.

(3) In this Part of this Act references to inducing somebody to accept a false instrument as genuine, or a copy of a false instrument as a copy of a genuine one, include references to inducing a machine to respond to the instrument or copy as if it were a genuine instrument or, as the case may be, a copy of a genuine one.

(4) Where subsection (3) above applies, the act or omission intended to be induced by the machine responding to the instrument or copy shall be treated as an act or omission to a person's prejudice.

(5) In this section 'loss' includes not getting what one might get as well as parting with what one has.

FRAUD ACT 2006

1. Fraud
(1) A person is guilty of fraud if he is in breach of any of the sections listed in subsection (2) (which provide for different ways of committing the offence).
(2) The sections are—
   (a) section 2 (fraud by false representation),
   (b) section 3 (fraud by failing to disclose information), and
   (c) section 4 (fraud by abuse of position).
(3) A person who is guilty of fraud is liable—
   (a) on summary conviction, to imprisonment for a term not exceeding 12 months or to a fine not exceeding the statutory maximum (or to both);
   (b) on conviction on indictment, to imprisonment for a term not exceeding 10 years or to a fine (or to both).
   ...

2. Fraud by false representation
(1) A person is in breach of this section if he—
   (a) dishonestly makes a false representation, and
   (b) intends, by making the representation—
      (i) to make a gain for himself or another, or
      (ii) to cause loss to another or to expose another to a risk of loss.
(2) A representation is false if—
   (a) it is untrue or misleading, and
   (b) the person making it knows that it is, or might be, untrue or misleading.
(3) 'Representation' means any representation as to fact or law, including a representation as to the state of mind of—
   (a) the person making the representation, or
   (b) any other person.
(4) A representation may be expressed or implied.
(5) For the purposes of this section a representation may be regarded as made if it (or anything implying it) is submitted in any form to any system or device designed to receive, convey or respond to communications (with or without human intervention).

3. Fraud by failing to disclose information
A person is in breach of this section if he—
(a) dishonestly fails to disclose to another person information which he is under a legal duty to disclose, and
(b) intends, by failing to disclose the information—
   (i) to make a gain for himself or another, or
   (ii) to cause loss to another or to expose another to a risk of loss.

4. Fraud by abuse of position
(1) A person is in breach of this section if he—
   (a) occupies a position in which he is expected to safeguard, or not to act against, the financial interests of another person,
   (b) dishonestly abuses that position, and
   (c) intends, by means of the abuse of that position—
      (i) to make a gain for himself or another, or
      (ii) to cause loss to another or to expose another to a risk of loss.
(2) A person may be regarded as having abused his position even though his conduct consisted of an omission rather than an act.

5. 'Gain' and 'loss'

(1) The references to gain and loss in sections 2 to 4 are to be read in accordance with this section.
(2) 'Gain' and 'loss'—
   (a) extend only to gain or loss in money or other property;
   (b) include any such gain or loss whether temporary or permanent;
   and 'property' means any property whether real or personal (including things in action and other intangible property).
(3) 'Gain' includes a gain by keeping what one has, as well as a gain by getting what one does not have.
(4) 'Loss' includes a loss by not getting what one might get, as well as a loss by parting with what one has.

6. Possession etc. of articles for use in frauds

(1) A person is guilty of an offence if he has in his possession or under his control any article for use in the course of or in connection with any fraud.
(2) A person guilty of an offence under this section is liable—
   (a) on summary conviction, to imprisonment for a term not exceeding 12 months or to a fine not exceeding the statutory maximum (or to both);
   (b) on conviction on indictment, to imprisonment for a term not exceeding 5 years or to a fine (or to both).
   …

7. Making or supplying articles for use in frauds

(1) A person is guilty of an offence if he makes, adapts, supplies or offers to supply any article—
   (a) knowing that it is designed or adapted for use in the course of or in connection with fraud, or
   (b) intending it to be used to commit, or assist in the commission of, fraud.
(2) A person guilty of an offence under this section is liable—
   (a) on summary conviction, to imprisonment for a term not exceeding 12 months or to a fine not exceeding the statutory maximum (or to both);
   (b) on conviction on indictment, to imprisonment for a term not exceeding 10 years or to a fine (or to both).
   …

8. 'Article'

(1) For the purposes of—
   (a) sections 6 and 7, and
   (b) the provisions listed in subsection (2), so far as they relate to articles for use in the course of or in connection with fraud,
   'article' includes any program or data held in electronic form.
(2) The provisions are—
   (a) section 1(7)(b) of the Police and Criminal Evidence Act 1984,
   (b) section 2(8)(b) of the Armed Forces Act 2001, and
   …
   (meaning of 'prohibited articles' for the purposes of stop and search powers).

9. Participating in fraudulent business carried on by sole trader etc.

(1) A person is guilty of an offence if he is knowingly a party to the carrying on of a business to which this section applies.
(2) This section applies to a business which is carried on—
   (a) by a person who is outside the reach of section 458 of the Companies Act 1985 …, and
   (b) with intent to defraud creditors of any person or for any other fraudulent purpose.
(3) The following are within the reach of section 458 of the 1985 Act—
   (a) a company (within the meaning of that Act;
   (b) a person to whom that section applies (with or without adaptations or modifications) as if the person were a company;

    (c) a person exempted from the application of that section.
    ...
(5) 'Fraudulent purpose' has the same meaning as in section 458 of the 1985 Act.
(6) A person guilty of an offence under this section is liable—
    (a) on summary conviction, to imprisonment for a term not exceeding 12 months or to a fine not exceeding the statutory maximum (or to both);
    (b) on conviction on indictment, to imprisonment for a term not exceeding 10 years or to a fine (or to both).
    ...

11. Obtaining services dishonestly

(1) A person is guilty of an offence under this section if he obtains services for himself or another—
    (a) by a dishonest act, and
    (b) in breach of subsection (2).
(2) A person obtains services in breach of this subsection if—
    (a) they are made available on the basis that payment has been, is being or will be made for or in respect of them,
    (b) he obtains them without any payment having been made for or in respect of them or without payment having been made in full, and
    (c) when he obtains them, he knows—
        (i) that they are being made available on the basis described in paragraph (a), or
        (ii) that they might be,
        but intends that payment will not be made, or will not be made in full.
(3) A person guilty of an offence under this section is liable—
    (a) on summary conviction, to imprisonment for a term not exceeding 12 months or to a fine not exceeding the statutory maximum (or to both);
    (b) on conviction on indictment, to imprisonment for a term not exceeding 5 years or to a fine (or to both).
    ...

12. Liability of company officers for offences by company

(1) Subsection (2) applies if an offence under this Act is committed by a body corporate.
(2) If the offence is proved to have been committed with the consent or connivance of—
    (a) a director, manager, secretary or other similar officer of the body corporate, or
    (b) a person who was purporting to act in any such capacity,
    he (as well as the body corporate) is guilty of the offence and liable to be proceeded against and punished accordingly.
(3) If the affairs of a body corporate are managed by its members, subsection (2) applies in relation to the acts and defaults of a member in connection with his functions of management as if he were a director of the body corporate.

GAMBLING ACT 2005

42. Cheating

(1) A person commits an offence if he—
    (a) cheats at gambling, or
    (b) does anything for the purpose of enabling or assisting another person to cheat at gambling.
(2) For the purposes of subsection (1) it is immaterial whether a person who cheats—
    (a) improves his chances of winning anything, or
    (b) wins anything.
(3) Without prejudice to the generality of subsection (1) cheating at gambling may, in particular, consist of actual or attempted deception or interference in connection with—

(a) the process by which gambling is conducted, or
(b) a real or virtual game, race or other event or process to which gambling relates.
(4) A person guilty of an offence under this section shall be liable—
    (a) on conviction on indictment, to imprisonment for a term not exceeding two years, to a fine or to both, or
    (b) on summary conviction, to imprisonment for a term not exceeding 51 weeks, to a fine not exceeding the statutory maximum or to both.
    ...
(6) Section 17 of the Gaming Act 1845 (winning by cheating) shall cease to have effect.

43. Chain-gift schemes

(1) A person commits an offence if he—
    (a) invites another to join a chain-gift scheme, or
    (b) knowingly participates in the promotion, administration or management of a chain-gift scheme.
(2) An arrangement is a 'chain-gift' scheme if—
    (a) in order to participate in the arrangement a person must make a payment to one or more other participants (a 'joining fee'), and
    (b) each person who participates in the arrangement—
        (i) is required or invited to invite others to participate, and
        (ii) is encouraged to believe that he will receive the joining fees, or part of the joining fees, of other participants, to an amount in excess of the joining fee paid by him.
(3) For the purposes of subsection (2)—
    (a) 'payment' means a payment of money or money's worth, but does not include the provision of goods or services, and
    (b) it is immaterial whether a payment is made directly or through a person responsible for managing or administering the scheme.
(4) A person guilty of an offence under this section shall be liable on summary conviction to—
    (a) imprisonment for a period not exceeding 51 weeks,
    (b) a fine not exceeding level 5 on the standard scale, or
    (c) both.
    ...

GENDER RECOGNITION ACT 2004

9. General

(1) Where a full gender recognition certificate is issued to a person, the person's gender becomes for all purposes the acquired gender (so that, if the acquired gender is the male gender, the person's sex becomes that of a man and, if it is the female gender, the person's sex becomes that of a woman).
(2) Subsection (1) does not affect things done, or events occurring, before the certificate is issued; but it does operate for the interpretation of enactments passed, and instruments and other documents made, before the certificate is issued (as well as those passed or made afterwards).
(3) Subsection (1) is subject to provision made by this Act or any other enactment or any subordinate legislation.

20. Gender-specific offences

(1) Where (apart from this subsection) a relevant gender-specific offence could be committed or attempted only if the gender of a person to whom a full gender recognition certificate has been issued were not the acquired gender, the fact that the person's gender has become the acquired gender does not prevent the offence being committed or attempted.
(2) An offence is a 'relevant gender-specific offence' if—
    (a) either or both of the conditions in subsection (3) are satisfied, and

(b) the commission of the offence involves the accused engaging in sexual activity.
(3) The conditions are—
   (a) that the offence may be committed only by a person of a particular gender, and
   (b) that the offence may be committed only on, or in relation to, a person of a particular gender, and the references to a particular gender include a gender identified by reference to the gender of the other person involved.

HEALTH ACT 2006

1. Introduction
(1) This Chapter makes provision for the prohibition of smoking in certain premises, places and vehicles which are smoke-free by virtue of this Chapter.
(2) In this Chapter—
   (a) 'smoking' refers to smoking tobacco or anything which contains tobacco, or smoking any other substance, and
   (b) smoking includes being in possession of lit tobacco or of anything lit which contains tobacco, or being in possession of any other lit substance in a form in which it could be smoked.
(3) In this Chapter, 'smoke' and other related expressions are to be read in accordance with subsection (2).

2. Smoke-free premises
(1) Premises are smoke-free if they are open to the public.
   But unless the premises also fall within subsection (2), they are smoke-free only when open to the public.
(2) Premises are smoke-free if they are used as a place of work—
   (a) by more than one person (even if the persons who work there do so at different times, or only intermittently), or
   (b) where members of the public might attend for the purpose of seeking or receiving goods or services from the person or persons working there (even if members of the public are not always present).
   They are smoke-free all the time.
(3) If only part of the premises is open to the public or (as the case may be) used as a place of work mentioned in subsection (2), the premises are smoke-free only to that extent.
(4) In any case, premises are smoke-free only in those areas which are enclosed or substantially enclosed.
(5) The appropriate national authority may specify in regulations what 'enclosed' and 'substantially enclosed' mean.
(6) Section 3 provides for some premises, or areas of premises, not to be smoke-free despite this section.
(7) Premises are 'open to the public' if the public or a section of the public has access to them, whether by invitation or not, and whether on payment or not.
(8) 'Work', in subsection (2), includes voluntary work.

3. Smoke-free premises: exemptions
(1) The appropriate national authority may make regulations providing for specified descriptions of premises, or specified areas within specified descriptions of premises, not to be smoke-free despite section 2.
(2) Descriptions of premises which may be specified under subsection (1) include, in particular, any premises where a person has his home, or is living whether permanently or temporarily (including hotels, care homes, and prisons and other places where a person may be detained).
(3) The power to make regulations under subsection (1) is not exercisable so as to specify any description of—

(a) premises in respect of which a premises licence under the Licensing Act 2003 authorising the sale by retail of alcohol for consumption on the premises has effect,
(b) premises in respect of which a club premises certificate (within the meaning of section 60 of that Act) has effect.

(4) But subsection (3) does not prevent the exercise of that power so as to specify any area, within a specified description of premises mentioned in subsection (3), where a person has his home, or is living whether permanently or temporarily.

(5) For the purpose of making provision for those participating as performers in a performance, or in a performance of a specified description, not to be prevented from smoking if the artistic integrity of the performance makes it appropriate for them to smoke—
(a) the power in subsection (1) also includes power to provide for specified descriptions of premises or specified areas within such premises not to be smoke-free in relation only to such performers, and
(b) subsection (3) does not prevent the exercise of that power as so extended.

(6) The regulations may provide, in relation to any description of premises or areas of premises specified in the regulations, that the premises or areas are not smoke-free—
(a) in specified circumstances,
(b) if specified conditions are satisfied, or
(c) at specified times,
or any combination of those.

(7) The conditions may include conditions requiring the designation in accordance with the regulations, by the person in charge of the premises, of any rooms in which smoking is to be permitted.

(8) For the purposes of subsection (5), the references to a performance—
(a) include, for example, the performance of a play, or a performance given in connection with the making of a film or television programme, and
(b) if the regulations so provide, include a rehearsal.

6. No-smoking signs

(1) It is the duty of any person who occupies or is concerned in the management of smoke-free premises to make sure that no-smoking signs complying with the requirements of this section are displayed in those premises in accordance with the requirements of this section.

(2) Regulations made by the appropriate national authority may provide for a duty corresponding to that mentioned in subsection (1) in relation to—
(a) places which are smoke-free by virtue of section 4,
(b) vehicles which are smoke-free by virtue of section 5.
The duty is to be imposed on persons, or on persons of a description, specified in the regulations.

(3) The signs must be displayed in accordance with any requirements contained in regulations made by the appropriate national authority.

(4) The signs must conform to any requirements specified in regulations made by the appropriate national authority (for example, requirements as to content, size, design, colour, or wording).

(5) A person who fails to comply with the duty in subsection (1), or any corresponding duty in regulations under subsection (2), commits an offence.

(6) It is a defence for a person charged with an offence under subsection (5) to show—
(a) that he did not know, and could not reasonably have been expected to know, that the premises were smoke-free (or, as the case may be, that the place or vehicle was smoke-free), or
(b) that he did not know, and could not reasonably have been expected to know, that no-smoking signs complying with the requirements of this section were not being displayed in accordance with the requirements of this section, or
(c) that on other grounds it was reasonable for him not to comply with the duty.

(7) If a person charged with an offence under subsection (5) relies on a defence in subsection (6), and evidence is adduced which is sufficient to raise an issue with respect to that defence, the court must assume that the defence is satisfied unless the prosecution proves beyond reasonable doubt that it is not.

(8) A person guilty of an offence under subsection (5) is liable on summary conviction to a fine not exceeding a level on the standard scale specified in regulations made by the Secretary of State.
(9) The references in this section, however expressed, to premises, places or vehicles which are smoke-free, are to those premises, places or vehicles so far as they are smoke-free under or by virtue of this Chapter (and references to smoke-free premises include premises which by virtue of regulations under section 3(5) are smoke-free except in relation to performers).

7. Offence of smoking in smoke-free place

(1) In this section, a 'smoke-free place' means any of the following—
   (a) premises, so far as they are smoke-free under or by virtue of sections 2 and 3 (including premises which by virtue of regulations under section 3(5) are smoke-free except in relation to performers),
   (b) a place, so far as it is smoke-free by virtue of section 4,
   (c) a vehicle, so far as it is smoke-free by virtue of section 5.
(2) A person who smokes in a smoke-free place commits an offence.
(3) But a person who smokes in premises which are not smoke-free in relation to performers by virtue of regulations under section 3(5) does not commit an offence if he is such a performer.
(4) It is a defence for a person charged with an offence under subsection (2) to show that he did not know, and could not reasonably have been expected to know, that it was a smoke-free place.
(5) If a person charged with an offence under this section relies on a defence in subsection (4), and evidence is adduced which is sufficient to raise an issue with respect to that defence, the court must assume that the defence is satisfied unless the prosecution proves beyond reasonable doubt that it is not.
(6) A person guilty of an offence under this section is liable on summary conviction to a fine not exceeding a level on the standard scale specified in regulations made by the Secretary of State.

8. Offence of failing to prevent smoking in smoke-free place

(1) It is the duty of any person who controls or is concerned in the management of smoke-free premises to cause a person smoking there to stop smoking.
(2) The reference in subsection (1) to a person smoking does not include a performer in relation to whom the premises are not smoke-free by virtue of regulations under section 3(5).
(3) Regulations made by the appropriate national authority may provide for a duty corresponding to that mentioned in subsection (1) in relation to—
   (a) places which are smoke-free by virtue of section 4,
   (b) vehicles which are smoke-free by virtue of section 5.
   The duty is to be imposed on persons, or on persons of a description, specified in the regulations.
(4) A person who fails to comply with the duty in subsection (1), or any corresponding duty in regulations under subsection (3), commits an offence.
(5) It is a defence for a person charged with an offence under subsection (4) to show—
   (a) that he took reasonable steps to cause the person in question to stop smoking, or
   (b) that he did not know, and could not reasonably have been expected to know, that the person in question was smoking, or
   (c) that on other grounds it was reasonable for him not to comply with the duty.
(6) If a person charged with an offence under this section relies on a defence in subsection (5), and evidence is adduced which is sufficient to raise an issue with respect to that defence, the court must assume that the defence is satisfied unless the prosecution proves beyond reasonable doubt that it is not.
(7) A person guilty of an offence under this section is liable on summary conviction to a fine not exceeding a level on the standard scale specified in regulations made by the Secretary of State.
(8) The references in this section, however expressed, to premises, places or vehicles which are smoke-free, are to those premises, places or vehicles so far as they are smoke-free under or by virtue of this Chapter (and references to smoke-free premises include premises which by virtue of regulations under section 3(5) are smoke-free except in relation to performers).

HOMICIDE ACT 1957

1. Abolition of 'constructive malice'
(1) Where a person kills another in the course or furtherance of some other offence, the killing shall not amount to murder unless done with the same malice aforethought (express or implied) as is required for a killing to amount to murder when not done in the course or furtherance of another offence.
(2) For the purposes of the foregoing subsection, a killing done in the course or for the purpose of resisting an officer of justice, or of resisting or avoiding or preventing a lawful arrest, or of effecting or assisting an escape or rescue from legal custody, shall be treated as a killing in the course or furtherance of an offence.

2. Persons suffering from diminished responsibility
(1) Where a person kills or is a party to the killing of another, he shall not be convicted of murder if he was suffering from such abnormality of mind (whether arising from a condition of arrested or retarded development of mind or any inherent causes or induced by disease or injury) as substantially impaired his mental responsibility for his acts and omissions in doing or being a party to the killing.
(2) On a charge of murder, it shall be for the defence to prove that the person charged is by virtue of this section not liable to be convicted of murder.
(3) A person who but for this section would be liable, whether as principal or as accessory, to be convicted of murder shall be liable instead to be convicted of manslaughter.
(4) The fact that one party to a killing is by virtue of this section not liable to be convicted of murder shall not affect the question whether the killing amounted to murder in the case of any other party to it.

3. Provocation
Where on a charge of murder there is evidence on which the jury can find that the person charged was provoked (whether by things done or by things said or by both together) to lose his self-control, the question whether the provocation was enough to make a reasonable man do as he did shall be left to be determined by the jury; and in determining that question the jury shall take into account everything both done and said according to the effect which, in their opinion, it would have on a reasonable man.

4. Suicide pacts
(1) It shall be manslaughter, and shall not be murder, for a person acting in pursuance of a suicide pact between him and another to kill the other or be a party to the other being killed by a third person.
(2) Where it is shown that a person charged with the murder of another killed the other or was a party to his being killed, it shall be for the defence to prove that the person charged was acting in pursuance of a suicide pact between him and the other.
(3) For the purposes of this section 'suicide pact' means a common agreement between two or more persons having for its object the death of all of them, whether or not each is to take his own life, but nothing done by a person who enters into a suicide pact shall be treated as done by him in pursuance of the pact unless it is done while he has the settled intention of dying in pursuance of the pact.

HUMAN FERTILISATION AND EMBRYOLOGY ACT 1990

1. Meaning of 'embryo', 'gamete' and associated expressions
(1) In this Act, except where otherwise stated—
    (a) embryo means a live human embryo where fertilisation is complete, and
    (b) references to an embryo include an egg in the process of fertilisation,
    and, for this purpose, fertilisation is not complete until the appearance of a two cell zygote.
(2) This Act, so far as it governs bringing about the creation of an embryo, applies only to bringing about the creation of an embryo outside the human body; and in this Act—
    (a) references to embryos the creation of which was brought about *in vitro* (in their application to those where fertilisation is complete) are to those where fertilisation began outside the human body whether or not it was completed there, and
    (b) references to embryos taken from a woman do not include embryos whose creation was brought about *in vitro*.
(3) This Act, so far as it governs the keeping or use of an embryo, applies only to keeping or using an embryo outside the human body.
(4) References in this Act to gametes, eggs or sperm, except where otherwise stated, are to live human gametes, eggs or sperm but references below in this Act to gametes or eggs do not include eggs in the process of fertilisation.
(5) For the purposes of this Act, sperm is to be treated as partner-donated sperm if the donor of the sperm and the recipient of the sperm declare that they have an intimate physical relationship.

2. Other terms
(1) In this Act—
    ...
    'licence' means a licence under Schedule 2 to this Act and, in relation to a licence, 'the person responsible' has the meaning given by section 17 of this Act, and
    'treatment services' means medical, surgical or obstetric services provided to the public or a section of the public for the purpose of assisting women to carry children.
(2) References in this Act to keeping, in relation to embryos or gametes, include keeping while preserved, in storage.
(2A) For the purposes of this Act, a person who, from any premises, controls the provision of services for transporting gametes or embryos is to be taken to distribute gametes or embryos on those premises.
    ...
(3) For the purposes of this Act, a woman is not to be treated as carrying a child until the embryo has become implanted.

3. Prohibitions in connection with embryos
(1) No person shall bring about the creation of an embryo except in pursuance of a licence.
(1A) No person shall keep or use an embryo except—
    (a) in pursuance of a licence, or
    (b) in the case of—
        (i) the keeping, without storage, of an embryo intended for human application, or
        (ii) the processing, without storage, of such an embryo,
        in pursuance of a third party agreement.
(1B) No person shall procure or distribute an embryo intended for human application except in pursuance of a licence or a third party agreement.
(2) No person shall place in a woman—
    (a) a live embryo other than a human embryo, or
    (b) any live gametes other than human gametes.

(3) A licence cannot authorise—
  (a) keeping or using an embryo after the appearance of the primitive streak,
  (b) placing an embryo in any animal,
  (c) keeping or using an embryo in any circumstances in which regulations prohibit its keeping or use, or
  (d) replacing a nucleus of a cell of an embryo with a nucleus taken from a cell of any person, embryo or subsequent development of an embryo.
(4) For the purposes of subsection (3)(a) above, the primitive streak is to be taken to have appeared in an embryo not later than the end of the period of 14 days beginning with the day when the gametes are mixed, not counting any time during which the embryo is stored.

3A. Prohibition in connection with germ cells
(1) No person shall, for the purpose of providing fertility services for any woman, use female germ cells taken or derived from an embryo or a foetus or use embryos created by using such cells.
(2) In this section—
  'female germ cells' means cells of the female germ line and includes such cells at any stage of maturity and accordingly includes eggs; and
  'fertility services' means medical, surgical or obstetric services provided for the purpose of assisting women to carry children.

4. Prohibitions in connection with gametes
(1) No person shall—
  (a) store any gametes, or
  (b) in the course of providing treatment services for any woman, use—
    (i) any sperm, other than partner-donated sperm which has been neither processed nor stored,
    (ii) the woman's eggs after processing or storage, or
    (iii) the eggs of any other woman, or
  (c) mix gametes with the live gametes of any animal, except in pursuance of a licence.
(1A) No person shall procure, test, process or distribute any gametes intended for human application except in pursuance of a license or a third party agreement.
(2) A licence cannot authorise storing or using gametes in any circumstances in which regulations prohibit their storage or use.
(3) No person shall place sperm and eggs in a woman in any circumstances specified in regulations except in pursuance of a licence.
(4) Regulations made by virtue of subsection (3) above may provide that, in relation to licences only to place sperm and eggs in a woman in such circumstances, sections 12 to 22 of this Act shall have effect with such modifications as may be specified in the regulations.
(5) Activities regulated by this section or section 3 of this Act are referred to in this Act as 'activities governed by this Act'.

41. Offences
(1) A person who—
  (a) contravenes sections 3(2), 3A or 4(1)(c) of this Act, or
  (b) does anything which, by virtue of section 3(3) of this Act, cannot be authorised by a licence,
  is guilty of an offence and liable on conviction on indictment to imprisonment for a term not exceeding ten years or a fine or both.
(2) A person who—
  (a) contravenes section 3(1) or (1A) of this Act, otherwise than by doing something which, by virtue of section 3(3) of this Act, cannot be authorised by a licence,
  (b) keeps any gametes in contravention of section 4(1)(a) of this Act,
  (ba) uses any gametes in contravention of section 4(1)(b),
  (c) contravenes section 4(3) of this Act, or
  (d) fails to comply with any directions given by virtue of section 24(7)(a) of this Act,
  is guilty of an offence.
(2A) A person who contravenes section 3(1B) or 4(1A) is guilty of an offence.

(3) If a person—
- (a) provides any information for the purposes of the grant of a licence, being information which is false or misleading in a material particular, and
- (b) either he knows the information to be false or misleading in a material particular or he provides the information recklessly,

he is guilty of an offence.

(4) A person guilty of an offence under subsection (2) or (3) above, other than an offence to which subsection (4B) applies, is liable—
- (a) on conviction on indictment, to imprisonment for a term not exceeding two years or a fine or both, and
- (b) on summary conviction, to imprisonment for a term not exceeding six months or a fine not exceeding the statutory maximum or both.

(4A) Subsection (4B) applies to—
- (a) an offence under subsection (2)(ba) or (d) or (3) committed in the course of providing basic partner treatment services or non-medical fertility services, or
- (b) an offence under subsection (2A).

(4B) A person guilty of an offence to which this subsection applies is liable—
- (a) on conviction on indictment, to imprisonment for a term not exceeding two years or a fine or both, and
- (b) on summary conviction, to imprisonment for a term not exceeding three months or a fine not exceeding the statutory maximum or both.

(5) A person who discloses any information in contravention of section 33 of this Act is guilty of an offence and liable—
- (a) on conviction on indictment, to imprisonment for a term not exceeding two years or a fine or both, and
- (b) on summary conviction, to imprisonment for a term not exceeding six months or a fine not exceeding the statutory maximum or both.

(6) A person who—
- (a) fails to comply with a requirement made by virtue of sections 39(1)(b) or (2)(b) or 40(2)(b)(ii) or (5)(b) of this Act, or
- (b) intentionally obstructs the exercise of any rights conferred by a warrant issued under section 40 of this Act,

is guilty of an offence.

(7) A person who without reasonable excuse fails to comply with a requirement imposed by regulations made by virtue of section 10(2)(a) of this Act is guilty of an offence.

(8) Where a person to whom a licence applies or the nominal licensee gives or receives any money or other benefit, not authorised by directions, in respect of any supply of gametes or embryos, he is guilty of an offence.

(9) A person guilty of an offence under subsection (6), (7) or (8) above is liable on summary conviction to imprisonment for a term not exceeding six months or a fine not exceeding level five on the standard scale or both.

(10) It is a defence for a person ('the defendant') charged with an offence of doing anything which, under sections 3(1) or 4(1) of this Act, cannot be done except in pursuance of a licence to prove—
- (a) that the defendant was acting under the direction of another, and
- (b) that the defendant believed on reasonable grounds—
  - (i) that the other person was at the material time the person responsible under a licence, a person designated by virtue of section 17(2)(b) of this Act as a person to whom a licence applied, or a person to whom directions had been given by virtue of section 24(9) of this Act, and
  - (ii) that the defendant was authorised by virtue of the licence or directions to do the thing in question.

(11) It is a defence for a person charged with an offence under this Act to prove—
- (a) that at the material time he was a person to whom a licence or third party agreement applied or to whom directions had been given, and

(b) that he took all such steps as were reasonable and exercised all due diligence to avoid committing the offence.

HUMAN RIGHTS ACT 1998

1. The Convention rights
(1) In this Act 'the Convention rights' means the rights and fundamental freedoms set out in—
(a) Articles 2 to 12 and 14 of the Convention,
(b) Articles 1 to 3 of the First Protocol, and
(c) Article 1 of the Thirteenth Protocol,
as read with Articles 16 to 18 of the Convention.
(2) Those Articles are to have effect for the purposes of this Act subject to any designated derogation or reservation (as to which see sections 14 and 15).
(3) The Articles are set out in Schedule 1.
...

2. Interpretation of Convention rights
(1) A court or tribunal determining a question which has arisen in connection with a Convention right must take into account any—
(a) judgment, decision, declaration or advisory opinion of the European Court of Human Rights,
(b) opinion of the Commission given in a report adopted under Article 31 of the Convention,
(c) decision of the Commission in connection with Article 26 or 27(2) of the Convention, or
(d) decision of the Committee of Ministers taken under Article 46 of the Convention, whenever made or given, so far as, in the opinion of the court or tribunal, it is relevant to the proceedings in which that question has arisen.
(2) Evidence of any judgment, decision, declaration or opinion of which account may have to be taken under this section is to be given in proceedings before any court or tribunal in such manner as may be provided by rules.
(3) In this section 'rules' means rules of court or, in the case of proceedings before a tribunal, rules made for the purposes of this section—
(a) by the Lord Chancellor or the Secretary of State, in relation to any proceedings outside Scotland;
...

3. Interpretation of legislation
(1) So far as it is possible to do so, primary legislation and subordinate legislation must be read and given effect in a way which is compatible with the Convention rights.
(2) This section—
(a) applies to primary legislation and subordinate legislation whenever enacted;
(b) does not affect the validity, continuing operation or enforcement of any incompatible primary legislation; and
(c) does not affect the validity, continuing operation or enforcement of any incompatible subordinate legislation if (disregarding any possibility of revocation) primary legislation prevents removal of the incompatibility.

4. Declaration of incompatibility
(1) Subsection (2) applies in any proceedings in which a court determines whether a provision of primary legislation is compatible with a Convention right.
(2) If the court is satisfied that the provision is incompatible with a Convention right, it may make a declaration of that incompatibility.
(3) Subsection (4) applies in any proceedings in which a court determines whether a provision of subordinate legislation, made in the exercise of a power conferred by primary legislation, is compatible with a Convention right.

(4) If the court is satisfied—
   (a) that the provision is incompatible with a Convention right, and
   (b) that (disregarding any possibility of revocation) the primary legislation concerned prevents removal of the incompatibility,
   it may make a declaration of that incompatibility.
(5) In this section 'court' means—
   (a) the House of Lords;
   (b) the Judicial Committee of the Privy Council;
   (c) the Courts-Martial Appeal Court;
   (d) in Scotland, the High Court of Justiciary sitting otherwise than as a trial court or the Court of Session;
   (e) in England and Wales or Northern Ireland, the High Court or the Court of Appeal.
   (f) the Court of Protection, in any matter being dealt with by the President of the Family Division, the Vice-Chancellor or a puisne judge of the High Court.
(6) A declaration under this section ('a declaration of incompatibility')—
   (a) does not affect the validity, continuing operation or enforcement of the provision in respect of which it is given; and
   (b) is not binding on the parties to the proceedings in which it is made.

SCHEDULE 1 | THE ARTICLES

| PART I THE CONVENTION

RIGHTS AND FREEDOMS

Article 2 Right to life
1. Everyone's right to life shall be protected by law. No one shall be deprived of his life intentionally save in the execution of a sentence of a court following his conviction of a crime for which this penalty is provided by law.
2. Deprivation of life shall not be regarded as inflicted in contravention of this Article when it results from the use of force which is no more than absolutely necessary:
   (a) in defence of any person from unlawful violence;
   (b) in order to effect a lawful arrest or to prevent the escape of a person lawfully detained;
   (c) in action lawfully taken for the purpose of quelling a riot or insurrection.

Article 3 Prohibition of torture
No one shall be subjected to torture or to inhuman or degrading treatment or punishment.

Article 4 Prohibition of slavery and forced labour
1. No one shall be held in slavery or servitude.
2. No one shall be required to perform forced or compulsory labour.
3. For the purpose of this Article the term 'forced or compulsory labour' shall not include:
   (a) any work required to be done in the ordinary course of detention imposed according to the provisions of Article 5 of this Convention or during conditional release from such detention;
   (b) any service of a military character or, in case of conscientious objectors in countries where they are recognised, service exacted instead of compulsory military service;
   (c) any service exacted in case of an emergency or calamity threatening the life or well-being of the community;
   (d) any work or service which forms part of normal civic obligations.

Article 5 Right to liberty and security
1. Everyone has the right to liberty and security of person. No one shall be deprived of his liberty save in the following cases and in accordance with a procedure prescribed by law:
   (a) the lawful detention of a person after conviction by a competent court;

(b) the lawful arrest or detention of a person for non-compliance with the lawful order of a court or in order to secure the fulfilment of any obligation prescribed by law;
(c) the lawful arrest or detention of a person effected for the purpose of bringing him before the competent legal authority on reasonable suspicion of having committed an offence or when it is reasonably considered necessary to prevent his committing an offence or fleeing after having done so;
(d) the detention of a minor by lawful order for the purpose of educational supervision or his lawful detention for the purpose of bringing him before the competent legal authority;
(e) the lawful detention of persons for the prevention of the spreading of infectious diseases, of persons of unsound mind, alcoholics or drug addicts or vagrants;
(f) the lawful arrest or detention of a person to prevent his effecting an unauthorised entry into the country or of a person against whom action is being taken with a view to deportation or extradition.
2. Everyone who is arrested shall be informed promptly, in a language which he understands, of the reasons for his arrest and of any charge against him.
3. Everyone arrested or detained in accordance with the provisions of paragraph 1(c) of this Article shall be brought promptly before a judge or other officer authorised by law to exercise judicial power and shall be entitled to trial within a reasonable time or to release pending trial. Release may be conditioned by guarantees to appear for trial.
4. Everyone who is deprived of his liberty by arrest or detention shall be entitled to take proceedings by which the lawfulness of his detention shall be decided speedily by a court and his release ordered if the detention is not lawful.
5. Everyone who has been the victim of arrest or detention in contravention of the provisions of this Article shall have an enforceable right to compensation.

Article 6 Right to a fair trial

1. In the determination of his civil rights and obligations or of any criminal charge against him, everyone is entitled to a fair and public hearing within a reasonable time by an independent and impartial tribunal established by law. Judgment shall be pronounced publicly but the press and public may be excluded from all or part of the trial in the interest of morals, public order or national security in a democratic society, where the interests of juveniles or the protection of the private life of the parties so require, or to the extent strictly necessary in the opinion of the court in special circumstances where publicity would prejudice the interests of justice.
2. Everyone charged with a criminal offence shall be presumed innocent until proved guilty according to law.
3. Everyone charged with a criminal offence has the following minimum rights:
    (a) to be informed promptly, in a language which he understands and in detail, of the nature and cause of the accusation against him;
    (b) to have adequate time and facilities for the preparation of his defence;
    (c) to defend himself in person or through legal assistance of his own choosing or, if he has not sufficient means to pay for legal assistance, to be given it free when the interests of justice so require;
    (d) to examine or have examined witnesses against him and to obtain the attendance and examination of witnesses on his behalf under the same conditions as witnesses against him;
    (e) to have the free assistance of an interpreter if he cannot understand or speak the language used in court.

Article 7 No punishment without law

1. No one shall be held guilty of any criminal offence on account of any act or omission which did not constitute a criminal offence under national or international law at the time when it was committed. Nor shall a heavier penalty be imposed than the one that was applicable at the time the criminal offence was committed.
2. This Article shall not prejudice the trial and punishment of any person for any act or omission which, at the time when it was committed, was criminal according to the general principles of law recognised by civilised nations.

Article 8 Right to respect for private and family life
1. Everyone has the right to respect for his private and family life, his home and his correspondence.
2. There shall be no interference by a public authority with the exercise of this right except such as is in accordance with the law and is necessary in a democratic society in the interests of national security, public safety or the economic well-being of the country, for the prevention of disorder or crime, for the protection of health or morals, or for the protection of the rights and freedoms of others.

Article 9 Freedom of thought, conscience and religion
1. Everyone has the right to freedom of thought, conscience and religion; this right includes freedom to change his religion or belief and freedom, either alone or in community with others and in public or private, to manifest his religion or belief, in worship, teaching, practice and observance.
2. Freedom to manifest one's religion or beliefs shall be subject only to such limitations as are prescribed by law and are necessary in a democratic society in the interests of public safety, for the protection of public order, health or morals, or for the protection of the rights and freedoms of others.

Article 10 Freedom of expression
1. Everyone has the right to freedom of expression. This right shall include freedom to hold opinions and to receive and impart information and ideas without interference by public authority and regardless of frontiers. This Article shall not prevent States from requiring the licensing of broadcasting, television or cinema enterprises.
2. The exercise of these freedoms, since it carries with it duties and responsibilities, may be subject to such formalities, conditions, restrictions or penalties as are prescribed by law and are necessary in a democratic society, in the interests of national security, territorial integrity or public safety, for the prevention of disorder or crime, for the protection of health or morals, for the protection of the reputation or rights of others, for preventing the disclosure of information received in confidence, or for maintaining the authority and impartiality of the judiciary.

Article 11 Freedom of assembly and association
1. Everyone has the right to freedom of peaceful assembly and to freedom of association with others, including the right to form and to join trade unions for the protection of his interests.
2. No restrictions shall be placed on the exercise of these rights other than such as are prescribed by law and are necessary in a democratic society in the interests of national security or public safety, for the prevention of disorder or crime, for the protection of health or morals or for the protection of the rights and freedoms of others. This Article shall not prevent the imposition of lawful restrictions on the exercise of these rights by members of the armed forces, of the police or of the administration of the State.

Article 12 Right to marry
Men and women of marriageable age have the right to marry and to found a family, according to the national laws governing the exercise of this right.

Article 14 Prohibition of discrimination
The enjoyment of the rights and freedoms set forth in this Convention shall be secured without discrimination on any ground such as sex, race, colour, language, religion, political or other opinion, national or social origin, association with a national minority, property, birth or other status.

Article 16 Restrictions on political activity of aliens
Nothing in Articles 10, 11 and 14 shall be regarded as preventing the High Contracting Parties from imposing restrictions on the political activity of aliens.

Article 17 Prohibition of abuse of rights
Nothing in this Convention may be interpreted as implying for any State, group or person any right to engage in any activity or perform any act aimed at the destruction of any of the rights and

freedoms set forth herein or at their limitation to a greater extent than is provided for in the Convention.

Article 18 Limitation on use of restrictions on rights
The restrictions permitted under this Convention to the said rights and freedoms shall not be applied for any purpose other than those for which they have been prescribed.

PART II THE FIRST PROTOCOL

Article 1 Protection of property
Every natural or legal person is entitled to the peaceful enjoyment of his possessions. No one shall be deprived of his possessions except in the public interest and subject to the conditions provided for by law and by the general principles of international law.

The preceding provisions shall not, however, in any way impair the right of a State to enforce such laws as it deems necessary to control the use of property in accordance with the general interest or to secure the payment of taxes or other contributions or penalties.

Article 2 Right to education
No person shall be denied the right to education. In the exercise of any functions which it assumes in relation to education and to teaching, the State shall respect the right of parents to ensure such education and teaching in conformity with their own religious and philosophical convictions.

Article 3 Right to free elections
The High Contracting Parties undertake to hold free elections at reasonable intervals by secret ballot, under conditions which will ensure the free expression of the opinion of the people in the choice of the legislature.

PART III ARTICLE 1 OF THE THIRTEENTH PROTOCOL

Abolition of the death penalty
The death penalty shall be abolished. No one shall be condemned to such penalty or executed.

HUNTING ACT 2004

1. Hunting wild mammals with dogs
A person commits an offence if he hunts a wild mammal with a dog, unless his hunting is exempt.

2. Exempt hunting
(1) Hunting is exempt if it is within a class specified in Schedule 1.
(2) The Secretary of State may by order amend Schedule 1 so as to vary a class of exempt hunting.

3. Hunting: assistance
(1) A person commits an offence if he knowingly permits land which belongs to him to be entered or used in the course of the commission of an offence under section 1.
(2) A person commits an offence if he knowingly permits a dog which belongs to him to be used in the course of the commission of an offence under section 1.

4. Hunting: defence
It is a defence for a person charged with an offence under section 1 in respect of hunting to show that he reasonably believed that the hunting was exempt.

5. Hare coursing
(1) A person commits an offence if he—
    (a) participates in a hare coursing event,

(b) attends a hare coursing event,
(c) knowingly facilitates a hare coursing event, or
(d) permits land which belongs to him to be used for the purposes of a hare coursing event.
(2) Each of the following persons commits an offence if a dog participates in a hare coursing event—
    (a) any person who enters the dog for the event,
    (b) any person who permits the dog to be entered, and
    (c) any person who controls or handles the dog in the course of or for the purposes of the event.
(3) A 'hare coursing event' is a competition in which dogs are, by the use of live hares, assessed as to skill in hunting hares.

6. Penalty

A person guilty of an offence under this Act shall be liable on summary conviction to a fine not exceeding level 5 on the standard scale.

11. Interpretation

(1) In this Act 'wild mammal' includes, in particular—
    (a) a wild mammal which has been bred or tamed for any purpose,
    (b) a wild mammal which is in captivity or confinement,
    (c) a wild mammal which has escaped or been released from captivity or confinement, and
    (d) any mammal which is living wild.
(2) For the purposes of this Act a reference to a person hunting a wild mammal with a dog includes, in particular, any case where—
    (a) a person engages or participates in the pursuit of a wild mammal, and
    (b) one or more dogs are employed in that pursuit (whether or not by him and whether or not under his control or direction).
(3) For the purposes of this Act land belongs to a person if he—
    (a) owns an interest in it,
    (b) manages or controls it, or
    (c) occupies it.
(4) For the purposes of this Act a dog belongs to a person if he—
    (a) owns it,
    (b) is in charge of it, or
    (c) has control of it.

SCHEDULE 1

SECTION 2 EXEMPT HUNTING

Stalking and flushing out

1
(1) Stalking a wild mammal, or flushing it out of cover, is exempt hunting if the conditions in this paragraph are satisfied.
(2) The first condition is that the stalking or flushing out is undertaken for the purpose of—
    (a) preventing or reducing serious damage which the wild mammal would otherwise cause—
        (i) to livestock,
        (ii) to game birds or wild birds (within the meaning of section 27 of the Wildlife and Countryside Act 1981),
        (iii) to food for livestock,
        (iv) to crops (including vegetables and fruit),
        (v) to growing timber,
        (vi) to fisheries,
        (vii) to other property, or

(viii) to the biological diversity of an area (within the meaning of the United Nations Environmental Programme Convention on Biological Diversity of 1992),
- (b) obtaining meat to be used for human or animal consumption, or
- (c) participation in a field trial.

(3) In subparagraph (2)(c) 'field trial' means a competition (other than a hare coursing event within the meaning of section 5) in which dogs—
- (a) flush animals out of cover or retrieve animals that have been shot (or both), and
- (b) are assessed as to their likely usefulness in connection with shooting.

(4) The second condition is that the stalking or flushing out takes place on land—
- (a) which belongs to the person doing the stalking or flushing out, or
- (b) which he has been given permission to use for the purpose by the occupier or, in the case of unoccupied land, by a person to whom it belongs.

(5) The third condition is that the stalking or flushing out does not involve the use of more than two dogs.

(6) The fourth condition is that the stalking or flushing out does not involve the use of a dog below ground otherwise than in accordance with paragraph 2 below.

(7) The fifth condition is that—
- (a) reasonable steps are taken for the purpose of ensuring that as soon as possible after being found or flushed out the wild mammal is shot dead by a competent person, and
- (b) in particular, each dog used in the stalking or flushing out is kept under sufficiently close control to ensure that it does not prevent or obstruct achievement of the objective in paragraph (a).

Use of dogs below ground to protect birds for shooting

2

(1) The use of a dog below ground in the course of stalking or flushing out is in accordance with this paragraph if the conditions in this paragraph are satisfied.

(2) The first condition is that the stalking or flushing out is undertaken for the purpose of preventing or reducing serious damage to game birds or wild birds (within the meaning of section 27 of the Wildlife and Countryside Act 1981) which a person is keeping or preserving for the purpose of their being shot.

(3) The second condition is that the person doing the stalking or flushing out—
- (a) has with him written evidence—
  - (i) that the land on which the stalking or flushing out takes place belongs to him, or
  - (ii) that he has been given permission to use that land for the purpose by the occupier or, in the case of unoccupied land, by a person to whom it belongs, and
- (b) makes the evidence immediately available for inspection by a constable who asks to see it.

(4) The third condition is that the stalking or flushing out does not involve the use of more than one dog below ground at any one time.

(5) In so far as stalking or flushing out is undertaken with the use of a dog below ground in accordance with this paragraph, paragraph 1 shall have effect as if for the condition in paragraph 1(7) there were substituted the condition that—
- (a) reasonable steps are taken for the purpose of ensuring that as soon as possible after being found the wild mammal is flushed out from below ground,
- (b) reasonable steps are taken for the purpose of ensuring that as soon as possible after being flushed out from below ground the wild mammal is shot dead by a competent person,
- (c) in particular, the dog is brought under sufficiently close control to ensure that it does not prevent or obstruct achievement of the objective in paragraph (b),
- (d) reasonable steps are taken for the purpose of preventing injury to the dog, and
- (e) the manner in which the dog is used complies with any code of practice which is issued or approved for the purpose of this paragraph by the Secretary of State.

Rats

3   The hunting of rats is exempt if it takes place on land—
- (a) which belongs to the hunter, or
- (b) which he has been given permission to use for the purpose by the occupier or, in the case of unoccupied land, by a person to whom it belongs.

Rabbits

4   The hunting of rabbits is exempt if it takes place on land—
    (a) which belongs to the hunter, or
    (b) which he has been given permission to use for the purpose by the occupier or, in the case of unoccupied land, by a person to whom it belongs.

Retrieval of hares

5   The hunting of a hare which has been shot is exempt if it takes place on land—
    (a) which belongs to the hunter, or
    (b) which he has been given permission to use for the purpose of hunting hares by the occupier or, in the case of unoccupied land, by a person to whom it belongs.

Falconry

6   Flushing a wild mammal from cover is exempt hunting if undertaken—
    (a) for the purpose of enabling a bird of prey to hunt the wild mammal, and
    (b) on land which belongs to the hunter or which he has been given permission to use for the purpose by the occupier or, in the case of unoccupied land, by a person to whom it belongs.

Recapture of wild mammal

7

(1) The hunting of a wild mammal which has escaped or been released from captivity or confinement is exempt if the conditions in this paragraph are satisfied.
(2) The first condition is that the hunting takes place—
    (a) on land which belongs to the hunter,
    (b) on land which he has been given permission to use for the purpose by the occupier or, in the case of unoccupied land, by a person to whom it belongs, or
    (c) with the authority of a constable.
(3) The second condition is that—
    (a) reasonable steps are taken for the purpose of ensuring that as soon as possible after being found the wild mammal is recaptured or shot dead by a competent person, and
    (b) in particular, each dog used in the hunt is kept under sufficiently close control to ensure that it does not prevent or obstruct achievement of the objective in paragraph (a).
(4) The third condition is that the wild mammal—
    (a) was not released for the purpose of being hunted, and
    (b) was not, for that purpose, permitted to escape.

Rescue of wild mammal

8

(1) The hunting of a wild mammal is exempt if the conditions in this paragraph are satisfied.
(2) The first condition is that the hunter reasonably believes that the wild mammal is or may be injured.
(3) The second condition is that the hunting is undertaken for the purpose of relieving the wild mammal's suffering.
(4) The third condition is that the hunting does not involve the use of more than two dogs.
(5) The fourth condition is that the hunting does not involve the use of a dog below ground.
(6) The fifth condition is that the hunting takes place—
    (a) on land which belongs to the hunter,
    (b) on land which he has been given permission to use for the purpose by the occupier or, in the case of unoccupied land, by a person to whom it belongs, or
    (c) with the authority of a constable.
(7) The sixth condition is that—
    (a) reasonable steps are taken for the purpose of ensuring that as soon as possible after the wild mammal is found appropriate action (if any) is taken to relieve its suffering, and
    (b) in particular, each dog used in the hunt is kept under sufficiently close control to ensure that it does not prevent or obstruct achievement of the objective in paragraph (a).
(8) The seventh condition is that the wild mammal was not harmed for the purpose of enabling it to be hunted in reliance upon this paragraph.

Research and observation

9

(1) The hunting of a wild mammal is exempt if the conditions in this paragraph are satisfied.
(2) The first condition is that the hunting is undertaken for the purpose of or in onnection with the observation or study of the wild mammal.
(3) The second condition is that the hunting does not involve the use of more than two dogs.
(4) The third condition is that the hunting does not involve the use of a dog below ground.
(5) The fourth condition is that the hunting takes place on land—
   (a) which belongs to the hunter, or
   (b) which he has been given permission to use for the purpose by the occupier or, in the case of unoccupied land, by a person to whom it belongs.
(6) The fifth condition is that each dog used in the hunt is kept under sufficiently close control to ensure that it does not injure the wild mammal.

IDENTITY CARDS ACT 2006

25. Possession of false identity documents etc.

(1) It is an offence for a person with the requisite intention to have in his possession or under his control—
   (a) an identity document that is false and that he knows or believes to be false;
   (b) an identity document that was improperly obtained and that he knows or believes to have been improperly obtained; or
   (c) an identity document that relates to someone else.
(2) The requisite intention for the purposes of subsection (1) is—
   (a) the intention of using the document for establishing registrable facts about himself; or
   (b) the intention of allowing or inducing another to use it for establishing, ascertaining or verifying registrable facts about himself or about any other person (with the exception, in the case of a document within paragraph (c) of that subsection, of the individual to whom it relates).
(3) It is an offence for a person with the requisite intention to make, or to have in his possession or under his control—
   (a) any apparatus which, to his knowledge, is or has been specially designed or adapted for the making of false identity documents; or
   (b) any article or material which, to his knowledge, is or has been specially designed or adapted to be used in the making of false identity documents.
(4) The requisite intention for the purposes of subsection (3) is the intention—
   (a) that he or another will make a false identity document; and
   (b) that the document will be used by somebody for establishing, ascertaining or verifying registrable facts about a person.
(5) It is an offence for a person to have in his possession or under his control, without reasonable excuse—
   (a) an identity document that is false;
   (b) an identity document that was improperly obtained;
   (c) an identity document that relates to someone else; or
   (d) any apparatus, article or material which, to his knowledge, is or has been specially designed or adapted for the making of false identity documents or to be used in the making of such documents.
(6) A person guilty of an offence under subsection (1) or (3) shall be liable, on conviction on indictment, to imprisonment for a term not exceeding ten years or to a fine, or to both.
(7) A person guilty of an offence under subsection (5) shall be liable—
   (a) on conviction on indictment, to imprisonment for a term not exceeding two years or to a fine, or to both;

(b) on summary conviction in England and Wales, to imprisonment for a term not exceeding twelve months or to a fine not exceeding the statutory maximum, or to both;

...

but, in relation to an offence committed before the commencement of section 154(1) of the Criminal Justice Act 2003, the reference in paragraph (b) to twelve months is to be read as a reference to six months.

(8) For the purposes of this section—
    (a) an identity document is false only if it is false within the meaning of Part 1 of the Forgery and Counterfeiting Act 1981 (see section 9(1) of that Act); and
    (b) an identity document was improperly obtained if false information was provided, in or in connection with the application for its issue or an application for its modification, to the person who issued it or (as the case may be) to a person entitled to modify it; and references to the making of a false identity document include references to the modification of an identity document so that it becomes false.

...

(10) In this section 'identity document' has the meaning given by section 26.

26. Identity documents for the purposes of section 25

(1) In section 25 'identity document' means any document that is, or purports to be—
    (a) an ID card;
    (b) a designated document;
    (c) an immigration document;
    (d) a United Kingdom passport (within the meaning of the Immigration Act 1971);
    (e) a passport issued by or on behalf of the authorities of a country or territory outside the United Kingdom or by or on behalf of an international organisation;
    (f) a document that can be used (in some or all circumstances) instead of a passport;
    (g) a UK driving licence; or
    (h) a driving licence issued by or on behalf of the authorities of a country or territory outside the United Kingdom.

(2) In subsection (1) 'immigration document' means—
    (a) a document used for confirming the right of a person under the Community Treaties in respect of entry or residence in the United Kingdom;
    (b) a document which is given in exercise of immigration functions and records information about leave granted to a person to enter or to remain in the United Kingdom; or
    (c) a registration card (within the meaning of section 26A of the Immigration Act 1971);
and in paragraph (b) 'immigration functions' means functions under the Immigration Acts (within the meaning of the Asylum and Immigration (Treatment of Claimants, etc.) Act 2004).

(3) In that subsection 'UK driving licence' means—
    (a) a licence to drive a motor vehicle granted under Part 3 of the Road Traffic Act 1988; or
    (b) a licence to drive a motor vehicle granted under Part 2 of the Road Traffic (Northern Ireland) Order 1981 (S.I. 1981/154 (N.I. 1)).

...

27. Unauthorised disclosure of information (NYIF)

(1) A person is guilty of an offence if, without lawful authority—
    (a) he provides any person with information that he is required to keep confidential; or
    (b) he otherwise makes a disclosure of any such information.

(2) For the purposes of this section a person is required to keep information confidential if it is information that is or has become available to him by reason of his holding an office or employment the duties of which relate, in whole or in part, to—
    (a) the establishment or maintenance of the Register;
    (b) the issue, manufacture, modification, cancellation or surrender of ID cards; or
    (c) the carrying out of the Commissioner's functions.

(3) For the purposes of this section information is provided or otherwise disclosed with lawful authority if, and only if the provision or other disclosure of the information—
    (a) is authorised by or under this Act or another enactment;

(b) is in pursuance of an order or direction of a court or of a tribunal established by or under any enactment;
(c) is in pursuance of a Community obligation; or
(d) is for the purposes of the performance of the duties of an office or employment of the sort mentioned in subsection (2).
(4) It is a defence for a person charged with an offence under this section to show that, at the time of the alleged offence, he believed, on reasonable grounds, that he had lawful authority to provide the information or to make the other disclosure in question.
(5) A person guilty of an offence under this section shall be liable, on conviction on indictment, to imprisonment for a term not exceeding two years or to a fine, or to both.

28. Providing false information (NYIF)

(1) A person is guilty of an offence if, in circumstances falling within subsection (2), he provides false information to any person —
    (a) for the purpose of securing the making or modification of an entry in the Register;
    (b) in confirming (with or without changes) the contents of an entry in the Register; or
    (c) for the purpose of obtaining for himself or another the issue or modification of an ID card.
(2) Those circumstances are that, at the time of the provision of the information he—
    (a) knows or believes the information to be false; or
    (b) is reckless as to whether or not it is false.
(3) A person guilty of an offence under this section shall be liable—
    (a) on conviction on indictment, to imprisonment for a term not exceeding two years or to a fine, or to both;
    (b) on summary conviction in England and Wales, to imprisonment for a term not exceeding twelve months or to a fine not exceeding the statutory maximum, or to both;
    (c) on summary conviction in Scotland or Northern Ireland, to imprisonment for a term not exceeding six months or to a fine not exceeding the statutory maximum, or to both;
    but, in relation to an offence committed before the commencement of section 154(1) of the Criminal Justice Act 2003, the reference in paragraph (b) to twelve months is to be read as a reference to six months.

29. Tampering with the Register etc. (NYIF)

(1) A person is guilty of an offence under this section if—
    (a) he engages in any conduct that causes an unauthorised modification of information recorded in the Register; and
    (b) at the time when he engages in the conduct, he has the requisite intent.
(2) For the purposes of this section a person has the requisite intent if he—
    (a) intends to cause a modification of information recorded in the Register; or
    (b) is reckless as to whether or not his conduct will cause such a modification.
(3) For the purposes of this section the cases in which conduct causes a modification of information recorded in the Register include—
    (a) where it contributes to a modification of such information; and
    (b) where it makes it more difficult or impossible for such information to be retrieved in a legible form from a computer on which it is stored by the Secretary of State, or contributes to making that more difficult or impossible.
(4) It is immaterial for the purposes of this section—
    (a) whether the conduct constituting the offence, or any of it, took place in the United Kingdom; or
    (b) in the case of conduct outside the United Kingdom, whether it is conduct of a British citizen.
(5) For the purposes of this section a modification is unauthorised, in relation to the person whose conduct causes it, if—
    (a) he is not himself entitled to determine if the modification may be made; and
    (b) he does not have a consent to the modification from a person who is so entitled.

(6) In proceedings against a person for an offence under this section in respect of conduct causing a modification of information recorded in the Register it is to be a defence for that person to show that, at the time of the conduct, he believed, on reasonable grounds—
   (a) that he was a person entitled to determine if that modification might be made; or
   (b) that consent to the modification had been given by a person so entitled.
(7) A person guilty of an offence under this section shall be liable—
   (a) on conviction on indictment, to imprisonment for a term not exceeding ten years or to a fine, or to both;
   (b) on summary conviction in England and Wales, to imprisonment for a term not exceeding twelve months or to a fine not exceeding the statutory maximum, or to both;
   ...
   but, in relation to an offence committed before the commencement of section 154(1) of the Criminal Justice Act 2003, the reference in paragraph (b) to twelve months is to be read as a reference to six months.
(8) In the case of an offence by virtue of this section in respect of conduct wholly or partly outside the United Kingdom—
   (a) proceedings for the offence may be taken at any place in the United Kingdom; and
   (b) the offence may for all incidental purposes be treated as having been committed at any such place.
(9) In this section—
   'conduct' includes acts and omissions; and
   'modification' includes a temporary modification.

INFANT LIFE (PRESERVATION) ACT 1929

1. Punishment for child destruction
(1) Subject as hereinafter in this subsection provided, any person who, with intent to destroy the life of a child capable of being born alive, by any wilful act causes a child to die before it has an existence independent of its mother, shall be guilty of felony, to wit, of child destruction, and shall be liable on conviction thereof on indictment to penal servitude for life:
   Provided that no person shall be found guilty of an offence under this section unless it is proved that the act which caused the death of the child was not done in good faith for the purpose only of preserving the life of the mother.
(2) For the purposes of this Act, evidence that a woman had at any material time been pregnant for a period of twenty-eight weeks or more shall be primâ facie proof that she was at that time pregnant of a child capable of being born alive.

2. Prosecution of offences
(2) Where upon the trial of any person for the murder or manslaughter of any child, or for infanticide, or for an offence under section 58 of the Offences against the Person Act 1861 (which relates to administering drugs or using instruments to procure abortion), the jury are of opinion that the person charged is not guilty of murder, manslaughter or infanticide, or of an offence under the said section 58, as the case may be, but that he is shown by the evidence to be guilty of the felony of child destruction, the jury may find him guilty of that felony, and thereupon the person convicted shall be liable to be punished as if he had been convicted upon an indictment for child destruction.
(3) Where upon the trial of any person for the felony of child destruction the jury are of opinion that the person charged is not guilty of that felony, but that he is shown by the evidence to be guilty of an offence under the said section 58 of the Offences against the Person Act 1861, the jury may find him guilty of that offence, and thereupon the person convicted shall be liable to be punished as if he had been convicted upon an indictment under that section.

INFANTICIDE ACT 1938

1. Offence of infanticide
(1) Where a woman by any wilful act or omission causes the death of her child being a child under the age of twelve months, but at the time of the act or omission the balance of her mind was disturbed by reason of her not having fully recovered from the effect of giving birth to the child or by reason of the effect of lactation consequent upon the birth of the child, then, notwithstanding that the circumstances were such that but for this Act the offence would have amounted to murder, she shall be guilty of felony, to wit of infanticide, and may for such offence be dealt with and punished as if she had been guilty of the offence of manslaughter of the child.
(2) Where upon the trial of a woman for the murder of her child, being a child under the age of twelve months, the jury are of opinion that she by any wilful act or omission caused its death, but that at the time of the act or omission the balance of her mind was disturbed by reason of her not having fully recovered from the effect of giving birth to the child or by reason of the effect of lactation consequent upon the birth of the child, then the jury may, notwithstanding that the circumstances were such that but for the provisions of this Act they might have returned a verdict of murder, return in lieu thereof a verdict of infanticide.
(3) Nothing in this Act shall affect the power of the jury upon an indictment for the murder of a child to return a verdict of manslaughter, or a verdict of guilty but insane.

INTERPRETATION ACT 1978

5. Definitions
In any Act, unless the contrary intention appears, words and expressions listed in Schedule 1 to this Act are to be construed according to that Schedule.

6. Gender and number
In any Act, unless the contrary intention appears,—
    (a) words importing the masculine gender include the feminine;
    (b) words importing the feminine gender include the masculine;
    (c) words in the singular include the plural and words in the plural include the singular.

15. Repeal of repeal
Where an Act repeals a repealing enactment, the repeal does not revive any enactment previously repealed unless words are added reviving it.

16. General savings
(1) Without prejudice to section 15, where an Act repeals an enactment, the repeal does not, unless the contrary intention appears,—
    (a) revive anything not in force or existing at the time at which the repeal takes effect;
    (b) affect the previous operation of the enactment repealed or anything duly done or suffered under that enactment;
    (c) affect any right, privilege, obligation or liability acquired, accrued or incurred under that enactment;
    (d) affect any penalty, forfeiture or punishment incurred in respect of any offence committed against that enactment;
    (e) affect any investigation, legal proceeding or remedy in respect of any such right, privilege, obligation, liability, penalty, forfeiture or punishment;
and any such investigation, legal proceeding or remedy may be instituted, continued or enforced, and any such penalty, forfeiture or punishment may be imposed, as if the repealing Act had not been passed.

(2) This section applies to the expiry of a temporary enactment as if it were repealed by an Act.

18. Duplicated offences
Where an act or omission constitutes an offence under two or more Acts, or both under an Act and at common law, the offender shall, unless the contrary intention appears, be liable to be prosecuted and punished under either or any of those Acts or at common law, but shall not be liable to be punished more than once for the same offence.

SCHEDULE 1 | SECTION 5, WORDS AND EXPRESSIONS DEFINED

DEFINITIONS
'Act' means an Act of Parliament ...
'The standard scale', with reference to a fine or penalty for an offence triable only summarily,—
    (a) in relation to England and Wales, has the meaning given by section 37 of the Criminal Justice Act 1982;
...
'Statutory maximum', with reference to a fine or penalty on summary conviction for an offence,—
    (a) in relation to England and Wales, means the prescribed sum within the meaning of section 32 of the Magistrates' Courts Act 1980;
...

CONSTRUCTION OF CERTAIN EXPRESSIONS RELATING TO OFFENCES
...
In relation to England and Wales—
    (a) 'indictable offence' means an offence which, if committed by an adult, is triable on indictment, whether it is exclusively so triable or triable either way;
    (b) 'summary offence' means an offence which, if committed by an adult, is triable only summarily;
    (c) 'offence triable either way' means an offence other than an offence triable on indictment only by virtue of Part V of the Criminal Justice Act 1988 which, if committed by an adult, is triable either on indictment or summarily; and the terms 'indictable', 'summary' and 'triable either way', in their application to offences, are to be construed accordingly.
In the above definitions references to the way or ways in which an offence is triable are to be construed without regard to the effect, if any, of section 22 of the Magistrates' Courts Act 1980 on the mode of trial in a particular case.

| INTOXICATING SUBSTANCES (SUPPLY) ACT 1985

1. Offence of supply of intoxicating substance
(1) It is an offence for a person to supply or offer to supply a substance other than a controlled drug—
    (a) to a person under the age of eighteen whom he knows, or has reasonable cause to believe, to be under that age; or
    (b) to a person—
        (i) who is acting on behalf of a person under that age; and
        (ii) whom he knows, or has reasonable cause to believe, to be so acting,
    if he knows or has reasonable cause to believe that the substance is, or its fumes are, likely to be inhaled by the person under the age of eighteen for the purpose of causing intoxication.

(2) In proceedings against any person for an offence under subsection (1) above it is a defence for him to show that at the time he made the supply or offer he was under the age of eighteen and was acting otherwise than in the course or furtherance of a business.
(3) A person guilty of an offence under this section shall be liable on summary conviction to imprisonment for a term not exceeding six months or to a fine not exceeding level 5 on the standard scale or to both.
(4) In this section 'controlled drug' has the same meaning as in the Misuse of Drugs Act 1971.

KNIVES ACT 1997

1. Unlawful marketing of knives
(1) A person is guilty of an offence if he markets a knife in a way which—
    (a) indicates, or suggests, that it is suitable for combat; or
    (b) is otherwise likely to stimulate or encourage violent behaviour involving the use of the knife as a weapon.
(2) 'Suitable for combat' and 'violent behaviour' are defined in section 10.
(3) For the purposes of this Act, an indication or suggestion that a knife is suitable for combat may, in particular, be given or made by a name or description—
    (a) applied to the knife;
    (b) on the knife or on any packaging in which it is contained; or
    (c) included in any advertisement which, expressly or by implication, relates to the knife.
(4) For the purposes of this Act, a person markets a knife if—
    (a) he sells or hires it;
    (b) he offers, or exposes, it for sale or hire; or
    (c) he has it in his possession for the purpose of sale or hire.
(5) A person who is guilty of an offence under this section is liable—
    (a) on summary conviction to imprisonment for a term not exceeding six months or to a fine not exceeding the statutory maximum, or to both;
    (b) on conviction on indictment to imprisonment for a term not exceeding two years or to a fine, or to both.

2. Publications
(1) A person is guilty of an offence if he publishes any written, pictorial or other material in connection with the marketing of any knife and that material—
    (a) indicates, or suggests, that the knife is suitable for combat; or
    (b) is otherwise likely to stimulate or encourage violent behaviour involving the use of the knife as a weapon.
(2) A person who is guilty of an offence under this section is liable—
    (a) on summary conviction to imprisonment for a term not exceeding six months or to a fine not exceeding the statutory maximum, or to both;
    (b) on conviction on indictment to imprisonment for a term not exceeding two years or to a fine, or to both.

3. Exempt trades
(1) It is a defence for a person charged with an offence under section 1 to prove that—
    (a) the knife was marketed—
        (i) for use by the armed forces of any country;
        (ii) as an antique or curio; or
        (iii) as falling within such other category (if any) as may be prescribed;
    (b) it was reasonable for the knife to be marketed in that way; and
    (c) there were no reasonable grounds for suspecting that a person into whose possession the knife might come in consequence of the way in which it was marketed would use it for an unlawful purpose.

(2) It is a defence for a person charged with an offence under section 2 to prove that—
   (a) the material was published in connection with marketing a knife—
      (i) for use by the armed forces of any country;
      (ii) as an antique or curio; or
      (iii) as falling within such other category (if any) as may be prescribed;
   (b) it was reasonable for the knife to be marketed in that way; and
   (c) there were no reasonable grounds for suspecting that a person into whose possession the knife might come in consequence of the publishing of the material would use it for an unlawful purpose.
   …

4. Other defences

(1) It is a defence for a person charged with an offence under section 1 to prove that he did not know or suspect, and had no reasonable grounds for suspecting, that the way in which the knife was marketed—
   (a) amounted to an indication or suggestion that the knife was suitable for combat; or
   (b) was likely to stimulate or encourage violent behaviour involving the use of the knife as a weapon.
(2) It is a defence for a person charged with an offence under section 2 to prove that he did not know or suspect, and had no reasonable grounds for suspecting, that the material—
   (a) amounted to an indication or suggestion that the knife was suitable for combat; or
   (b) was likely to stimulate or encourage violent behaviour involving the use of the knife as a weapon.
(3) It is a defence for a person charged with an offence under section 1 or 2 to prove that he took all reasonable precautions and exercised all due diligence to avoid committing the offence.

9. Offences by bodies corporate

(1) If an offence under this Act committed by a body corporate is proved—
   (a) to have been committed with the consent or connivance of an officer, or
   (b) to be attributable to any neglect on his part, he as well as the body corporate is guilty of the offence and liable to be proceeded against and punished accordingly.
(2) In subsection (1) 'officer', in relation to a body corporate, means a director, manager, secretary or other similar officer of the body, or a person purporting to act in any such capacity.
(3) If the affairs of a body corporate are managed by its members, subsection (1) applies in relation to the acts and defaults of a member in connection with his functions of management as if he were a director of the body corporate.
   …

10. Interpretation

In this Act—
   'the court' means
   (a) in relation to England and Wales … the Crown Court or a magistrate's court;
   (b) …
      'knife' means an instrument which has a blade or is sharply pointed;
      'marketing' and related expressions are to be read with section 1(4);
      'publication' includes a publication in electronic form and, in the case of a publication which is, or may be, produced from electronic data, any medium on which the data are stored;
      'suitable for combat' means suitable for use as a weapon for inflicting injury on a person or causing a person to fear injury;
      'violent behaviour' means an unlawful act inflicting injury on a person or causing a person to fear injury.

LAW REFORM (YEAR AND A DAY RULE) ACT 1996

1. Abolition of 'year and a day rule'

The rule known as the 'year and a day rule' (that is, the rule that, for the purposes of offences involving death and of suicide, an act or omission is conclusively presumed not to have caused a person's death if more than a year and a day elapsed before he died) is abolished for all purposes.

2. Restriction on institution of proceedings for a fatal offence

(1) Proceedings to which this section applies may only be instituted by or with the consent of the Attorney General.
(2) This section applies to proceedings against a person for a fatal offence if—
    (a) the injury alleged to have caused the death was sustained more than three years before the death occurred, or
    (b) the person has previously been convicted of an offence committed in circumstances alleged to be connected with the death.
(3) In subsection (2) 'fatal offence' means—
    (a) murder, manslaughter, infanticide or any other offence of which one of the elements is causing a person's death,
    (b) the offence of aiding, abetting, counselling or procuring a person's suicide, or
    (c) an offence under section 5 of the Domestic Violence, Crime and Victims Act 2004 (causing or allowing the death of a child or vulnerable adult).
(4) No provision that proceedings may be instituted only by or with the consent of the Director of Public Prosecutions shall apply to proceedings to which this section applies.

3. Short title, commencement and extent

...
(2) Section 1 does not affect the continued application of the rule referred to in that section to a case where the act or omission (or the last of the acts or omissions) which caused the death occurred before the day on which this Act is passed.

LICENSING ACT 2003

141. Sale of alcohol to a person who is drunk

(1) A person to whom subsection (2) applies commits an offence if, on relevant premises, he knowingly—
    (a) sells or attempts to sell alcohol to a person who is drunk, or
    (b) allows alcohol to be sold to such a person.
(2) This subsection applies—
    (a) to any person who works at the premises in a capacity, whether paid or unpaid, which gives him authority to sell the alcohol concerned,
    (b) in the case of licensed premises, to—
        (i) the holder of a premises licence in respect of the premises, and
        (ii) the designated premises supervisor (if any) under such a licence,
    (c) in the case of premises in respect of which a club premises certificate has effect, to any member or officer of the club which holds the certificate who at the time the sale (or attempted sale) takes place is present on the premises in a capacity which enables him to prevent it, and
    (d) in the case of premises which may be used for a permitted temporary activity by virtue of Part 5, to the premises user in relation to the temporary event notice in question.

(3) This section applies in relation to the supply of alcohol by or on behalf of a club to or to the order of a member of the club as it applies in relation to the sale of alcohol.
(4) A person guilty of an offence under this section is liable on summary conviction to a fine not exceeding level 3 on the standard scale.

142. Obtaining alcohol for a person who is drunk
(1) A person commits an offence if, on relevant premises, he knowingly obtains or attempts to obtain alcohol for consumption on those premises by a person who is drunk.
(2) A person guilty of an offence under this section is liable on summary conviction to a fine not exceeding level 3 on the standard scale.

MAGISTRATES COURTS ACT 1980

44. Aiders and abettors
(1) A person who aids, abets, counsels or procures the commission by another person of a summary offence shall be guilty of the like offence and may be tried (whether or not he is charged as a principal) either by a court having jurisdiction to try that other person or by a court having by virtue of his own offence jurisdiction to try him.
(2) Any offence consisting in aiding, abetting, counselling or procuring the commission of an offence triable either way (other than an offence listed in Schedule 1 to this Act) shall by virtue of this subsection be triable either way.

45. (repealed)

MALICIOUS COMMUNICATIONS ACT 1988

1. Offence of sending letters etc. with intent to cause distress or anxiety
(1) Any person who sends to another person—
   (a) a letter, electronic communication or article of any description which conveys—
      (i) a message which is indecent or grossly offensive;
      (ii) a threat; or
      (iii) information which is false and known or believed to be false by the sender; or
   (b) any article or electronic communication which is, in whole or part, of an indecent or grossly offensive nature, is guilty of an offence if his purpose, or one of his purposes, in sending it is that it should, so far as falling within paragraph (a) or (b) above, cause distress or anxiety to the recipient or to any other person to whom he intends that it or its contents or nature should be communicated.
(2) A person is not guilty of an offence by virtue of subsection (1)(a)(ii) above if he shows—
   (a) that the threat was used to reinforce a demand made by him on reasonable grounds; and
   (b) that he believed, and had reasonable grounds for believing, that the use of the threat was a proper means of reinforcing the demand.
(2A) In this section 'electronic communication' includes—
   (a) any oral or other communication by means of an electronic communication network; and
   (b) any communication (however sent) that is in electronic form.
(3) In this section references to sending include references to delivering or transmitting and to causing to be sent, delivered or transmitted and 'sender' shall be construed accordingly.
(4) A person guilty of an offence under this section shall be liable on summary conviction to imprisonment for a term not exceeding six months or to a fine not exceeding level 5 on the standard scale, or to both.

MENTAL CAPACITY ACT 2005

2. People who lack capacity
(1) For the purposes of this Act, a person lacks capacity in relation to a matter if at the material time he is unable to make a decision for himself in relation to the matter because of an impairment of, or a disturbance in the functioning of, the mind or brain.
(2) It does not matter whether the impairment or disturbance is permanent or temporary.
(3) A lack of capacity cannot be established merely by reference to—
   (a) a person's age or appearance, or
   (b) a condition of his, or an aspect of his behaviour, which might lead others to make unjustified assumptions about his capacity.
(4) In proceedings under this Act or any other enactment, any question whether a person lacks capacity within the meaning of this Act must be decided on the balance of probabilities.
...

3. Inability to make decisions
(1) For the purposes of section 2, a person is unable to make a decision for himself if he is unable—
   (a) to understand the information relevant to the decision,
   (b) to retain that information,
   (c) to use or weigh that information as part of the process of making the decision, or
   (d) to communicate his decision (whether by talking, using sign language or any other means).
(2) A person is not to be regarded as unable to understand the information relevant to a decision if he is able to understand an explanation of it given to him in a way that is appropriate to his circumstances (using simple language, visual aids or any other means).
(3) The fact that a person is able to retain the information relevant to a decision for a short period only does not prevent him from being regarded as able to make the decision.
(4) The information relevant to a decision includes information about the reasonably foreseeable consequences of—
   (a) deciding one way or another, or
   (b) failing to make the decision.

44. Ill-treatment or neglect
(1) Subsection (2) applies if a person ('D')—
   (a) has the care of a person ('P') who lacks, or whom D reasonably believes to lack, capacity,
   (b) is the donee of a lasting power of attorney, or an enduring power of attorney (within the meaning of Schedule 4), created by P, or
   (c) is a deputy appointed by the court for P.
(2) D is guilty of an offence if he ill-treats or wilfully neglects P.
(3) A person guilty of an offence under this section is liable—
   (a) on summary conviction, to imprisonment for a term not exceeding 12 months or a fine not exceeding the statutory maximum or both;
   (b) on conviction on indictment, to imprisonment for a term not exceeding 5 years or a fine or both.

62. Scope of the Act
For the avoidance of doubt, it is hereby declared that nothing in this Act is to be taken to affect the law relating to murder or manslaughter or the operation of section 2 of the Suicide Act 1961 (assisting suicide).

MISUSE OF DRUGS ACT 1971

2. Controlled drugs and their classification for purposes of this Act
(1) In this Act—
   (a) the expression 'controlled drug' means any substance or product for the time being specified in Part I, II, or III of Schedule 2 to this Act; and
   (b) the expressions 'Class A drug', 'Class B drug' and 'Class C drug' mean any of the substances and products for the time being specified respectively in Part I, Part II and Part III of that Schedule;
   and the provisions of Part IV of that Schedule shall have effect with respect to the meanings of expressions used in that Schedule.

3. Restriction of importation and exportation of controlled drugs
(1) Subject to subsection (2) below—
   (a) the importation of a controlled drug; and
   (b) the exportation of a controlled drug,
   are hereby prohibited.
(2) Subsection (1) above does not apply—
   (a) to the importation or exportation of a controlled drug which is for the time being excepted from paragraph (a) or, as the case may be, paragraph (b) of subsection (1) above by regulations under section 7 of this Act; or
   (b) to the importation or exportation of a controlled drug under and in accordance with the terms of a licence issued by the Secretary of State and in compliance with any conditions attached thereto.

4. Restriction of production and supply of controlled drugs
(1) Subject to any regulations under section 7 of this Act for the time being in force, it shall not be lawful for a person—
   (a) to produce a controlled drug; or
   (b) to supply or offer to supply a controlled drug to another.
(2) Subject to section 28 of this Act, it is an offence for a person—
   (a) to produce a controlled drug in contravention of subsection (1) above; or
   (b) to be concerned in the production of such a drug in contravention of that subsection by another.
(3) Subject to section 28 of this Act, it is an offence for a person—
   (a) to supply or offer to supply a controlled drug to another in contravention of subsection (1) above; or
   (b) to be concerned in the supplying of such a drug to another in contravention of that subsection; or
   (c) to be concerned in the making to another in contravention of that subsection of an offer to supply such a drug.

4A. Aggravation of offence of supply of controlled drug
(1) This section applies if—
   (a) a court is considering the seriousness of an offence under section 4(3) of this Act, and
   (b) at the time the offence was committed the offender had attained the age of 18.
(2) If either of the following conditions is met the court—
   (a) must treat the fact that the condition is met as an aggravating factor (that is to say, a factor that increases the seriousness of the offence), and
   (b) must state in open court that the offence is so aggravated.
(3) The first condition is that the offence was committed on or in the vicinity of school premises at a relevant time.
(4) The second condition is that in connection with the commission of the offence the offender used a courier who, at the time the offence was committed, was under the age of 18.
(5) In subsection (3), a relevant time is—

(a) any time when the school premises are in use by persons under the age of 18;
(b) one hour before the start and one hour after the end of any such time.
(6) For the purposes of subsection (4), a person uses a courier in connection with an offence under section 4(3) of this Act if he causes or permits another person (the courier)—
(a) to deliver a controlled drug to a third person, or
(b) to deliver a drug related consideration to himself or a third person.
(7) For the purposes of subsection (6), a drug related consideration is a consideration of any description which—
(a) is obtained in connection with the supply of a controlled drug, or
(b) is intended to be used in connection with obtaining a controlled drug.
(8) In this section—
'school premises' means land used for the purposes of a school excluding any land occupied solely as a dwelling by a person employed at the school; and
'school' has the same meaning—
(a) in England and Wales, as in section 4 of the Education Act 1996;
…

5. Restriction of possession of controlled drugs

(1) Subject to any regulations under section 7 of this Act for the time being in force, it shall not be lawful for a person to have a controlled drug in his possession.
(2) Subject to section 28 of this Act and to subsection (4) below, it is an offence for a person to have a controlled drug in his possession in contravention of subsection (1) above.
(3) Subject to section 28 of this Act, it is an offence for a person to have a controlled drug in his possession, whether lawfully or not, with intent to supply it to another in contravention of section 4(1) of this Act.
(4) In any proceedings for an offence under subsection (2) above in which it is proved that the accused had a controlled drug in his possession, it shall be a defence for him to prove—
(a) that, knowing or suspecting it to be a controlled drug, he took possession of it for the purpose of preventing another from committing or continuing to commit an offence in connection with that drug and that as soon as possible after taking possession of it he took all such steps as were reasonably open to him to destroy the drug or to deliver it into the custody of a person lawfully entitled to take custody of it; or
(b) that, knowing or suspecting it to be a controlled drug, he took possession of it for the purpose of delivering it into the custody of a person lawfully entitled to take custody of it and that as soon as possible after taking possession of it he took all such steps as were reasonably open to him to deliver it into the custody of such a person.
(4A) In any proceedings for an offence under subsection (3) above, if it is proved that the accused had an amount of a controlled drug in his possession which is not less than the prescribed amount, the court or jury must assume that he had the drug in his possession with the intent to supply it as mentioned in subsection (3). **(NYIF)**
(4B) Subsection (4A) above does not apply if evidence is adduced which is sufficient to raise an issue that the accused may not have had the drug in his possession with that intent. **(NYIF)**
(4C) Regulations under subsection (4A) above have effect only in relation to proceedings for an offence committed after the regulations come into force. **(NYIF)**
(6) Nothing in subsection (4) or (5) above shall prejudice any defence which it is open to a person charged with an offence under this section to raise apart from that subsection.

6. Restriction of cultivation of cannabis plant

(1) Subject to any regulations under section 7 of this Act for the time being in force, it shall not be lawful for a person to cultivate any plant of the genus *Cannabis*.
(2) Subject to section 28 of this Act, it is an offence to cultivate any such plant in contravention subsection (1) above.

7. Authorisation of activities otherwise unlawful under foregoing provisions

(1) The Secretary of State may by regulations—
(a) except from sections 3(1)(a) or (b), 4(1)(a) or (b) or 5(1) of this Act such controlled drugs as may be specified in the regulations; and

(b) make such other provision as he thinks fit for the purpose of making it lawful for persons to do things which under any of the following provisions of this Act, that is to say sections 4(1), 5(1) and 6(1), it would otherwise be unlawful for them to do.
(2) Without prejudice to the generality of paragraph (b) of subsection (1) above, regulations under that subsection authorising the doing of any such thing as is mentioned in that paragraph may in particular provide for the doing of that thing to be lawful—
   (a) if it is done under and in accordance with the terms of a licence or other authority issued by the Secretary of State and in compliance with any conditions attached thereto; or
   (b) if it is done in compliance with such conditions as may be prescribed.
(3) Subject to subsection (4) below, the Secretary of State shall so exercise his power to make regulations under subsection (1) above as to secure—
   (a) that it is not unlawful under section 4(1) of this Act for a doctor, dentist, veterinary practitioner or veterinary surgeon, acting in his capacity as such, to prescribe, administer, manufacture, compound or supply a controlled drug, or for a pharmacist or a person lawfully conducting a retail pharmacy business, acting in either case in his capacity as such, to manufacture, compound or supply a controlled drug; and
   (b) that it is not unlawful under section 5(1) of this Act for a doctor, dentist, veterinary practitioner, veterinary surgeon, pharmacist or person lawfully conducting a retail pharmacy business to have a controlled drug in his possession for the purpose of acting in his capacity as such.
(4) If in the case of any controlled drug the Secretary of State is of the opinion that it is in the public interest—
   (a) for production, supply and possession of that drug to be either wholly unlawful or unlawful except for purposes of research or other special purposes; or
   (b) for it to be unlawful for practitioners, pharmacists and persons lawfully conducting retail pharmacy businesses to do in relation to that drug any of the things mentioned in subsection (3) above except under a licence or other authority issued by the Secretary of State,
   he may by order designate that drug as a drug to which this subsection applies; and while there is in force an order under this subsection designating a controlled drug as one to which this subsection applies, subsection (3) above shall not apply as regards that drug.
   ...
(8) References in this section to a person's 'doing' things include references to his having things in his possession.
   ...

8. Occupiers etc. of premises to be punishable for permitting certain activities to take place there

A person commits an offence if, being the occupier or concerned in the management of any premises, he knowingly permits or suffers any of the following activities to take place on those premises, that is to say—
   (a) producing or attempting to produce a controlled drug in contravention of section 4(1) of this Act;
   (b) supplying or attempting to supply a controlled drug to another in contravention of section 4(1) of this Act, or offering to supply a controlled drug to another in contravention of section 4(1);
   (c) preparing opium for smoking;
   (d) smoking cannabis, cannabis resin or prepared opium.

9. Prohibition of certain activities etc. relating to opium

Subject to section 28 of this Act, it is an offence for a person—
   (a) to smoke or otherwise use prepared opium; or
   (b) to frequent a place used for the purpose of opium smoking; or
   (c) to have in his possession—
      (i) any pipes or other utensils made or adapted for use in connection with the smoking of opium, being pipes or utensils which have been used by him or with his knowledge and permission in that connection or which he intends to use or permit others to use in that connection; or

(ii) any utensils which have been used by him or with his knowledge and permission in connection with the preparation of opium for smoking.

9A. Prohibition of supply etc. of articles for administering or preparing controlled drugs

(1) A person who supplies or offers to supply any article which may be used or adapted to be used (whether by itself or in combination with another article or other articles) in the administration by any person of a controlled drug to himself or another, believing that the article (or the article as adapted) is to be so used in circumstances where the administration is unlawful, is guilty of an offence.

(2) It is not an offence under subsection (1) above to supply or offer to supply a hypodermic syringe, or any part of one.

(3) A person who supplies or offers to supply any article which may be used to prepare a controlled drug for administration by any person to himself or another believing that the article is to be so used in circumstances where the administration is unlawful is guilty of an offence.

(4) For the purposes of this section, any administration of a controlled drug is unlawful except—
   (a) the administration by any person of a controlled drug to another in circumstances where the administration of the drug is not unlawful under section 4(1) of this Act, or
   (b) the administration by any person of a controlled drug to himself in circumstances where having the controlled drug in his possession is not unlawful under section 5(1) of this Act.

(5) In this section, references to administration by any person of a controlled drug to himself include a reference to his administering it to himself with the assistance of another.

28. Proof of lack of knowledge etc. to be a defence in proceedings for certain offences

(1) This section applies to offences under any of the following provisions of this Act, that is to say section 4(2) and (3), section 5(2) and (3), section 6(2) and section 9.

(2) Subject to subsection (3) below, in any proceedings for an offence to which this section applies it shall be a defence for the accused to prove that he neither knew of nor suspected nor had reason to suspect the existence of some fact alleged by the prosecution which it is necessary for the prosecution to prove if he is to be convicted of the offence charged.

(3) Where in any proceedings for an offence to which this section applies it is necessary, if the accused is to be convicted of the offence charged, for the prosecution to prove that some substance or product involved in the alleged offence was the controlled drug which the prosecution alleges it to have been, and it is proved that the substance or product in question was that controlled drug, the accused—
   (a) shall not be acquitted of the offence charged by reason only of proving that he neither knew nor suspected nor had reason to suspect that the substance or product in question was the particular controlled drug alleged; but
   (b) shall be acquitted thereof—
      (i) if he proves that he neither believed nor suspected nor had reason to suspect that the substance or product in question was a controlled drug; or
      (ii) if he proves that he believed the substance or product in question to be a controlled drug, or a controlled drug of a description, such that, if it had in fact been that controlled drug or a controlled drug of that description, he would not at the material time have been committing any offence to which this section applies.

(4) Nothing in this section shall prejudice any defence which it is open to a person charged with an offence to which this section applies to raise apart from this section.

37. Interpretation

(1) In this Act, except in so far as the context otherwise requires, the following expressions have the meanings hereby assigned to them respectively, that is to say:—

   …

   'cannabis' (except in the expression 'cannabis resin') means any plant of the genus *Cannabis* or any part of any such plant (by whatever name designated) except that it does not include cannabis resin or any of the following products after separation from the rest of the plant, namely—
   (a) mature stalk of any such plant,

(b) fibre produced from mature stalk of any such plant, and
(c) seed of any such plant;
'cannabis resin' means the separated resin, whether crude or purified, obtained from any plant of the genus *Cannabis*;

...

'controlled drug' has the meaning assigned by section 2 of this Act;

...

'prepared opium' means opium prepared for smoking and includes dross and any other residues remaining after opium has been smoked;

...

'produce', where the reference is to producing a controlled drug, means producing it by manufacture, cultivation or any other method, and 'production' has a corresponding meaning;
'supplying' including distributing;

...

(2) References in this Act to misusing a drug are references to misusing it by taking it; and the reference in the foregoing provision to the taking of a drug is a reference to the taking of it by a human being by way of any form of self-administration, whether or not involving assistance by another.

(3) For the purposes of this Act the things which a person has in his possession shall be taken to include any thing subject to his control which is in the custody of another.

SCHEDULE 2 | SECTION 2, CONTROLLED DRUGS

PART I CLASS A DRUGS

1. The following substances and products, namely—

(a) Acetorphine
Alfentanil
Allylprodine
Alphacetylmethadol
Alphameprodine
Alphamethadol
Alphaprodine
Anileridine
Benzethidine
Benzylmorphine
(3-benzylmorphine)
Betacetylmethadol
Betameprodine
Betamethadol
Betaprodine
Bezitramide
Bufotenine
Carfentanil
Clonitazene
Coca leaf
Cocaine
Desomorphine
Dextromoramide
Diamorphine

Diampromide
Diethylthiambutene
Difenoxin
Dihydrocodeinone
O-carboxymethyloxime
Dihydroetorphine
Dihydromorphine
Dimenoxadole
Dimepheptanol
Dimethylthiambutene
Dioxaphetyl butyrate
Diphenoxylate
Dipipanone
Drotebanol
Ecgonine, and any
    derivative of ecgonine
    which is convertible to
    ecgonine or to cocaine
Ethylmethylthiambutene
Etricyclidine
Etonitazene
Etorphine
Etoxeridine
Etryptamine
Fentanyl

Fungus (of any kind which contains psilocin or an ester of psilocin)
Furethidine
Hydrocodone
Hydromorphinol
Hydromorphone
Hydroxypethidine
Isomethadone
Ketobemidone
Levomethorphan
Levomoramide
Levophenacylmorphan
Levorphanol
Lofentanil
Lysergamide
Lysergide and any other
    N-alkyl derivatives of
    lysergamide
Mescaline
Metazocine
Methadone
Methadyl acetate
Methlamphetamine
Methyldesorphine

Methyldihydromorphine
(6-methyldihydromorphine)
Metopon
Morpheridine
Morphine
Morphine methobromide, morphine N-oxide and other pentavalent nitrogen morphine derivatives
Myrophine
Nicomorphine
Noracymethadol
Norlevorphanol
Normethadone
Normorphine
Norpipanone
Opium, whether raw, prepared, or medicinal
Oxycodone
Oxymorphone
Pethidine
Phenadoxone
Phenampromide
Phenazocine
Phencyclidine
Phenomorphan
Phenoperidine
Piminodine
Piritramide
Poppy-straw and concentrate of poppy-straw
Proheptazine
Properidine
Psilocin
Racemethorphan
Racemoramide
Racemorphan
Remifentanil
Rolicyclidine
Sufentanil
Tenocyclidine
Thebacon
Thebaine
Tilidate
Trimeperidine
4-Bromo-2,5-dimethoxy-a-methylphenethylamine
4-Cyano-2-dimethylamino-4
4-diphenylbutane
4-Cyano-1-methyl-4-phenyl-piperidine
N,N-Diethyltryptamine
N,N-Dimethyltryptamine
2,5-Dimethoxy-a, 4-dimethylphenethylamine
N-Hydroxy-tenamphetamine
1-Methyl-4-phenylpiperidine-4-carboxylic acid
2-Methyl-3-morpholino-1, 1-diphenylpropanecarboxylic acid
4-Methyl-aminorex
4-Phenylpiperidine-4-carboxylic acid ethyl ester

(b) any compound (not being a compound for the time being specified in sub-paragraph (a) above) structurally derived from tryptamine or from a ring-hydroxy tryptamine by substitution at the nitrogen atom of the sidechain with one or more alkyl substituents but no other substituent;

(ba)...

(c) any compound (not being methoxyphenamine or a compound for the time being specified in sub-paragraph (a) above) structurally derived from phenethylamine an N-alkylphenethylamine, a-methylphenethylamine, an N-alkyl-a-methylphenethylamine, a-ethylphenethylamine, or an N-alkyl-a-ethylphenethylamine by substitution in the ring to any extent with alkyl, alkoxy, alkylenedioxy or halide substituents, whether or not further substituted in the ring by one or more other univalent substituents.

(d) any compound (not being a compound for the time being specified in sub-paragraph (a) above) structurally derived from fentanyl by modification in any of the following ways, that is to say,
   (i) by replacement of the phenyl portion of the phenethyl group by any heteromonocycle whether or not further substituted in the heterocycle;
   (ii) by substitution in the phenethyl group with alkyl, alkenyl, alkoxy, hydroxy, halogeno, haloalkyl, amino or nitro groups;
   (iii) by substitution in the piperidine ring with alkyl or alkenyl groups;
   (iv) by substitution in the aniline ring with alkyl, alkoxy, alkylenedioxy, halogeno or haloalkyl groups;
   (v) by substitution at the 4-position of the piperidine ring with any alkoxycarbonyl or alkoxyalkyl or acyloxy group;
   (vi) by replacement of the N-propionyl group by another acyl group;

(e) any compound (not being a compound for the time being specified in sub-paragraph (a) above) structurally derived from pethidine by modification in any of the following ways, that is to say,
   (i) by replacement of the 1-methyl group by an acyl, alkyl whether or not unsaturated, benzyl or phenethyl group, whether or not further substituted;

(ii) by substitution in the piperidine ring with alkyl or alkenyl groups or with a propano bridge, whether or not further substituted;
(iii) by substitution in the 4-phenyl ring wiith alkyl, alkoxy, aryloxy, halogeno or haloalkyl groups;
(iv) by replacement of the 4-ethoxycarbonyl by any other alkoxycarbonyl or any alkoxyalkyl or acyloxy group;
(v) by formation of an *N*-oxide or of a quaternary base.

2. Any stereoisomeric form of a substance for the time being specified in paragraph 1 above not being dextromethorphan or dextrorphan.
3. Any ester or ether of a substance for the time being specified in paragraph 1 or 2 above not being a substance for the time being specified in Part II of this Schedule.
4. Any salt of a substance for the time being specified in any of paragraphs 1 to 3 above.
5. Any preparation or other product containing a substance or product for the time being specified in any of paragraphs 1 to 4 above.
6. Any preparation designed for administration by injection which includes a substance or product for the time being specified in any of paragraphs 1 to 3 of Part II of this Schedule.

PART II CLASS B DRUGS

1. The following substances and products, namely—

(a) Acetyldihydrocodeine
Amphetamine
Codeine
Dihydrocodeine
Ethylmorphine (3-ethylmorphine)
Glutethimide
Lefetamine
Mecloqualone
Methaqualone
Methcathinone
Methylphenidate
a-Methylphenethylhydroxylamine

Methylphenobarbitone
Nicodine
Nicodicodine
(6-nicotinoyldihydrocodeine)
Norcodeine
Pentazocine
Phenmetrazine
Pholcodine
Propiram
Zipeprol
(b) any 5,5 disubstituted barbituric acid.

2. Any stereoisomeric form of a substance for the time being specified in paragraph 1 of this Part of this Schedule.
3. Any salt of a substance for the time being specified in paragraph 1 or 2 of this Part of this Schedule.
4. Any preparation or other product containing a substance or product for the time being specified in any of paragraphs 1 to 3 of this Part of this Schedule, not being a preparation falling within paragraph 6 of Part I of this Schedule.

PART III CLASS C DRUGS

1. The following substances, namely—

(a) Alprazolam
Aminorex
Benzphetamine
Bromazepam
Brotizolam
Buprenorphine
Camazepam
Cannabinol
Cannabinol derivatives

Cannabis and cannabis resin
Cathine
Cathinone
Chlordiazepoxide
Chlorphentermine
Clobazam
Clonazepam
Clorazepic acid
Clotiazepam

Cloxazolam
Delorazepam
Dextropropoxyphene
Diazepam
Diethylpropion
Estazolam
Ethchlorvynol
Ethinamate
Ethyl loflazepate

Fencamfamin	Prazepam	Methandriol
Fenethylline	Pyrovalerone	Methenolone
Fenproporex	Temazepam	Methyltestosterone
Fludiazepam	Tetrazepam	Metribolone
Flunitrazepam	Triazolam	Mibolerone
Flurazepam	N-Ethylamphetamine	Nandrolone
Halazepam	Zolpidem	19-Nor-4-Androstene-3, 17-dione
Haloxazolam	(b) 4-Androstene-3, 17-dione	
4-Hydroxy-n-butyric acid	5-Androstene-3, 17-diol	19-Nor-5-Andrastene-3, 17-diol
Ketamine	Atamestane	
Ketazolam	Bolandiol	Norboletone
Loprazolam	Bolasterone	Norclostebol
Lorazepam	Bolazine	Norethandrolone
Lormetazepam	Boldenone	Ovandrotone
Mazindol	Bolenol	Oxabolone
Medazepam	Bolmantalate	Oxandrolone
Mefenorex	Calusterone	Oxymesterone
Mephentermine	4-Chloromethandienone	Oxymetholone
Meprobamate	Clostebol	Prasterone
Mesocarb	Drostanolone	Propetandrol
Methyprylone	Enestebol	Quinbolone
Midazolam	Epitiostanol	Roxibolone
Nimetazepam	Ethyloestrenol	Silandrone
Nitrazepam	Fluoxymesterone	Stanolone
Nordazepam	Formebolone	Stanozolol
Oxazepam	Furazabol	Stenbolone
Oxazolam	Mebolazine	Testosterone
Pemoline	Mepitiostane	Thiomesterone
Phendimetrazine	Mesabolone	Trenbolone.
Phentermine	Mestanolone	
Pinazepam	Mesterolone	
Pipradrol	Methandienone	

(c) any compound (not being Trilostane or a compound for the time being specified in sub-paragraph (b) above) structurally derived from 17-hydroxyandrostan-3-one or from 17-hydroxyestran-3-one by modification in any of the following ways, that is to say,
  (i) by further substitution at position 17 by a methyl or ethyl group;
  (ii) by substitution to any extent at one or more of positions 1, 2, 4, 6, 7, 9, 11 or 16, but at no other position;
  (iii) by unsaturation in the carbocyclic ring system to any extent, provided that there are no more than two ethylenic bonds in any one carbocyclic ring;
  (iv) by fusion of ring A with a heterocyclic system;
(d) any substance which is an ester or ether (or, where more than one hydroxyl function is available, both an ester and an ether) of a substance specified in sub-paragraph (b) or described in sub-paragraph (c) above or of cannahiol or a cannihiol derivative;
(e) Chorionic Gonadotrophin (HCG); Clenbuterol; Non-human chorionic gonadotrophin; Somatotropin; Somatrem; Somatropin.
...

MOBILE TELEPHONE (RE-PROGRAMMING ACT) 2002

1. Re-programming mobile telephone etc.

(1) A person commits an offence if—
  (a) he changes a unique device identifier,
  (b) he interferes with the operation of a unique device identifier,
  (c) he offers or agrees to change, or interfere with the operation of, a unique device identifier, or
  (d) he offers or agrees to arrange for another person to change, or interfere with the operation of, a unique device identifier.

(2) A unique device identifier is an electronic equipment identifier which is unique to a mobile wireless communications device.

(3) But a person does not commit an offence under this section if—
  (a) he is the manufacturer of the device, or
  (b) he does the act mentioned in subsection (1) with the written consent of the manufacturer of the device.

(4) A person guilty of an offence under this section is liable—
  (a) on summary conviction, to imprisonment for a term not exceeding 6 months or to a fine not exceeding the statutory maximum or to both, or
  (b) on conviction on indictment, to imprisonment for a term not exceeding 5 years or to a fine or to both.

2. Possession or supply of anything for re-programming purposes

(1) A person commits an offence if—
  (a) he has in his custody or under his control anything which may be used for the purpose of changing or interfering with the operation of a unique device identifier, and
  (b) he intends to use the thing unlawfully for that purpose or to allow it to be used unlawfully for that purpose.

(2) A person commits an offence if—
  (a) he supplies anything which may be used for the purpose of changing or interfering with the operation of a unique device identifier, and
  (b) he knows or believes that the person to whom the thing is supplied intends to use it unlawfully for that purpose or to allow it to be used unlawfully for that purpose.

(3) A person commits an offence if—
  (a) he offers to supply anything which may be used for the purpose of changing or interfering with the operation of a unique device identifier, and
  (b) he knows or believes that the person to whom the thing is offered intends if it is supplied to him to use it unlawfully for that purpose or to allow it to be used unlawfully for that purpose.

(4) A unique device identifier is an electronic equipment identifier which is unique to a mobile wireless communications device.

(5) A thing is used by a person unlawfully for a purpose if in using it for that purpose he commits an offence under section 1.

(6) A person guilty of an offence under this section is liable—
  (a) on summary conviction, to imprisonment for a term not exceeding 6 months or to a fine not exceeding the statutory maximum or to both, or
  (b) on conviction on indictment, to imprisonment for a term not exceeding 5 years or to a fine or to both.

MURDER (ABOLITION OF DEATH PENALTY) ACT 1965

1. Abolition of death penalty for murder

(1) No person shall suffer death for murder, and a person convicted of murder shall ... be sentenced to imprisonment for life.

...

(3) For the purpose of any proceedings on or subsequent to a person's trial on a charge of capital murder, that charge and any plea or finding of guilty of capital murder shall be treated as being or having been a charge, or a plea or finding of guilty, of murder only; and if at the commencement of this Act a person is under sentence of death for murder, the sentence shall have effect as a sentence of imprisonment for life.

(4) In the foregoing subsections any reference to murder shall include an offence of or corresponding to murder under section 70 of the Army Act 1955 or of the Air Force Act 1955 or under section 42 of the Naval Discipline Act 1957, and any reference to capital murder shall be construed accordingly...

OFFENCES AGAINST THE PERSON ACT 1861

4. Soliciting to commit murder

Whosoever shall solicit, encourage, persuade, or endeavour to persuade, or shall propose to any person, to murder any other person, whether he be a subject of Her Majesty or not, and whether he be within the Queen's dominions or not, shall be guilty of an offence, and being convicted thereof shall be liable to imprisonment for life.

9. Murder or manslaughter abroad

Where any murder or manslaughter shall be committed on land out of the United Kingdom, whether within the Queen's dominions or without, and whether the person killed were a subject of Her Majesty or not, every offence committed by any subject of Her Majesty in respect of any such case, whether the same shall amount to the offence of murder or of manslaughter, may be dealt with, inquired of, tried, determined, and punished in England or Ireland ...

16. Threats to kill

A person who without lawful excuse makes to another a threat, intending that that other would fear it would be carried out, to kill that other or a third person shall be guilty of an offence and liable on conviction on indictment to imprisonment for a term not exceeding ten years.

18. Wounding, or causing grievous bodily harm with intent to do grievous bodily harm, or to resist apprehension

Whosoever shall unlawfully and maliciously by any means whatsoever wound or cause any grievous bodily harm to any person with intent to do some grievous bodily harm to any person, or with intent to resist or prevent the lawful apprehension or detainer of any person, shall be guilty of an offence, and being convicted thereof shall be liable to imprisonment for life.

20. Wounding or inflicting grievous bodily harm

Whosoever shall unlawfully and maliciously wound or inflict any grievous bodily harm upon any other person, either with or without any weapon or instrument, shall be guilty of an offence, and being convicted thereof shall be liable ... to imprisonment for not more than five years.

21. Attempting to choke, etc., in order to commit or assist in the committing of any indictable offence

Whosoever shall, by any means whatsoever, attempt to choke, suffocate, or strangle any other person, or shall by any means calculated to choke, suffocate, or strangle, attempt to render any other person insensible, unconscious, or incapable of resistance, with intent in any of such cases thereby to enable himself or any other person to commit, or with intent in any of such cases thereby to assist any other person in committing any indictable offence, shall be guilty of an offence, and being convicted thereof shall be liable to imprisonment for life.

22. Using chloroform, etc., to commit or assist in the committing of any indictable offence

Whosoever shall unlawfully apply or administer to or cause to be taken by, or attempt to apply or administer to or attempt to cause to be administered to or taken by, any person, any chloroform, laudanum, or other stupefying or overpowering drug, matter, or thing, with intent in any of such cases thereby to enable himself or any other person to commit, or with intent in any of such cases thereby to assist any other person in committing, any indictable offence, shall be guilty of an offence, and being convicted thereof shall be liable to imprisonment for life.

23. Maliciously administering poison, etc., so as to endanger life or inflict grievous bodily harm

Whosoever shall unlawfully and maliciously administer to or cause to be administered to or taken by any other person any poison or other destructive or noxious thing, so as thereby to endanger the life of such person, or so as thereby to inflict upon such person any grievous bodily harm, shall be guilty of an offence, and being convicted thereof shall be liable to imprisonment for a term not exceeding ten years.

24. Maliciously administering poison, etc., with intent to injure, aggrieve, or annoy any other person

Whosoever shall unlawfully and maliciously administer to or cause to be administered to or taken by any other person any poison or other destructive or noxious thing, with intent to injure, aggrieve, or annoy such person, shall be guilty of an offence, and being convicted thereof shall be liable to imprisonment for a term not exceeding five years.

28. Causing bodily injury by gunpowder

Whosoever shall unlawfully and maliciously, by the explosion of gunpowder or other explosive substance, burn, maim, disfigure, disable, or do any grievous bodily harm to any person, shall be guilty of an offence, and being convicted thereof shall be liable, at the discretion of the court, to imprisonment for life.

29. Causing gunpowder to explode, or sending to any person an explosive substance, or throwing corrosive fluid on a person, with intent to do grievous bodily harm

Whosoever shall unlawfully and maliciously cause any gunpowder or other explosive substance to explode, or send or deliver to or cause to be taken or received by any person any explosive substance or any other dangerous or noxious thing, or put or lay at any place, or cast or throw at or upon or otherwise apply to any person, any corrosive fluid or any destructive or explosive substance, with intent in any of the cases aforesaid to burn, maim, disfigure, or disable any person, or to do some grievous bodily harm to any person, shall, whether any bodily injury be effected or not, be guilty of an offence, and being convicted thereof shall be liable, at the discretion of the court, to imprisonment for life.

30. Placing gunpowder near a building, with intent to do bodily injury to any person

Whosoever shall unlawfully and maliciously place or throw in, into, upon, against, or near any building, ship, or vessel any gunpowder or other explosive substance, with intent to do any bodily injury to any person, shall, whether or not any explosion take place, and whether or not any bodily injury be effected, be guilty of an offence, and being convicted thereof shall be liable, at the discretion of the court, to imprisonment for any term not exceeding fourteen years.

32. Placing wood, etc., on a railway, with intent to endanger passengers

Whosoever shall unlawfully and maliciously put or throw upon or across any railway any wood, stone, or other matter or thing, or shall unlawfully and maliciously take up, remove, or displace any rail, sleeper, or other matter or thing belonging to any railway, or shall unlawfully and maliciously turn, move, or divert any points or other machinery belonging to any railway, or shall unlawfully and maliciously make or show, hide or remove, any signal or light upon or near to any railway, or shall unlawfully and maliciously do or cause to be done any other matter or thing, with intent, in any of the cases aforesaid, to endanger the safety of any person travelling or being upon such railway, shall be guilty of an offence, and being convicted thereof shall be liable, at the discretion of the court, to imprisonment for life.

33. Casting stone, etc. upon a railway carriage, with intent to endanger the safety of any person therein

Whosoever shall unlawfully and maliciously throw, or cause to fall or strike, at, against, into, or upon any engine, tender, carriage, or truck used upon any railway, any wood, stone, or other matter or thing, with intent to injure or endanger the safety of any person being in or upon such engine, tender, carriage, or truck, or in or upon any other engine, tender, carriage, or truck of any train of which such first-mentioned engine, tender, carriage, or truck shall form part, shall be guilty of an offence, and being convicted thereof shall be liable ... to imprisonment for life.

38. Assault with intent to resist arrest

Whosoever shall assault any person with intent to resist or prevent the lawful apprehension or detainer of himself or of any other person for any offence, shall be guilty of an offence, and being convicted thereof shall be liable, at the discretion of the court, to be imprisoned for any term not exceeding two years.

47. Assault occasioning bodily harm

Whosoever shall be convicted upon an indictment of any assault occasioning actual bodily harm shall be liable to be imprisoned for any term not exceeding five years.

57. Bigamy

Whosoever, being married, shall marry any other person during the life of the former husband or wife, whether the second marriage shall have taken place in England or Ireland or elsewhere, shall be guilty of felony, and being convicted thereof shall be liable to a term of imprisonment not exceeding seven years ... : Provided, that nothing in this section contained shall extend to any second marriage contracted elsewhere than in England and Ireland by any other than a subject of Her Majesty, or to any person marrying a second time whose husband or wife shall have been continually absent from such person for the space of seven years then last past, and shall not have been known by such person to be living within that time, or shall extend to any person who, at the time of such second marriage, shall have been divorced from the bond of the first marriage, or to any person whose former marriage shall have been declared void by the sentence of any court of competent jurisdiction.

58. Administering drugs or using instruments to procure abortion

Every woman, being with child, who, with intent to procure her own miscarriage, shall unlawfully administer to herself any poison or other noxious thing, or shall unlawfully use any instrument or other means whatsoever with the like intent, and whosoever, with intent to procure the miscarriage of any woman, whether she be or be not with child, shall unlawfully administer to her or cause to be taken by her any poison or other noxious thing, or shall unlawfully use any instrument or other means whatsoever with the like intent, shall be guilty of an offence, and being convicted thereof shall be liable to imprisonment for life ...

59. Procuring drugs, etc., to cause abortion

Whosoever shall unlawfully supply or procure any poison or other noxious thing, or any instrument or thing whatsoever, knowing that the same is intended to be unlawfully used or employed with intent to procure the miscarriage of any woman, whether she be or be not with child, shall be guilty of an offence, and being convicted thereof shall be liable to a term of imprisonment not exceeding five years.

60. Concealing the birth of a child

If any woman shall be delivered of a child, every person who shall, by any secret disposition of the dead body of the said child, whether such child died before, at, or after its birth, endeavour to conceal the birth thereof, shall be guilty of an offence, and being convicted thereof shall be liable, at the discretion of the court, to be imprisoned for any term not exceeding two years.

64. Making or having gunpowder, etc., with intent to commit an offence in this Act
Whosoever shall knowingly have in his possession, or make or manufacture, any gunpowder, explosive substance, or any dangerous or noxious thing, or any machine, engine, instrument, or thing, with intent by means thereof to commit, or for the purpose of enabling any other person to commit, any of the offences in this Act mentioned shall be guilty of an offence, and being convicted thereof shall be liable, at the discretion of the court, to be imprisoned for any term not exceeding two years.

PERJURY ACT 1911

1. Perjury
(1) If any person lawfully sworn as a witness or as an interpreter in a judicial proceeding wilfully makes a statement material in that proceeding, which he knows to be false or does not believe to be true, he shall be guilty of perjury, and shall, on conviction thereof on indictment, be liable to imprisonment for a term not exceeding seven years, or to a fine or to both imprisonment and fine.
(2) The expression 'judicial proceeding' includes a proceeding before any court, tribunal, or person having by law power to hear, receive, and examine evidence on oath.
(3) Where a statement made for the purposes of a judicial proceeding is not made before the tribunal itself, but is made on oath before a person authorised by law to administer an oath to the person who makes the statement, and to record or authenticate the statement, it shall, for the purposes of this section, be treated as having been made in a judicial proceeding.
(4) A statement made by a person lawfully sworn in England for the purposes of a judicial proceeding—
 (a) in another part of His Majesty's dominions; or
 (b) in a British tribunal lawfully constituted in any place by sea or land outside Her Majesty's dominions; or
 (c) in a tribunal of any foreign state,
 shall, for the purposes of this section, be treated as a statement made in a judicial proceeding in England.
(5) Where, for the purposes of a judicial proceeding in England, a person is lawfully sworn under the authority of an Act of Parliament—
 (a) in any other part of His Majesty's dominions; or
 (b) before a British tribunal or a British officer in a foreign country, or within the jurisdiction of the Admiralty of England;
 a statement made by such person so sworn as aforesaid (unless the Act of Parliament under which it was made otherwise specifically provides) shall be treated for the purposes of this section as having been made in the judicial proceeding in England for the purposes whereof it was made.
(6) The question whether a statement on which perjury is assigned was material is a question of law to be determined by the court of trial.

1A. False unsworn statement under Evidence (Proceedings in Other Jurisdictions) Act 1975
If any person, in giving any testimony (either orally or in writing) otherwise than on oath, where required to do so by an order under section 2 of the Evidence (Proceedings in Other Jurisdictions) Act 1975, makes a statement—
 (a) which he knows to be false in a material particular, or
 (b) which is false in a material particular and which he does not believe to be true,
 he shall be guilty of an offence and shall be liable on conviction on indictment to imprisonment for a term not exceeding two years or a fine or both.

7. Aiders, abettors, suborners, etc.

(1) Every person who aids, abets, counsels, procures, or suborns another person to commit an offence against this Act shall be liable to be proceeded against, indicted, tried and punished as if he were a principal offender.
(2) Every person who incites another person to commit an offence against this Act shall be guilty of a misdemeanour, and, on conviction thereof on indictment, shall be liable to imprisonment, or to a fine, or to both such imprisonment and fine.

13. Corroboration

A person shall not be liable to be convicted of any offence against this Act, or of any offence declared by any other Act to be perjury or subornation of perjury, or to be punishable as perjury or subornation of perjury, solely upon the evidence of one witness as to the falsity of any statement alleged to be false.

POLICE ACT 1996

89. Assaults on constables

(1) Any person who assaults a constable in the execution of his duty, or a person assisting a constable in the execution of his duty, shall be guilty of an offence and liable on summary conviction to imprisonment for a term not exceeding six months or to a fine not exceeding level 5 on the standard scale, or to both.
(2) Any person who resists or wilfully obstructs a constable in the execution of his duty, or a person assisting a constable in the execution of his duty, shall be guilty of an offence and liable on summary conviction to imprisonment for a term not exceeding one month or to a fine not exceeding level 3 on the standard scale, or to both.
(3) This section also applies to a constable who is a member of a police force maintained in Scotland or Northern Ireland when he is executing a warrant, or otherwise acting in England or Wales, by virtue of any enactment conferring powers on him in England and Wales.
(4) In this section references to a person assisting a constable in the execution of his duty include references to any person who is neither a constable nor in the company of a constable but who—
    (a) is a member of an international joint investigation team that is led by a member of a police force or by a member of the National Criminal Intelligence Service or of the National Crime Squad; and
    (b) is carrying out his functions as a member of that team.
(5) In this section 'international joint investigation team' means any investigation team formed in accordance with—
    (a) any framework decision on joint investigation teams adopted under Article 34 of the Treaty on European Union;
    (b) the Convention on Mutual Assistance in Criminal Matters between the Member States of the European Union, and the Protocol to that Convention, established in accordance with that Article of that Treaty; or
    (c) any international agreement to which the United Kingdom is a party and which is specified for the purposes of this section in an order made by the Secretary of State.
(6) A statutory instrument containing an order under subsection (5) shall be subject to annulment in pursuance of a resolution of either House of Parliament.

90. Impersonation, etc.

(1) Any person who with intent to deceive impersonates a member of a police force or special constable, or makes any statement or does any act calculated falsely to suggest that he is such a member or constable, shall be guilty of an offence and liable on summary conviction to imprisonment for a term not exceeding six months or to a fine not exceeding level 5 on the standard scale, or to both.

(2) Any person who, not being a constable, wears any article of police uniform in circumstances where it gives him an appearance so nearly resembling that of a member of a police force as to be calculated to deceive shall be guilty of an offence and liable on summary conviction to a fine not exceeding level 3 on the standard scale.

(3) Any person who, not being a member of a police force or special constable, has in his possession any article of police uniform shall, unless he proves that he obtained possession of that article lawfully and has possession of it for a lawful purpose, be guilty of an offence and liable on summary conviction to a fine not exceeding level 1 on the standard scale.

(4) In this section—
  (a) 'article of police uniform' means any article of uniform or any distinctive badge or mark or document of identification usually issued to members of police forces or special constables, or anything having the appearance of such an article, badge, mark or document,
  (aa) 'member of a police force' includes a member of the British Transport Police Force,
  (ab) 'member of a police force' includes a member of the staff of the National Policing Improvement Agency who is a constable, and
  (b) 'special constable' means a special constable appointed for a police area.

91. Causing disaffection

(1) Any person who causes, or attempts to cause, or does any act calculated to cause, disaffection amongst the members of any police force, or induces or attempts to induce, or does any act calculated to induce, any member of a police force to withhold his services, shall be guilty of an offence and liable—
  (a) on summary conviction, to imprisonment for a term not exceeding six months or to a fine not exceeding the statutory maximum, or to both;
  (aa) members of the staff of the National Policing Improvement Agency who are constables,
  (b) on conviction on indictment, to imprisonment for a term not exceeding two years or to a fine, or to both.

(2) This section applies in the case of—
  (a) special constables appointed for a police area,
  (aa) members of the staff of the National Policing Improvement Agency who are constables,
  (b) members of the Civil Nuclear Constabulary, and
  (c) members of the British Transport Police Force,
  as it applies in the case of members of a police force.

(3) Liability under subsection (1) for any behaviour is in addition to any civil liability for that behaviour.

PREVENTION OF CRIME ACT 1953

1. Prohibition of the carrying of offensive weapons without lawful authority or reasonable excuse

(1) Any person who without lawful authority or reasonable excuse, the proof whereof shall lie on him, has with him in any public place any offensive weapon shall be guilty of an offence, and shall be liable—
  (a) on summary conviction, to imprisonment for a term not exceeding six months or a fine not exceeding the prescribed sum, or both;
  (b) on conviction on indictment, to imprisonment for a term not exceeding four years or a fine or both.

(2) Where any person is convicted of an offence under subsection (1) of this section the court may make an order for the forfeiture or disposal of any weapon in respect of which the offence was committed.

(4) In this section 'public place' includes any highway, or other premises or place to which at the material time the public have or are permitted to have access, whether on payment or otherwise; and 'offensive weapon' means any article made or adapted for use for causing injury to the person, or intended by the person having it with him for such use by him or by some other person.

PROTECTION FROM HARASSMENT ACT 1997

1. Prohibition of harassment
(1) A person must not pursue a course of conduct—
   (a) which amounts to harassment of another, and
   (b) which he knows or ought to know amounts to harassment of the other.
(1A) A person must not pursue a course of conduct—
   (a) which involves harassment of two or more persons, and
   (b) which he knows or ought to know involves harassment of those persons, and
   (c) by which he intends to persuade any person (whether or not one of those mentioned above)—
      (i) not to do something that he is entitled or required to do, or
      (ii) to do something that he is not under any obligation to do.
(2) For the purposes of this section, the person whose course of conduct is in question ought to know that it amounts to or involves harassment of another if a reasonable person in possession of the same information would think the course of conduct amounted to or involved harassment of the other.
(3) Subsection (1) or (1A) does not apply to a course of conduct if the person who pursued it shows—
   (a) that it was pursued for the purpose of preventing or detecting crime,
   (b) that it was pursued under any enactment or rule of law or to comply with any condition or requirement imposed by any person under any enactment, or
   (c) that in the particular circumstances the pursuit of the course of conduct was reasonable.

2. Offence of harassment
(1) A person who pursues a course of conduct in breach of section 1(1) or (1A) is guilty of an offence.
(2) A person guilty of an offence under this section is liable on summary conviction to imprisonment for a term not exceeding six months, or a fine not exceeding level 5 on the standard scale, or both.

4. Putting people in fear of violence
(1) A person whose course of conduct causes another to fear, on at least two occasions, that violence will be used against him is guilty of an offence if he knows or ought to know that his course of conduct will cause the other so to fear on each of those occasions.
(2) For the purposes of this section, the person whose course of conduct is in question ought to know that it will cause another to fear that violence will be used against him on any occasion if a reasonable person in possession of the same information would think the course of conduct would cause the other so to fear on that occasion.
(3) It is a defence for a person charged with an offence under this section to show that—
   (a) his course of conduct was pursued for the purpose of preventing or detecting crime,
   (b) his course of conduct was pursued under any enactment or rule of law or to comply with any condition or requirement imposed by any person under any enactment, or
   (c) the pursuit of his course of conduct was reasonable for the protection of himself or another or for the protection of his or another's property.
(4) A person guilty of an offence under this section is liable—
   (a) on conviction on indictment, to imprisonment for a term not exceeding five years, or a fine, or both, or
   (b) on summary conviction, to imprisonment for a term not exceeding six months, or a fine not exceeding the statutory maximum, or both.

7. Interpretation of this group of sections
(1) This section applies for the interpretation of sections 1 to 5A.
(2) References to harassing a person include alarming the person or causing the person distress.

(3) A 'course of conduct' must involve—
   (a) in the case of conduct in relation to a single person (see section 1(1)), conduct on at least two occasions in relation to that person, or
   (b) in the case of conduct in relation to two or more persons (see section 1(1A)), conduct on at least one occasion in relation to each of those persons.
(3A) A person's conduct on any occasion shall be taken, if aided, abetted, counselled or procured by another—
   (a) to be conduct on that occasion of the other (as well as conduct of the person whose conduct it is); and
   (b) to be conduct in relation to which the other's knowledge and purpose, and what he ought to have known, are the same as they were in relation to what was contemplated or reasonably foreseeable at the time of the aiding, abetting, counselling or procuring.
(4) 'Conduct' includes speech.
(5) References to a person, in the context of the harassment of a person, are references to a person who is an individual.

PROTECTION OF CHILDREN ACT 1978

1. Indecent photographs of children

(1) Subject to sections 1A and 1B it is an offence for a person—
   (a) to take, or permit to be taken or to make, any indecent photograph or pseudo- photograph of a child; or
   (b) to distribute or show such indecent photographs or pseudo-photographs; or
   (c) to have in his possession such indecent photographs or pseudo-photographs, with a view to their being distributed or shown by himself or others; or
   (d) to publish or cause to be published any advertisement likely to be understood as conveying that the advertiser distributes or shows such indecent photographs or pseudo-photographs, or intends to do so.
(2) For purposes of this Act, a person is to be regarded as distributing an indecent photograph or pseudo-photograph if he parts with possession of it to, or exposes or offers it for acquisition by, another person.
(3) Proceedings for an offence under this Act shall not be instituted except by or with the consent of the Director of Public Prosecutions.
(4) Where a person is charged with an offence under subsection (1)(b) or (c), it shall be a defence for him to prove—
   (a) that he had a legitimate reason for distributing or showing the photographs or pseudo-photographs or (as the case may be) having them in his possession; or
   (b) that he had not himself seen the photographs or pseudo-photographs and did not know, nor had any cause to suspect, them to be indecent.

1A. Marriage and other relationships

(1) This section applies where, in proceedings for an offence under section 1(1)(a) of taking or making an indecent photograph of a child, or for an offence under section 1(1)(b) or (c) relating to an indecent photograph of a child, the defendant proves that the photograph was of the child aged 16 or over, and that at the time of the offence charged the child and he—
   (a) were married or civil partners of each other, or
   (b) lived together as partners in an enduring family relationship.
(2) Subsections (5) and (6) also apply where, in proceedings for an offence under section 1(1)(b) or (c) relating to an indecent photograph of a child,
   the defendant proves that the photograph was of the child aged 16 or over, and that at the time when he obtained it the child and he—
   (a) were married or civil partners of each other, or
   (b) lived together as partners in an enduring family relationship.

(3) This section applies whether the photograph showed the child alone or with the defendant, but not if it showed any other person.
(4) In the case of an offence under section 1(1)(a), if sufficient evidence is adduced to raise an issue as to whether the child consented to the photograph being taken or made, or as to whether the defendant reasonably believed that the child so consented, the defendant is not guilty of the offence unless it is proved that the child did not so consent and that the defendant did not reasonably believe that the child so consented.
(5) In the case of an offence under section 1(1)(b), the defendant is not guilty of the offence unless it is proved that the showing or distributing was to a person other than the child.
(6) In the case of an offence under section 1(1)(c), if sufficient evidence is adduced to raise an issue both—
    (a) as to whether the child consented to the photograph being in the defendant's possession, or as to whether the defendant reasonably believed that the child so consented, and
    (b) as to whether the defendant had the photograph in his possession with a view to its being distributed or shown to anyone other than the child,
the defendant is not guilty of the offence unless it is proved either that the child did not so consent and that the defendant did not reasonably believe that the child so consented, or that the defendant had the photograph in his possession with a view to its being distributed or shown to a person other than the child.

1B. Exception for criminal proceedings, investigations etc.

(1) In proceedings for an offence under section 1(1)(a) of making an indecent photograph or pseudo-photograph of a child, the defendant is not guilty of the offence if he proves that—
    (a) it was necessary for him to make the photograph or pseudo-photograph for the purposes of the prevention, detection or investigation of crime, or for the purposes of criminal proceedings, in any part of the world,
    (b) at the time of the offence charged he was a member of the Security Service or the Secret Intelligence Service, and it was necessary for him to make the photograph or pseudo-photograph for the exercise of any of the functions of that Service, or
    (c) at the time of the offence charged he was a member of GCHQ, and it was necessary for him to make the photograph or pseudo-photograph for the exercise of any of the functions of GCHQ.
(2) In this section 'GCHQ' has the same meaning as in the Intelligence Services Act 1994.

2. Evidence

(3) In proceedings under this Act relating to indecent photographs of children a person is to be taken as having been a child at any material time if it appears from the evidence as a whole that he was then under the age of 18.

6. Punishments

(1) Offences under this Act shall be punishable either on conviction on indictment or on summary conviction.
(2) A person convicted on indictment of any offence under this Act shall be liable to imprisonment for a term of not more than ten years, or to a fine or to both.
(3) A person convicted summarily of any offence under this Act shall be liable—
    (a) to imprisonment for a term not exceeding six months; or
    (b) to a fine not exceeding the prescribed sum for the purposes of section 32 of the Magistrates' Courts Act 1980 ... or to both.

7. Interpretation

(1) The following subsections apply for the interpretation of this Act.
(2) References to an indecent photograph include an indecent film, a copy of an indecent photograph or film, and an indecent photograph comprised in a film.
(3) Photographs (including those comprised in a film) shall, if they show children and are indecent, be treated for all purposes of this Act as indecent photographs of children and so as respects pseudo-photographs.

(4) References to a photograph include—
 (a) the negative as well as the positive version; and
 (b) data stored on a computer disc or by other electronic means which is capable of conversion into a photograph.
(4A) References to a photograph also include—
 (a) a tracing or other image, whether made by electronic or other means (of whatever nature)—
  (i) which is not itself a photograph or pseudo-photograph, but
  (ii) which is derived from the whole or part of a photograph or pseudo- photograph (or a combination of either or both); and
 (b) data stored on a computer disc or by other electronic means which is capable of conversion into an image within paragraph (a);
 and subsection (8) applies in relation to such an image as it applies in relation to a pseudo-photograph.
(5) 'Film' includes any form of video-recording.
(6) 'Child', subject to subsection (8), means a person under the age of 18.
(7) 'Pseudo-photograph' means an image, whether made by computer-graphics or otherwise howsoever, which appears to be a photograph.
(8) If the impression conveyed by a pseudo-photograph is that the person shown is a child, the pseudo-photograph shall be treated for all purposes of this Act as showing a child and so shall a pseudo-photograph where the predominant impression conveyed is that the person shown is a child notwithstanding that some of the physical characteristics shown are those of an adult.
(9) References to an indecent pseudo-photograph include—
 (a) a copy of an indecent pseudo-photograph; and
 (b) data stored on a computer disc or by other electronic means which is capable of conversion into an indecent pseudo-photograph.

PUBLIC ORDER ACT 1986

1. Riot
(1) Where 12 or more persons who are present together use or threaten unlawful violence for a common purpose and the conduct of them (taken together) is such as would cause a person of reasonable firmness present at the scene to fear for his personal safety, each of the persons using unlawful violence for the common purpose is guilty of riot.
(2) It is immaterial whether or not the 12 or more use or threaten unlawful violence simultaneously.
(3) The common purpose may be inferred from conduct.
(4) No person of reasonable firmness need actually be, or be likely to be, present at the scene.
(5) Riot may be committed in private as well as in public places.
(6) A person guilty of riot is liable on conviction on indictment to imprisonment for a term not exceeding ten years or a fine or both.

2. Violent disorder
(1) Where 3 or more persons who are present together use or threaten unlawful violence and the conduct of them (taken together) is such as would cause a person of reasonable firmness present at the scene to fear for his personal safety, each of the persons using or threatening unlawful violence is guilty of violent disorder.
(2) It is immaterial whether or not the 3 or more use or threaten unlawful violence simultaneously.
(3) No person of reasonable firmness need actually be, or be likely to be, present at the scene.
(4) Violent disorder may be committed in private as well as in public places.
(5) A person guilty of violent disorder is liable on conviction on indictment to imprisonment for a term not exceeding 5 years or a fine or both, or on summary conviction to imprisonment for a term not exceeding 6 months or a fine not exceeding the statutory maximum or both.

3. Affray

(1) A person is guilty of affray if he uses or threatens unlawful violence towards another and his conduct is such as would cause a person of reasonable firmness present at the scene to fear for his personal safety.
(2) Where 2 or more persons use or threaten the unlawful violence, it is the conduct of them taken together that must be considered for the purposes of subsection (1).
(3) For the purposes of this section a threat cannot be made by the use of words alone.
(4) No person of reasonable firmness need actually be, or be likely to be, present at the scene.
(5) Affray may be committed in private as well as in public places.
(7) A person guilty of affray is liable on conviction on indictment to imprisonment for a term not exceeding 3 years or a fine or both, or on summary conviction to imprisonment for a term not exceeding 6 months or a fine not exceeding the statutory maximum or both.

4. Fear or provocation of violence

(1) A person is guilty of an offence if he—
    (a) uses towards another person threatening, abusive or insulting words or behaviour, or
    (b) distributes or displays to another person any writing, sign or other visible representation which is threatening, abusive or insulting,
  with intent to cause that person to believe that immediate unlawful violence will be used against him or another by any person, or to provoke the immediate use of unlawful violence by that person or another, or whereby that person is likely to believe that such violence will be used or it is likely that such violence will be provoked.
(2) An offence under this section may be committed in a public or a private place, except that no offence is committed where the words or behaviour are used, or the writing, sign or other visible representation is distributed or displayed, by a person inside a dwelling and the other person is also inside that or another dwelling.
(4) A person guilty of an offence under this section is liable on summary conviction to imprisonment for a term not exceeding 6 months or a fine not exceeding level 5 on the standard scale or both.

4A. Intentional harassment, alarm or distress

(1) A person is guilty of an offence if, with intent to cause a person harassment, alarm or distress, he—
    (a) uses threatening, abusive or insulting words or behaviour, or disorderly behaviour, or
    (b) displays any writing, sign or other visible representation which is threatening, abusive or insulting, thereby causing that or another person harassment, alarm or distress.
(2) An offence under this section may be committed in a public or a private place, except that no offence is committed where the words or behaviour are used, or the writing, sign or other visible representation is displayed, by a person inside a dwelling and the person who is harassed, alarmed or distressed is also inside that or another dwelling.
(3) It is a defence for the accused to prove—
    (a) that he was inside a dwelling and had no reason to believe that the words or behaviour used, or the writing, sign or other visible representation displayed, would be heard or seen by a person outside that or any other dwelling, or
    (b) that his conduct was reasonable.
(5) A person guilty of an offence under this section is liable on summary conviction to imprisonment for a term not exceeding 6 months or a fine not exceeding level 5 on the standard scale or both.

5. Harassment, alarm or distress

(1) A person is guilty of an offence if he—
    (a) uses threatening, abusive or insulting words or behaviour, or disorderly behaviour, or
    (b) displays any writing, sign or other visible representation which is threatening, abusive or insulting, within the hearing or sight of a person likely to be caused harassment, alarm or distress thereby.

(2) An offence under this section may be committed in a public or a private place, except that no offence is committed where the words or behaviour are used, or the writing, sign or other visible representation is displayed, by a person inside a dwelling and the other person is also inside that or another dwelling.

(3) It is a defence for the accused to prove—
  (a) that he had no reason to believe that there was any person within hearing or sight who was likely to be caused harassment, alarm or distress, or
  (b) that he was inside a dwelling and had no reason to believe that the words or behaviour used, or the writing, sign or other visible representation displayed, would be heard or seen by a person outside that or any other dwelling, or
  (c) that his conduct was reasonable.

(6) A person guilty of an offence under this section is liable on summary conviction to a fine not exceeding level 3 on the standard scale.

6. Mental element: miscellaneous

(1) A person is guilty of riot only if he intends to use violence or is aware that his conduct may be violent.

(2) A person is guilty of violent disorder or affray only if he intends to use or threaten violence or is aware that his conduct may be violent or threaten violence.

(3) A person is guilty of an offence under section 4 only if he intends his words or behaviour, or the writing, sign or other visible representation, to be threatening, abusive or insulting, or is aware that it may be threatening, abusive or insulting.

(4) A person is guilty of an offence under section 5 only if he intends his words or behaviour, or the writing, sign or other visible representation, to be threatening, abusive or insulting, or is aware that it may be threatening, abusive or insulting or (as the case may be) he intends his behaviour to be or is aware that it may be disorderly.

(5) For the purposes of this section a person whose awareness is impaired by intoxication shall be taken to be aware of that of which he would be aware if not intoxicated, unless he shows either that his intoxication was not self-induced or that it was caused solely by the taking or administration of a substance in the course of medical treatment.

(6) In subsection (5) 'intoxication' means any intoxication, whether caused by drink, drugs or other means, or by a combination of means.

(7) Subsections (1) and (2) do not affect the determination for the purposes of riot or violent disorder of the number of persons who use or threaten violence.

7. Procedure: miscellaneous

(1) No prosecution for an offence of riot may be instituted except by or with the consent of the Director of Public Prosecutions.

(2) For the purposes of the rules against charging more than one offence in the same count or information, each of sections 1 to 5 creates one offence.

(3) If on the trial on indictment of a person charged with violent disorder or affray the jury find him not guilty of the offence charged, they may (without prejudice to section 6(3) of the Criminal Law Act 1967) find him guilty of an offence under section 4.

(4) The Crown Court has the same powers and duties in relation to a person who is by virtue of subsection (3) convicted before it of an offence under section 4 as a magistrates' court would have on convicting him of the offence.

8. Interpretation

In this Part—
  'dwelling' means any structure or part of a structure occupied as a person's home or as other living accommodation (whether the occupation is separate or shared with others) but does not include any part not so occupied, and for this purpose 'structure' includes a tent, caravan, vehicle, vessel or other temporary or movable structure;
  'violence' means any violent conduct, so that—
    (a) except in the context of affray, it includes violent conduct towards property as well as violent conduct towards persons, and

(b) it is not restricted to conduct causing or intended to cause injury or damage but includes any other violent conduct (for example, throwing at or towards a person a missile of a kind capable of causing injury which does not hit or falls short).

17. Meaning of 'racial hatred'

In this Part 'racial hatred' means hatred against a group of persons ... defined by reference to colour, race, nationality (including citizenship) or ethnic or national origins.

18. Use of words or behaviour or display of written material

(1) A person who uses threatening, abusive or insulting words or behaviour, or displays any written material which is threatening, abusive or insulting, is guilty of an offence if—
    (a) he intends thereby to stir up racial hatred, or
    (b) having regard to all the circumstances racial hatred is likely to be stirred up thereby.
(2) An offence under this section may be committed in a public or a private place, except that no offence is committed where the words or behaviour are used, or the written material is displayed, by a person inside a dwelling and are not heard or seen except by other persons in that or another dwelling.
(4) In proceedings for an offence under this section it is a defence for the accused to prove that he was inside a dwelling and had no reason to believe that the words or behaviour used, or the written material displayed, would be heard or seen by a person outside that or any other dwelling.
(5) A person who is not shown to have intended to stir up racial hatred is not guilty of an offence under this section if he did not intend his words or behaviour, or the written material, to be, and was not aware that it might be, threatening, abusive or insulting.
(6) This section does not apply to words or behaviour used, or written material displayed, solely for the purpose of being included in a programme included in a programme service.

19. Publishing or distributing written material

(1) A person who publishes or distributes written material which is threatening, abusive or insulting is guilty of an offence if—
    (a) he intends thereby to stir up racial hatred, or
    (b) having regard to all the circumstances racial hatred is likely to be stirred up thereby.
(2) In proceedings for an offence under this section it is a defence for an accused who is not shown to have intended to stir up racial hatred to prove that he was not aware of the content of the material and did not suspect, and had no reason to suspect, that it was threatening, abusive or insulting.
(3) References in this Part to the publication or distribution of written material are to its publication or distribution to the public or a section of the public.

29. Interpretation

In this Part—
> 'distribute', and related expressions, shall be construed in accordance with section 19(3)(written material) and section 21(2)(recordings);
> 'dwelling' means any structure or part of a structure occupied as a person's home or other living accommodation (whether the occupation is separate or shared with others) but does not include any part not so occupied, and for this purpose 'structure' includes a tent, caravan, vehicle, vessel or other temporary or movable structure;
> 'programme' means any item which is included in a programme service;
> 'programme service' has the same meaning as in the Broadcasting Act 1990;
> 'publish', and related expressions, in relation to written material, shall be construed in accordance with section 19 (3);
> 'racial hatred' has the meaning given by section 17;
> 'recording' has the meaning given by section 21(2), and 'play' and 'show', and related expressions, in relation to a recording, shall be construed in accordance with that provision;
> 'written material' includes any sign or other visible representation.

29A. Meaning of 'religious hatred'

In this Part 'religious hatred' means hatred against a group of persons defined by reference to religious belief or lack of religious belief.

29B. Use of words or behaviour or display of written material

(1) A person who uses threatening words or behaviour, or displays any written material which is threatening, is guilty of an offence if he intends thereby to stir up religious hatred.

(2) An offence under this section may be committed in a public or a private place, except that no offence is committed where the words or behaviour are used, or the written material is displayed, by a person inside a dwelling and are not heard or seen except by other persons in that or another dwelling.

(4) In proceedings for an offence under this section it is a defence for the accused to prove that he was inside a dwelling and had no reason to believe that the words or behaviour used, or the written material displayed, would be heard or seen by a person outside that or any other dwelling.

(5) This section does not apply to words or behaviour used, or written material displayed, solely for the purpose of being included in a programme service.

29C. Publishing or distributing written material

(1) A person who publishes or distributes written material which is threatening is guilty of an offence if he intends thereby to stir up religious hatred.

(2) References in this Part to the publication or distribution of written material are to its publication or distribution to the public or a section of the public.

29D. Public performance of play

(1) If a public performance of a play is given which involves the use of threatening words or behaviour, any person who presents or directs the performance is guilty of an offence if he intends thereby to stir up religious hatred

(2) This section does not apply to a performance given solely or primarily for one or more of the following purposes—
  (a) rehearsal,
  (b) making a recording of the performance, or
  (c) enabling the performance to be included in a programme service; but if it is proved that the performance was attended by persons other than those directly connected with the giving of the performance or the doing in relation to it of the things mentioned in paragraph (b) or (c), the performance shall, unless the contrary is shown, be taken not to have been given solely or primarily for the purpose mentioned above.

(3) For the purposes of this section—
  (a) a person shall not be treated as presenting a performance of a play by reason only of his taking part in it as a performer,
  (b) a person taking part as a performer in a performance directed by another shall be treated as a person who directed the performance if without reasonable excuse he performs otherwise than in accordance with that person's direction, and
  (c) a person shall be taken to have directed a performance of a play given under his direction notwithstanding that he was not present during the performance; and a person shall not be treated as aiding or abetting the commission of an offence under this section by reason only of his taking part in a performance as a performer.

(4) In this section 'play' and 'public performance' have the same meaning as in the Theatres Act 1968.

29E. Distributing, showing or playing a recording

(1) A person who distributes, or shows or plays, a recording of visual images or sounds which are threatening is guilty of an offence if he intends thereby to stir up religious hatred.

(2) In this Part 'recording' means any record from which visual images or sounds may, by any means, be reproduced; and references to the distribution, showing or playing of a recording are to its distribution, showing or playing to the public or a section of the public.

(3) This section does not apply to the showing or playing of a recording solely for the purpose of enabling the recording to be included in a programme service.

29F. Broadcasting or including programme in programme service

(1) If a programme involving threatening visual images or sounds is included in a programme service, each of the persons mentioned in subsection (2) is guilty of an offence if he intends thereby to stir up religious hatred
(2) The persons are—
   (a) the person providing the programme service,
   (b) any person by whom the programme is produced or directed, and
   (c) any person by whom offending words or behaviour are used.

29G. Possession of inflammatory material

(1) A person who has in his possession written material which is threatening, or a recording of visual images or sounds which are threatening, with a view to—
   (a) in the case of written material, its being displayed, published, distributed, or included in a programme service whether by himself or another, or
   (b) in the case of a recording, its being distributed, shown, played, or included in a programme service, whether by himself or another, is guilty of an offence if he intends thereby to stir up religious hatred.
(2) For this purpose regard shall be had to such display, publication, distribution, showing, playing, or inclusion in a programme service as he has, or it may be reasonably be inferred that he has, in view.

29J. Protection of freedom of expression

Nothing in this Part shall be read or given effect in a way which prohibits or restricts discussion, criticism or expressions of antipathy, dislike, ridicule, insult or abuse of particular religions or the beliefs or practices of their adherents, or of any other belief system or the beliefs or practices of its adherents, or proselytising or urging adherents of a different religion or belief system to cease practising their religion or belief system.

29JA. Protection of freedom of expression (sexual orientation)

In this Part, for the avoidance of doubt, the discussion or criticism of sexual conduct or practices or the urging of persons to refrain from or modify such conduct or practices shall not be taken of itself to be threatening or intended to stir up hatred.

29K. Savings for reports of parliamentary or judicial proceedings

(1) Nothing in this Part applies to a fair and accurate report of proceedings in Parliament …
(2) Nothing in this Part applies to a fair and accurate report of proceedings publicly heard before a court or tribunal exercising judicial authority where the report is published contemporaneously with the proceedings or, if it is not reasonably practicable or would be unlawful to publish a report of them contemporaneously, as soon as publication is reasonably practicable and lawful.

29L. Procedure and punishment

(1) No proceedings for an offence under this Part may be instituted except by or with the consent of the Attorney General.
(2) For the purposes of the rules against charging more than one offence in the same count or information, each of sections 29B to 29G creates one offence.
(3) A person guilty of an offence under this Part is liable—
   (a) on conviction on indictment to imprisonment for a term not exceeding seven years or a fine or both;
   (b) on summary conviction to imprisonment for a term not exceeding 12 months or a fine not exceeding the statutory maximum or both.
(4) In subsection (3)(b) the reference to 12 months shall be read as a reference to 6 months in relation to an offence committed before the commencement of section 154(i)g of the Criminal Justice Act 2003.

29M. Offences by corporations

(1) Where a body corporate is guilty of an offence under this Part and it is shown that the offence was committed with the consent or connivance of a director, manager, secretary or other similar officer of the body, or a person purporting to act in any such capacity, he as well as the body corporate is guilty of the offence and liable to be proceeded against and punished accordingly.

(2) Where the affairs of a body corporate are managed by its members, subsection (1) applies in relation to the acts and defaults of a member in connection with his functions of management as it applies to a director.

29N. Interpretation

In this Part—

'distribute', and related expressions, shall be construed in accordance with section 29C(2)(written material) and section 29E(2)(recordings);

'dwelling' means any structure or part of a structure occupied as a person's home or other living accommodation (whether the occupation is separate or shared with others) but does not include any part not so occupied, and for this purpose 'structure' includes a tent, caravan, vehicle, vessel or other temporary or movable structure;

'programme' means any item which is included in a programme service;

'programme service' has the same meaning as in the Broadcasting Act 1990;

'publish', and related expressions, in relation to written material, shall be construed in accordance with section 29C(2);

'religious hatred' has the meaning given by section 29A;

'recording' has the meaning given by section 29E(2), and 'play' and 'show', and related expressions, in relation to a recording, shall be construed in accordance with that provision;

'written material' includes any sign or other visible representation.

SERIOUS CRIME ACT 2007

44. Intentionally encouraging or assisting an offence (NYIF)

(1) A person commits an offence if—
   (a) he does an act capable of encouraging or assisting the commission of an offence; and
   (b) he intends to encourage or assist its commission.

(2) But he is not to be taken to have intended to encourage or assist the commission of an offence merely because such encouragement or assistance was a foreseeable consequence of his act.

45. Encouraging or assisting an offence believing it will be committed (NYIF)

A person commits an offence if—
   (a) he does an act capable of encouraging or assisting the commission of an offence; and
   (b) he believes—
      (i) that the offence will be committed; and
      (ii) that his act will encourage or assist its commission.

46. Encouraging or assisting offences believing one or more will be committed (NYIF)

(1) A person commits an offence if—
   (a) he does an act capable of encouraging or assisting the commission of one or more of a number of offences; and
   (b) he believes—
      (i) that one or more of those offences will be committed (but has no belief as to which); and
      (ii) that his act will encourage or assist the commission of one or more of them.

(2) It is immaterial for the purposes of subsection (1)(b)(ii) whether the person has any belief as to which offence will be encouraged or assisted.

(3) If a person is charged with an offence under subsection (1)—
    (a) the indictment must specify the offences alleged to be the 'number of offences' mentioned in paragraph (a) of that subsection; but
    (b) nothing in paragraph (a) requires all the offences potentially comprised in that number to be specified.
(4) In relation to an offence under this section, reference in this Part to the offences specified in the indictment is to the offences specified by virtue of subsection (3)(a).

47. Proving an offence under this Part (NYIF)

(1) Sections 44, 45 and 46 are to be read in accordance with this section.
(2) If it is alleged under section 44(1)(b) that a person (D) intended to encourage or assist the commission of an offence, it is sufficient to prove that he intended to encourage or assist the doing of an act which would amount to the commission of that offence.
(3) If it is alleged under section 45(b) that a person (D) believed that an offence would be committed and that his act would encourage or assist its commission, it is sufficient to prove that he believed—
    (a) that an act would be done which would amount to the commission of that offence; and
    (b) that his act would encourage or assist the doing of that act.
(4) If it is alleged under section 46(1)(b) that a person (D) believed that one or more of a number of offences would be committed and that his act would encourage or assist the commission of one or more of them, it is sufficient to prove that he believed—
    (a) that one or more of a number of acts would be done which would amount to the commission of one or more of those offences; and
    (b) that his act would encourage or assist the doing of one or more of those acts.
(5) In proving for the purposes of this section whether an act is one which, if done, would amount to the commission of an offence—
    (a) if the offence is one requiring proof of fault, it must be proved that—
        (i) D believed that, were the act to be done, it would be done with that fault;
        (ii) D was reckless as to whether or not it would be done with that fault; or
        (iii) D's state of mind was such that, were he to do it, it would be done with that fault; and
    (b) if the offence is one requiring proof of particular circumstances or consequences (or both), it must be proved that—
        (i) D believed that, were the act to be done, it would be done in those circumstances or with those consequences; or
        (ii) D was reckless as to whether or not it would be done in those circumstances or with those consequences.
(6) For the purposes of subsection (5)(a)(iii), D is to be assumed to be able to do the act in question.
(7) In the case of an offence under section 44—
    (a) subsection (5)(b)(i) is to be read as if the reference to 'D believed' were a reference to 'D intended or believed'; but
    (b) D is not to be taken to have intended that an act would be done in particular circumstances or with particular consequences merely because its being done in those circumstances or with those consequences was a foreseeable consequence of his act of encouragement or assistance.
(8) Reference in this section to the doing of an act includes reference to—
    (a) a failure to act;
    (b) the continuation of an act that has already begun;
    (c) an attempt to do an act (except an act amounting to the commission of the offence of attempting to commit another offence).
(9) In the remaining provisions of this Part (unless otherwise provided) a reference to the anticipated offence is—
    (a) in relation to an offence under section 44, a reference to the offence mentioned in subsection (2); and
    (b) in relation to an offence under section 45, a reference to the offence mentioned in subsection (3).

48. Proving an offence under section 46 (NYIF)

(1) This section makes further provision about the application of section 47 to an offence under section 46.
(2) It is sufficient to prove the matters mentioned in section 47(5) by reference to one offence only.
(3) The offence or offences by reference to which those matters are proved must be one of the offences specified in the indictment.
(4) Subsection (3) does not affect any enactment or rule of law under which a person charged with one offence may be convicted of another and is subject to section 57.

49. Supplemental provisions (NYIF)

(1) A person may commit an offence under this Part whether or not any offence capable of being encouraged or assisted by his act is committed.
(2) If a person's act is capable of encouraging or assisting the commission of a number of offences—
    (a) section 44 applies separately in relation to each offence that he intends to encourage or assist to be committed; and
    (b) section 45 applies separately in relation to each offence that he believes will be encouraged or assisted to be committed.
(3) A person may, in relation to the same act, commit an offence under more than one provision of this Part.
(4) In reckoning whether—
    (a) for the purposes of section 45, an act is capable of encouraging or assisting the commission of an offence; or
    (b) for the purposes of section 46, an act is capable of encouraging or assisting the commission of one or more of a number of offences; offences under this Part and listed offences are to be disregarded.
(5) 'Listed offence' means—
    (a) in England and Wales, an offence listed in Part 1, 2 or 3 of Schedule 3; and
    ...
(7) For the purposes of sections 45(b)(i) and 46(1)(b)(i) it is sufficient for the person concerned to believe that the offence (or one or more of the offences) will be committed if certain conditions are met.

50. Defence of acting reasonably (NYIF)

(1) A person is not guilty of an offence under this Part if he proves—
    (a) that he knew certain circumstances existed; and
    (b) that it was reasonable for him to act as he did in those circumstances.
(2) A person is not guilty of an offence under this Part if he proves—
    (a) that he believed certain circumstances to exist;
    (b) that his belief was reasonable; and
    (c) that it was reasonable for him to act as he did in the circumstances as he believed them to be.
(3) Factors to be considered in determining whether it was reasonable for a person to act as he did include—
    (a) the seriousness of the anticipated offence (or, in the case of an offence under section 46, the offences specified in the indictment);
    (b) any purpose for which he claims to have been acting;
    (c) any authority by which he claims to have been acting.

55. Mode of trial (NYIF)

(1) An offence under section 44 or 45 is triable in the same way as the anticipated offence.
(2) An offence under section 46 is triable on indictment.

56. Persons who may be perpetrators or encouragers etc. (NYIF)

(1) In proceedings for an offence under this Part ('the inchoate offence') the defendant may be convicted if—

(a) it is proved that he must have committed the inchoate offence or the anticipated offence; but
(b) it is not proved which of those offences he committed.
(2) For the purposes of this section, a person is not to be treated as having committed the anticipated offence merely because he aided, abetted, counselled or procured its commission.
(3) In relation to an offence under section 46, a reference in this section to the anticipated offence is to be read as a reference to an offence specified in the indictment.

57. Alternative verdicts and guilty pleas (NYIF)

(1) If in proceedings on indictment for an offence under section 44 or 45 a person is not found guilty of that offence by reference to the specified offence, he may be found guilty of that offence by reference to an alternative offence.
(2) If in proceedings for an offence under section 46 a person is not found guilty of that offence by reference to any specified offence, he may be found guilty of that offence by reference to one or more alternative offences.
(3) If in proceedings for an offence under section 46 a person is found guilty of the offence by reference to one or more specified offences, he may also be found guilty of it by reference to one or more other alternative offences.
(4) For the purposes of this section, an offence is an alternative offence if—
   (a) it is an offence of which, on a trial on indictment for the specified offence, an accused may be found guilty; or
   (b) it is an indictable offence, or one to which section 40 of the Criminal Justice Act 1988 applies (power to include count for common assault etc. in indictment), and the condition in subsection (5) is satisfied.
(5) The condition is that the allegations in the indictment charging the person with the offence under this Part amount to or include (expressly or by implication) an allegation of that offence by reference to it.
(6) Subsection (4)(b) does not apply if the specified offence, or any of the specified offences, is murder or treason.
(7) In the application of subsection (5) to proceedings for an offence under section 44, the allegations in the indictment are to be taken to include an allegation of that offence by reference to the offence of attempting to commit the specified offence.
(8) Section 49(4) applies to an offence which is an alternative offence in relation to a specified offence as it applies to that specified offence.
(9) In this section—
   (a) in relation to a person charged with an offence under section 44 or 45, 'the specified offence' means the offence specified in the indictment as the one alleged to be the anticipated offence;
   (b) in relation to a person charged with an offence under section 46, 'specified offence' means an offence specified in the indictment (within the meaning of subsection (4) of that section), and related expressions are to be read accordingly.
(10) A person arraigned on an indictment for an offence under this Part may plead guilty to an offence of which he could be found guilty under this section on that indictment.
(11) This section applies to an indictment containing more than one count as if each count were a separate indictment.
(12) This section is without prejudice to—
   (a) section 6(1)(b) and (3) of the Criminal Law Act 1967;
   (b) ...

58. Penalties (NYIF)

(1) Subsections (2) and (3) apply if—
   (a) a person is convicted of an offence under section 44 or 45; or
   (b) a person is convicted of an offence under section 46 by reference to only one offence ('the reference offence').
(2) If the anticipated or reference offence is murder, he is liable to imprisonment for life.

(3) In any other case he is liable to any penalty for which he would be liable on conviction of the anticipated or reference offence.
(4) Subsections (5) to (7) apply if a person is convicted of an offence under section 46 by reference to more than one offence ('the reference offences').
(5) If one of the reference offences is murder, he is liable to imprisonment for life.
(6) If none of the reference offences is murder but one or more of them is punishable with imprisonment, he is liable—
   (a) to imprisonment for a term not exceeding the maximum term provided for any one of those offences (taking the longer or the longest term as the limit for the purposes of this paragraph where the terms provided differ); or
   (b) to a fine.
(7) In any other case he is liable to a fine.
(8) Subsections (3), (6) and (7) are subject to any contrary provision made by or under—
   (a) an Act; or
   ...
(9) In the case of an offence triable either way, the reference in subsection (6) to the maximum term provided for that offence is a reference to the maximum term so provided on conviction on indictment.

59. Abolition of common law replaced by this Part (NYIF)
The common law offence of inciting the commission of another offence is abolished.

64. Encouraging or assisting the commission of an offence (NYIF)
A reference in this Part to encouraging or assisting the commission of an offence is to be read in accordance with section 47.

65. Being capable of encouraging or assisting (NYIF)
(1) A reference in this Part to a person's doing an act that is capable of encouraging the commission of an offence includes a reference to his doing so by threatening another person or otherwise putting pressure on another person to commit the offence.
(2) A reference in this Part to a person's doing an act that is capable of encouraging or assisting the commission of an offence includes a reference to his doing so by—
   (a) taking steps to reduce the possibility of criminal proceedings being brought in respect of that offence;
   (b) failing to take reasonable steps to discharge a duty.
(3) But a person is not to be regarded as doing an act that is capable of encouraging or assisting the commission of an offence merely because he fails to respond to a constable's request for assistance in preventing a breach of the peace.

66. Indirectly encouraging or assisting (NYIF)
If a person (D1) arranges for a person (D2) to do an act that is capable of encouraging or assisting the commission of an offence, and D2 does the act, D1 is also to be treated for the purposes of this Part as having done it.

SCHEDULE 1

PART 1 SERIOUS OFFENCES IN ENGLAND AND WALES

1 Drug trafficking
(1) An offence under any of the following provisions of the Misuse of Drugs Act 1971—
   (a) section 4(2) or (3) (unlawful production or supply of controlled drugs);
   (b) section 5(3) (possession of controlled drug with intent to supply);
   (c) section 8 (permitting etc. certain activities relating to controlled drugs);
   (d) section 20 (assisting in or inducing the commission outside the United Kingdom of an offence punishable under a corresponding law).

(2) An offence under any of the following provisions of the Customs and Excise Management Act 1979 if it is committed in connection with a prohibition or restriction on importation or exportation which has effect by virtue of section 3 of the Misuse of Drugs Act 1971—
    (a) section 50(2) or (3) (improper importation of goods);
    (b) section 68(2) (exportation of prohibited or restricted goods);
    (c) section 170 (fraudulent evasion of duty etc.).
(3) An offence under either of the following provisions of the Criminal Justice (International Co-operation) Act 1990—
    (a) section 12 (manufacture or supply of a substance for the time being specified in Schedule 2 to that Act);
    (b) section 19 (using a ship for illicit traffic in controlled drugs).

2 People trafficking

(1) An offence under sections 25, 25A or 25B of the Immigration Act 1971 (assisting unlawful immigration etc.).
(2) An offence under any of sections 57 to 59 of the Sexual Offences Act 2003 (trafficking for sexual exploitation).
(3) An offence under section 4 of the Asylum and Immigration (Treatment of Claimants, etc.) Act 2004 (trafficking people for exploitation).

3 Arms trafficking

(1) An offence under either of the following provisions of the Customs and Excise Management Act 1979 if it is committed in connection with a firearm or ammunition—
    (a) section 68(2) (exportation of prohibited or restricted goods);
    (b) section 170 (fraudulent evasion of duty etc.).
(2) An offence under section 3(1) of the Firearms Act 1968 (dealing etc. in firearms or ammunition by way of trade or business without being registered).
(3) In this paragraph 'firearm' and 'ammunition' have the same meanings as in section 57 of the Firearms Act 1968.

4 Prostitution and child sex

(1) An offence under section 33A of the Sexual Offences Act 1956 (keeping a brothel used for prostitution).
(2) An offence under any of the following provisions of the Sexual Offences Act 2003—
    (a) section 14 (arranging or facilitating commission of a child sex offence);
    (b) section 48 (causing or inciting child prostitution or pornography);
    (c) section 49 (controlling a child prostitute or a child involved in pornography);
    (d) section 50 (arranging or facilitating child prostitution or pornography);
    (e) section 52 (causing or inciting prostitution for gain);
    (f) section 53 (controlling prostitution for gain).

5 Armed Robbery etc

(1) An offence under section 8(1) of the Theft Act 1968 (robbery) where the use or threat of force involves a firearm, an imitation firearm or an offensive weapon.
(2) An offence at common law of an assault with intent to rob where the assault involves a firearm, imitation firearm or an offensive weapon.
(3) In this paragraph—
    'firearm' has the meaning given by section 57(1) of the Firearms Act 1968;
    'imitation firearm' has the meaning given by section 57(4) of that Act;
    'offensive weapon' means any weapon to which section 141 of the Criminal Justice Act 1988 (offensive weapons) applies.

6 Money laundering

An offence under any of the following provisions of the Proceeds of Crime Act 2002—
    (a) section 327 (concealing etc. criminal property);
    (b) section 328 (facilitating the acquisition etc. of criminal property by or on behalf of another);
    (c) section 329 (acquisition, use and possession of criminal property).

7 Fraud

(1) An offence under section 17 of the Theft Act 1968 (false accounting).
(2) An offence under any of the following provisions of the Fraud Act 2006—
    (a) section 1 (fraud by false representation, failing to disclose information or abuse of position);
    (b) section 6 (possession etc. of articles for use in frauds);
    (c) section 7 (making or supplying articles for use in frauds);
    (d) section 9 (participating in fraudulent business carried on by sole trader etc.);
    (e) section 11 (obtaining services dishonestly).
(3) An offence at common law of conspiracy to defraud.

8 Offences in relation to public revenue

(1) An offence under section 170 of the Customs and Excise Management Act 1979 (fraudulent evasion of duty etc.) so far as not falling within paragraph 1(2)(c) or 3(1)(b) above.
(2) An offence under section 72 of the Value Added Tax Act 1994 (fraudulent evasion of VAT etc.).
(3) An offence under section 144 of the Finance Act 2000 (fraudulent evasion of income tax).
(4) An offence under section 35 of the Tax Credits Act 2002 (tax credit fraud).
(5) An offence at common law of cheating in relation to the public revenue.

9 Corruption and bribes

(1) An offence under section 1 of the Public Bodies Corrupt Practices Act 1889 (corruption in public office).
(2) An offence which is the first or second offence under section 1(1) of the Prevention of Corruption Act 1906 (corrupt transactions with agents other than those of giving or using false etc. documents which intended to mislead principal).
(3) An offence at common law of bribery.

10 Counterfeiting

An offence under any of the following provisions of the Forgery and Counterfeiting Act 1981—
    (a) section 14 (making counterfeit notes or coins);
    (b) section 15 (passing etc. counterfeit notes or coins);
    (c) section 16 (having custody or control of counterfeit notes or coins);
    (d) section 17 (making or having custody or control of counterfeiting materials or implements).

11 Blackmail

(1) An offence under section 21 of the Theft Act 1968 (blackmail).
(2) An offence under section 12(1) or (2) of the Gangmasters (Licensing) Act 2004 (acting as a gangmaster other than under the authority of a licence, possession of false documents, etc.).

12 Intellectual property

(1) An offence under any of the following provisions of the Copyright, Designs and Patents Act 1988—
    (a) section 107(1)(a), (b), (d)(iv) or (e)(making, importing or distributing an article which infringes copyright);
    (b) section 198(1)(a), (b) or (d)(iii)(making, importing or distributing an illicit recording);
    (c) section 297A (making or dealing etc. in unauthorised decoders).
(2) An offence under section 92(1), (2) or (3) of the Trade Marks Act 1994 (unauthorised use of trade mark etc.).

13 Environment

(1) An offence under section 1 of the Salmon and Freshwater Fisheries Act 1975 (fishing for salmon, trout or freshwater fish with prohibited implements etc.).
(2) An offence under section 14 of the Wildlife and Countryside Act 1981 (introduction of new species etc.).
(3) An offence under section 33 of the Environmental Protection Act 1990 (prohibition on unauthorised or harmful deposit, treatment or disposal etc. of waste).

(4) An offence under regulation 8 of the Control of Trade in Endangered Species (Enforcement) Regulations 1997 (S.I. 1997/1372) (purchase and sale etc. of endangered species and provision of false statements and certificates).

14 Inchoate offences
(1) An offence of attempting or conspiring the commission of an offence specified or described in this Part of this Schedule.
(2) An offence under Part 2 of this Act (encouraging or assisting) where the offence (or one of the offences) which the person in question intends or believes would be committed is an offence specified or described in this Part of this Schedule.
(3) An offence of aiding, abetting, counselling or procuring the commission of an offence specified or described in this Part of this Schedule.
(4) The references in sub-paragraphs (1) to (3) to offences specified or described in this Part of this Schedule do not include the offence at common law of conspiracy to defraud.

15 Earlier offences
(1) This Part of this Schedule (apart from paragraph 14(2)) has effect, in its application to conduct before the passing of this Act, as if the offences specified or described in this Part included any corresponding offences under the law in force at the time of the conduct.
(2) Paragraph 14(2) has effect, in its application to conduct before the passing of this Act or before the coming into force of section 59 of this Act, as if the offence specified or described in that provision were an offence of inciting the commission of an offence specified or described in this Part of this Schedule.

16 Scope of offences
Where this Part of this Schedule refers to offences which are offences under the law of England and Wales and another country, the reference is to be read as limited to the offences so far as they are offences under the law of England and Wales.

SCHEDULE 3 (NYIF)

PART 1 OFFENCES COMMON TO ENGLAND AND WALES AND NORTHERN IRELAND

Offences Against the Person Act 1861
1 An offence under section 4 of the Offences against the Person Act 1861 (solicitation etc. of murder).
2 An offence under section 21 of that Act (attempting to choke etc. in order to commit or assist in the committing of any indictable offence) so far as it may be committed with the intention of enabling any other person to commit, or assisting any other person in the commission of, an indictable offence.
3 An offence under section 22 of that Act (using chloroform etc. to commit or assist in the committing of any indictable offence) so far as it may be committed with the intention of enabling any other person to commit, or assisting any other person in the commission of, an indictable offence.

Alien Restriction (Amendment) Act 1919
4 But references in paragraphs 2 and 3 to any other person do not include reference to the person whose act is capable of encouraging or assisting the commission of the offence under section 21 or, as the case may be, section 22 of that Act.
5 An offence under section 3(1) of the Aliens Restriction (Amendment) Act 1919 (acts calculated or likely to cause sedition or disaffection amongst HM forces etc.) consisting in attempting an act calculated or likely to cause sedition or disaffection in contravention of that subsection.
6 An offence under section 3(2) of that Act (promoting or attempting to promote industrial unrest) consisting in attempting to promote industrial unrest in contravention of that subsection.

Official Secrets Act 1920
7 An offence under section 7 of the Official Secrets Act 1920 (soliciting etc. commission of an offence under that Act or the Official Secrets Act 1911).

Incitement to Disaffection Act 1934
8 An offence under section 1 of the Incitement to Disaffection Act 1934 (endeavouring to seduce members of HM forces from their duty or allegiance).

Misuse of Drugs Act 1971
9 An offence under section 19 of the Misuse of Drugs Act 1971 (inciting any other offence under that Act).

10 An offence under section 20 of that Act (assisting or inducing commission outside United Kingdom of offence punishable under corresponding law).

Immigration Act 1971
11 An offence under section 25 of the Immigration Act 1971 (assisting unlawful immigration to a member State).

12 An offence under section 25B of that Act (assisting entry to the United Kingdom in breach of deportation or exclusion order).

Representation of the People Act 1982
13 An offence under section 97(1) of the Representation of the People Act 1983 (public meetings) consisting in the incitement of others to act in a disorderly manner for the purpose of preventing at a lawful public meeting to which that section applies the transaction of the

Computer Misuse Act 1990
14 An offence under section 3A(1) of the Computer Misuse Act 1990 (making etc. Article intending it to be used to commit, or to assist in the commission of, an offence under section 1 or 3 of that Act).

15 An offence under section 3A(2) of that Act (supply or offer to supply article believing it is likely to be used to commit, or to assist in the commission of, an offence under section 1 or 3 of that Act).

16 An offence under section 3A(3) of that Act (obtaining an article with a view to its being supplied for use to commit, or to assist in the commission of, an offence under section 1 or 3 of that Act).

Criminal Justice Act 1993
17 An offence under section 52(2)(a) of the Criminal Justice Act 1993 (encouraging insider dealing).

Reserve Forces Act 1996
18 An offence under section 101 of the Reserve Forces Act 1996 (inducing a person to desert or absent himself).

Landmines Act 1998
19 An offence under section 2(2) of the Landmines Act 1998 (encouraging, assisting or inducing an offence under section 2(1) of that Act).

Terrorism Act 2006
20 An offence under section 1(2) of the Terrorism Act 2006 (encouraging terrorism).

21 An offence under section 2(1) of that Act (disseminating terrorist publications).

22 An offence under section 5 of that Act (engaging in conduct in preparation for giving effect to intention to commit or assisting another to commit acts of terrorism).

23 An offence under section 6(1) of that Act (provision of instruction or training knowing that a person trained or instructed intends to use the skills obtained for or in connection with the commission of acts of terrorism or for assisting the commission or preparation of such acts by others).

24 An offence under section 6(2) of that Act as a result of paragraph (b)(ii) of that subsection (receipt of instruction or training intending to use the skills obtained for assisting the commission or preparation of acts of terrorism by others).

SERIOUS ORGANISED CRIME AND POLICE ACT 2005

128. Offence of trespassing on designated site

(1) A person commits an offence if he enters, or is on, any protected site in England and Wales or Northern Ireland as a trespasser.

(1A) In this section 'protected site' means—
   (a) a nuclear site; or
   (b) a designated site.

(1B) In this section 'nuclear site' means—
   (a) so much of any premises in respect of which a nuclear site licence (within the meaning of the Nuclear Installations Act 1965) is for the time being in force as lies within the outer perimeter of the protection provided for those premises; and
   (b) so much of any other premises of which premises falling within paragraph (a) form a part as lies within that outer perimeter.

(1C) For this purpose—
   (a) the outer perimeter of the protection provided for any premises is the line of the outermost fences, walls or other obstacles provided or relied on for protecting those premises from intruders; and
   (b) that line shall be determined on the assumption that every gate, door or other barrier across a way through a fence, wall or other obstacle is closed.

(2) A 'designated site' means a site—
   (a) specified or described (in any way) in an order made by the Secretary of State, and
   (b) designated for the purposes of this section by the order.

(3) The Secretary of State may only designate a site for the purposes of this section if—
   (a) it is comprised in Crown land; or
   (b) it is comprised in land belonging to Her Majesty in Her private capacity or to the immediate heir to the Throne in his private capacity; or
   (c) it appears to the Secretary of State that it is appropriate to designate the site in the interests of national security.

(4) It is a defence for a person charged with an offence under this section to prove that he did not know, and had no reasonable cause to suspect, that the site in relation to which the offence is alleged to have been committed was a protected site.

(5) A person guilty of an offence under this section is liable on summary conviction—
   (a) to imprisonment for a term not exceeding 51 weeks, or
   (b) to a fine not exceeding level 5 on the standard scale, or to both.

(6) No proceedings for an offence under this section may be instituted against any person—
   (a) in England and Wales, except by or with the consent of the Attorney General, or
   ...

(7) For the purposes of this section a person who is on any protected site as a trespasser does not cease to be a trespasser by virtue of being allowed time to leave the site.

(8) In this section—
   (a) 'site' means the whole or part of any building or buildings, or any land, or both;
   (b) 'Crown land' means land in which there is a Crown interest or a Duchy interest.

(9) For this purpose—
   'Crown interest' means an interest belonging to Her Majesty in right of the Crown, and
   'Duchy interest' means an interest belonging to Her Majesty in right of the Duchy of Lancaster or belonging to the Duchy of Cornwall.

132. Demonstrating without authorisation in designated area

(1) Any person who—
   (a) organises a demonstration in a public place in the designated area, or
   (b) takes part in a demonstration in a public place in the designated area, or

(c) carries on a demonstration by himself in a public place in the designated area,

is guilty of an offence if, when the demonstration starts, authorisation for the demonstration has not been given under section 134(2).

(2) It is a defence for a person accused of an offence under subsection (1) to show that he reasonably believed that authorisation had been given.
(3) Subsection (1) does not apply if the demonstration is—
   (a) a public procession of which notice is required to be given under subsection (1) of section 11 of the Public Order Act 1986, or of which (by virtue of subsection (2) of that section) notice is not required to be given, or
   (b) a public procession for the purposes of sections 12 or 13 of that Act.
(4) Subsection (1) also does not apply in relation to any conduct which is lawful under section 220 of the Trade Union and Labour Relations (Consolidation) Act 1992.
(5) If subsection (1) does not apply by virtue of subsection (3) or (4), nothing in sections 133 to 136 applies either.
(6) Section 14 of the Public Order Act 1986 (imposition of conditions on public assemblies) does not apply in relation to a public assembly which is also a demonstration in a public place in the designated area.
(7) In this section and in sections 133 to 136—
   (a) 'the designated area' means the area specified in an order under section 138,
   (b) 'public place' means any highway or any place to which at the material time the public or any section of the public has access, on payment or otherwise, as of right or by virtue of express or implied permission,
   (c) references to any person organising a demonstration include a person participating in its organisation,
   (d) references to any person organising a demonstration do not include a person carrying on a demonstration by himself,
   (e) references to any person or persons taking part in a demonstration (except in subsection (1) of this section) include a person carrying on a demonstration by himself.

138. The designated area

(1) The Secretary of State may by order specify an area as the designated area for the purposes of sections 132 to 137.
(2) The area may be specified by description, by reference to a map or in any other way.
(3) No point in the area so specified may be more than one kilometre in a straight line from the point nearest to it in Parliament Square.

145. Interference with contractual relationships so as to harm animal research organisation

(1) A person (A) commits an offence if, with the intention of harming an animal research organisation, he—
   (a) does a relevant act, or
   (b) threatens that he or somebody else will do a relevant act,
   in circumstances in which that act or threat is intended or likely to cause a second person (B) to take any of the steps in subsection (2).
(2) The steps are—
   (a) not to perform any contractual obligation owed by B to a third person (C) (whether or not such non-performance amounts to a breach of contract);
   (b) to terminate any contract B has with C;
   (c) not to enter into a contract with C.
(3) For the purposes of this section, a 'relevant act' is—
   (a) an act amounting to a criminal offence, or
   (b) a tortious act causing B to suffer loss or damage of any description;
   but paragraph (b) does not include an act which is actionable on the ground only that it induces another person to break a contract with B.
(4) For the purposes of this section, 'contract' includes any other arrangement (and 'contractual' is to be read accordingly).

(5) For the purposes of this section, to 'harm' an animal research organisation means—
    (a) to cause the organisation to suffer loss or damage of any description, or
    (b) to prevent or hinder the carrying out by the organisation of any of its activities.
(6) This section does not apply to any act done wholly or mainly in contemplation or furtherance of a trade dispute.
(7) In subsection (6) 'trade dispute' has the same meaning as in Part 4 of the Trade Union and Labour Relations (Consolidation) Act 1992, except that section 218 of that Act shall be read as if—
    (a) it made provision corresponding to section 244(4) of that Act, and
    (b) in subsection (5), the definition of 'worker' included any person falling within paragraph (b) of the definition of 'worker' in section 244(5).

146. Intimidation of persons connected with animal research organisation

(1) A person (A) commits an offence if, with the intention of causing a second person (B) to abstain from doing something which B is entitled to do (or to do something which B is entitled to abstain from doing)—
    (a) A threatens B that A or somebody else will do a relevant act, and
    (b) A does so wholly or mainly because B is a person falling within subsection (2).
(2) A person falls within this subsection if he is—
    (a) an employee or officer of an animal research organisation;
    (b) a student at an educational establishment that is an animal research organisation;
    (c) a lessor or licensor of any premises occupied by an animal research organisation;
    (d) a person with a financial interest in, or who provides financial assistance to, an animal research organisation;
    (e) a customer or supplier of an animal research organisation;
    (f) a person who is contemplating becoming someone within paragraph (c), (d) or (e);
    (g) a person who is, or is contemplating becoming, a customer or supplier of someone within paragraph (c), (d), (e) or (f);
    (h) an employee or officer of someone within paragraph (c), (d), (e), (f) or (g);
    (i) a person with a financial interest in, or who provides financial assistance to, someone within paragraph (c), (d), (e), (f) or (g);
    (j) a spouse, civil partner, friend or relative of, or a person who is known personally to, someone within any of paragraphs (a) to (i);
    (k) a person who is, or is contemplating becoming, a customer or supplier of someone within paragraph (a), (b), (h), (i) or (j); or
    (l) an employer of someone within paragraph (j).
(3) For the purposes of this section, an 'officer' of an animal research organisation or a person includes—
    (a) where the organisation or person is a body corporate, a director, manager or secretary;
    (b) where the organisation or person is a charity, a charity trustee (within the meaning of the Charities Act 1993;
    (c) where the organisation or person is a partnership, a partner.
(4) For the purposes of this section—
    (a) a person is a customer or supplier of another person if he purchases goods, services or facilities from, or (as the case may be) supplies goods, services or facilities to, that other; and
    (b) 'supplier' includes a person who supplies services in pursuance of any enactment that requires or authorises such services to be provided.
(5) For the purposes of this section, a 'relevant act' is—
    (a) an act amounting to a criminal offence, or
    (b) a tortious act causing B or another person to suffer loss or damage of any description.
(6) The Secretary of State may by order amend this section so as to include within subsection (2) any description of persons framed by reference to their connection with—
    (a) an animal research organisation, or
    (b) any description of persons for the time being mentioned in that subsection.
(7) This section does not apply to any act done wholly or mainly in contemplation or furtherance of a trade dispute.

(8) In subsection (7) 'trade dispute' has the meaning given by section 145(7).

147. Penalty for offences under sections 145 and 146
(1) A person guilty of an offence under sections 145 or 146 is liable—
    (a) on summary conviction, to imprisonment for a term not exceeding 12 months or to a fine not exceeding the statutory maximum, or to both;
    (b) on conviction on indictment, to imprisonment for a term not exceeding five years or to a fine, or to both.
(2) No proceedings for an offence under either of those sections may be instituted except by or with the consent of the Director of Public Prosecutions.

148. Animal research organisations
(1) For the purposes of sections 145 and 146 'animal research organisation' means any person or organisation falling within subsection (2) or (3).
(2) A person or organisation falls within this subsection if he or it is the owner, lessee or licensee of premises constituting or including—
    (a) a place specified in a licence granted under sections 4 or 5 of the 1986 Act,
    (b) a scientific procedure establishment designated under section 6 of that Act, or
    (c) a breeding or supplying establishment designated under section 7 of that Act.
(3) A person or organisation falls within this subsection if he or it employs, or engages under a contract for services, any of the following in his capacity as such—
    (a) the holder of a personal licence granted under section 4 of the 1986 Act,
    (b) the holder of a project licence granted under section 5 of that Act,
    (c) a person specified under section 6(5) of that Act, or
    (d) a person specified under section 7(5) of that Act.
(4) The Secretary of State may by order amend this section so as to include a reference to any description of persons whom he considers to be involved in, or to have a direct connection with persons who are involved in, the application of regulated procedures.
(5) In this section—
    'the 1986 Act' means the Animals (Scientific Procedures) Act 1986;
    'organisation' includes any institution, trust, undertaking or association of persons;
    'premises' includes any place within the meaning of the 1986 Act;
    'regulated procedures' has the meaning given by section 2 of the 1986 Act.

149. Extension of sections 145 to 147
(1) The Secretary of State may by order provide for sections 145, 146 and 147 to apply in relation to persons or organisations of a description specified in the order as they apply in relation to animal research organisations.
(2) The Secretary of State may, however, only make an order under this section if satisfied that a series of acts has taken place and—
    (a) that those acts were directed at persons or organisations of the description specified in the order or at persons having a connection with them, and
    (b) that, if those persons or organisations had been animal research organisations, those acts would have constituted offences under sections 145 or 146.
(3) In this section 'organisation' and 'animal research organisation' have the meanings given by section 148.

SEXUAL OFFENCES ACT 1956

33. Keeping a brothel
It is an offence for a person to keep a brothel, or to manage, or act or assist in the management of, a brothel.

33A. Keeping a brothel used for prostitution

(1) It is an offence for a person to keep a brothel, or to manage, or act or assist in the management of, a brothel to which people resort for practices involving prostitution (whether or not also for other practices).
(2) In this section 'prostitution' has the meaning given by section 51(2) of the Sexual Offences Act 2003.

34. Landlord letting premises for use as brothel

It is an offence for the lessor or landlord of any premises or his agent to let the whole or part of the premises with the knowledge that it is to be used, in whole or in part, as a brothel, or, where the whole or part of the premises is used as a brothel, to be wilfully a party to that use continuing.

35. Tenant permitting premises to be used as brothel

(1) It is an offence for the tenant or occupier, or person in charge, of any premises knowingly to permit the whole or part of the premises to be used as a brothel.
(2) Where the tenant or occupier of any premises is convicted (whether under this section or, for an offence committed before the commencement of this Act, under section thirteen of the Criminal Law Amendment Act 1885) of knowingly permitting the whole or part of the premises to be used as a brothel, the First Schedule to this Act shall apply to enlarge the rights of the lessor or landlord with respect to the assignment or determination of the lease or other contract under which the premises are held by the person convicted.
(3) Where the tenant or occupier of any premises is so convicted, or was so convicted under the said section thirteen before the commencement of this Act, and either—
   (a) the lessor or landlord, after having the conviction brought to his notice, fails or failed to exercise his statutory rights in relation to the lease or contract under which the premises are or were held by the person convicted; or
   (b) the lessor or landlord, after exercising his statutory rights so as to determine that lease or contract, grants or granted a new lease or enters or entered into a new contract of tenancy of the premises to, with or for the benefit of the same person, without having all reasonable provisions to prevent the recurrence of the offence inserted in the new lease or contract;
   then, if subsequently an offence under this section is committed in respect of the premises during the subsistence of the lease or contract referred to in paragraph (a) of this subsection or (where paragraph (b) applies) during the subsistence of the new lease or contract, the lessor or landlord shall be deemed to be a party to that offence unless he shows that he took all reasonable steps to prevent the recurrence of the offence.
   References in this subsection to the statutory rights of a lessor or landlord refer to his rights under the First Schedule to this Act or under subsection (1) of section five of the Criminal Law Amendment Act 1912 (the provision replaced for England and Wales by that Schedule).

36. Tenant permitting premises to be used for prostitution

It is an offence for the tenant or occupier of any premises knowingly to permit the whole or part of the premises to be used for the purposes of habitual prostitution (whether any prostitute involved is male or female).

SEXUAL OFFENCES ACT 1967

6. Premises resorted to for homosexual practices

Premises shall be treated for purposes of sections 33 to 35 of the Act of 1956 as a brothel if people resort to it for the purpose of lewd homosexual practices in circumstances in which resort thereto for lewd heterosexual practices would have led to its being treated as a brothel for the purposes of those sections.

SEXUAL OFFENCES ACT 1985

1. Kerb-crawling
(1) A person commits an offence if he solicits another person (or different persons) for the purpose of prostitution—
   (a) from a motor vehicle while it is in a street or public place; or
   (b) in a street or public place while in the immediate vicinity of a motor vehicle that he has just got out of or off, persistently or in such manner or in such circumstances as to be likely to cause annoyance to the person (or any of the persons) solicited, or nuisance to other persons in the neighbourhood.
(2) A person guilty of an offence under this section shall be liable on summary conviction to a fine not exceeding level 3 on the standard scale.
(3) In this section 'motor vehicle' has the same meaning as in the Road Traffic Act 1988.

2. Persistent soliciting
(1) A person commits an offence if in a street or public place he persistently solicits another person (or different persons) for the purpose of prostitution.
(2) A person guilty of an offence under this section shall be liable on summary conviction to a fine not exceeding level 3 on the standard scale.

4. Interpretation
(1) References in this Act to a person soliciting another person for the purpose of prostitution are references to his soliciting that person for the purpose of obtaining that person's services as a prostitute.
(4) For the purposes of this Act 'street' includes any bridge, road, lane, footway, subway, square, court, alley or passage, whether a thoroughfare or not, which is for the time being open to the public; and the doorways and entrances of premises abutting on a street (as hereinbefore defined), and any ground adjoining and open to a street, shall be treated as forming part of the street.

SEXUAL OFFENCES ACT 1993

1. Abolition of presumption of sexual incapacity
The presumption of criminal law that a boy under the age of fourteen is incapable of sexual intercourse (whether natural or unnatural) is hereby abolished.

SEXUAL OFFENCES ACT 2003

1. Rape
(1) A person (A) commits an offence if—
   (a) he intentionally penetrates the vagina, anus or mouth of another person (B) with his penis,
   (b) B does not consent to the penetration, and
   (c) A does not reasonably believe that B consents.
(2) Whether a belief is reasonable is to be determined having regard to all the circumstances, including any steps A has taken to ascertain whether B consents.
(3) Sections 75 and 76 apply to an offence under this section.
(4) A person guilty of an offence under this section is liable, on conviction on indictment, to imprisonment for life.

2. Assault by penetration

(1) A person (A) commits an offence if—
   (a) he intentionally penetrates the vagina or anus of another person (B) with a part of his body or anything else,
   (b) the penetration is sexual,
   (c) B does not consent to the penetration, and
   (d) A does not reasonably believe that B consents.
(2) Whether a belief is reasonable is to be determined having regard to all the circumstances, including any steps A has taken to ascertain whether B consents.
(3) Sections 75 and 76 apply to an offence under this section.
(4) A person guilty of an offence under this section is liable, on conviction on indictment, to imprisonment for life.

3. Sexual assault

(1) A person (A) commits an offence if—
   (a) he intentionally touches another person (B),
   (b) the touching is sexual,
   (c) B does not consent to the touching, and
   (d) A does not reasonably believe that B consents.
(2) Whether a belief is reasonable is to be determined having regard to all the circumstances, including any steps A has taken to ascertain whether B consents.
(3) Sections 75 and 76 apply to an offence under this section.
(4) A person guilty of an offence under this section is liable—
   (a) on summary conviction, to imprisonment for a term not exceeding 6 months or a fine not exceeding the statutory maximum or both;
   (b) on conviction on indictment, to imprisonment for a term not exceeding 10 years.

4. Causing a person to engage in sexual activity without consent

(1) A person (A) commits an offence if—
   (a) he intentionally causes another person (B) to engage in an activity,
   (b) the activity is sexual,
   (c) B does not consent to engaging in the activity, and
   (d) A does not reasonably believe that B consents.
(2) Whether a belief is reasonable is to be determined having regard to all the circumstances, including any steps A has taken to ascertain whether B consents.
(3) Sections 75 and 76 apply to an offence under this section.
(4) A person guilty of an offence under this section, if the activity caused involved—
   (a) penetration of B's anus or vagina,
   (b) penetration of B's mouth with a person's penis,
   (c) penetration of a person's anus or vagina with a part of B's body or by B with anything else, or
   (d) penetration of a person's mouth with B's penis,
   is liable, on conviction on indictment, to imprisonment for life.
(5) Unless subsection (4) applies, a person guilty of an offence under this section is liable—
   (a) on summary conviction, to imprisonment for a term not exceeding 6 months or to a fine not exceeding the statutory maximum or both;
   (b) on conviction on indictment, to imprisonment for a term not exceeding 10 years.

5. Rape of a child under 13

(1) A person commits an offence if—
   (a) he intentionally penetrates the vagina, anus or mouth of another person with his penis, and
   (b) the other person is under 13.
(2) A person guilty of an offence under this section is liable, on conviction on indictment, to imprisonment for life.

6. Assault of a child under 13 by penetration

(1) A person commits an offence if—
   (a) he intentionally penetrates the vagina or anus of another person with a part of his body or anything else,
   (b) the penetration is sexual, and
   (c) the other person is under 13.
(2) A person guilty of an offence under this section is liable, on conviction on indictment, to imprisonment for life.

7. Sexual assault of a child under 13

(1) A person commits an offence if—
   (a) he intentionally touches another person,
   (b) the touching is sexual, and
   (c) the other person is under 13.
(2) A person guilty of an offence under this section is liable—
   (a) on summary conviction, to imprisonment for a term not exceeding 6 months or a fine not exceeding the statutory maximum or both;
   (b) on conviction on indictment, to imprisonment for a term not exceeding 14 years.

8. Causing or inciting a child under 13 to engage in sexual activity

(1) A person commits an offence if—
   (a) he intentionally causes or incites another person (B) to engage in an activity,
   (b) the activity is sexual, and
   (c) B is under 13.
(2) A person guilty of an offence under this section, if the activity caused or incited involved—
   (a) penetration of B's anus or vagina,
   (b) penetration of B's mouth with a person's penis,
   (c) penetration of a person's anus or vagina with a part of B's body or by B with anything else, or
   (d) penetration of a person's mouth with B's penis,
   is liable, on conviction on indictment, to imprisonment for life.
(3) Unless subsection (2) applies, a person guilty of an offence under this section is liable—
   (a) on summary conviction, to imprisonment for a term not exceeding 6 months or to a fine not exceeding the statutory maximum or both;
   (b) on conviction on indictment, to imprisonment for a term not exceeding 14 years.

9. Sexual activity with a child

(1) A person aged 18 or over (A) commits an offence if—
   (a) he intentionally touches another person (B),
   (b) the touching is sexual, and
   (c) either—
      (i) B is under 16 and A does not reasonably believe that B is 16 or over, or
      (ii) B is under 13.
(2) A person guilty of an offence under this section, if the touching involved—
   (a) penetration of B's anus or vagina with a part of A's body or anything else,
   (b) penetration of B's mouth with A's penis,
   (c) penetration of A's anus or vagina with a part of B's body, or
   (d) penetration of A's mouth with B's penis,
   is liable, on conviction on indictment, to imprisonment for a term not exceeding 14 years.
(3) Unless subsection (2) applies, a person guilty of an offence under this section is liable—
   (a) on summary conviction, to imprisonment for a term not exceeding 6 months or to a fine not exceeding the statutory maximum or both;
   (b) on conviction on indictment, to imprisonment for a term not exceeding 14 years.

10. Causing or inciting a child to engage in sexual activity

(1) A person aged 18 or over (A) commits an offence if—

(a) he intentionally causes or incites another person (B) to engage in an activity,
(b) the activity is sexual, and
(c) either—
    (i) B is under 16 and A does not reasonably believe that B is 16 or over, or
    (ii) B is under 13.
(2) A person guilty of an offence under this section, if the activity caused or incited involved—
(a) penetration of B's anus or vagina,
(b) penetration of B's mouth with a person's penis,
(c) penetration of a person's anus or vagina with a part of B's body or by B with anything else, or
(d) penetration of a person's mouth with B's penis,
is liable, on conviction on indictment, to imprisonment for a term not exceeding 14 years.
(3) Unless subsection (2) applies, a person guilty of an offence under this section is liable—
(a) on summary conviction, to imprisonment for a term not exceeding 6 months or to a fine not exceeding the statutory maximum or both;
(b) on conviction on indictment, to imprisonment for a term not exceeding 14 years.

11. Engaging in sexual activity in the presence of a child

(1) A person aged 18 or over (A) commits an offence if—
(a) he intentionally engages in an activity,
(b) the activity is sexual,
(c) for the purpose of obtaining sexual gratification, he engages in it—
    (i) when another person (B) is present or is in a place from which A can be observed, and
    (ii) knowing or believing that B is aware, or intending that B should be aware, that he is engaging in it, and
(d) either—
    (i) B is under 16 and A does not reasonably believe that B is 16 or over, or
    (ii) B is under 13.
(2) A person guilty of an offence under this section is liable—
(a) on summary conviction, to imprisonment for a term not exceeding 6 months or a fine not exceeding the statutory maximum or both;
(b) on conviction on indictment, to imprisonment for a term not exceeding 10 years.

12. Causing a child to watch a sexual act

(1) A person aged 18 or over (A) commits an offence if—
(a) for the purpose of obtaining sexual gratification, he intentionally causes another person (B) to watch a third person engaging in an activity, or to look at an image of any person engaging in an activity,
(b) the activity is sexual, and
(c) either—
    (i) B is under 16 and A does not reasonably believe that B is 16 or over, or
    (ii) B is under 13.
(2) A person guilty of an offence under this section is liable—
(a) on summary conviction, to imprisonment for a term not exceeding 6 months or a fine not exceeding the statutory maximum or both;
(b) on conviction on indictment, to imprisonment for a term not exceeding 10 years.

13. Child sex offences committed by children or young persons

(1) A person under 18 commits an offence if he does anything which would be an offence under any of sections 9 to 12 if he were aged 18.
(2) A person guilty of an offence under this section is liable—
(a) on summary conviction, to imprisonment for a term not exceeding 6 months or a fine not exceeding the statutory maximum or both;
(b) on conviction on indictment, to imprisonment for a term not exceeding 5 years.

14. Arranging or facilitating commission of a child sex offence

(1) A person commits an offence if—
  (a) he intentionally arranges or facilitates something that he intends to do, intends another person to do, or believes that another person will do, in any part of the world, and
  (b) doing it will involve the commission of an offence under any of sections 9 to 13.
(2) A person does not commit an offence under this section if—
  (a) he arranges or facilitates something that he believes another person will do, but that he does not intend to do or intend another person to do, and
  (b) any offence within subsection (1)(b) would be an offence against a child for whose protection he acts.
(3) For the purposes of subsection (2), a person acts for the protection of a child if he acts for the purpose of—
  (a) protecting the child from sexually transmitted infection,
  (b) protecting the physical safety of the child,
  (c) preventing the child from becoming pregnant, or
  (d) promoting the child's emotional well-being by the giving of advice,
  and not for the purpose of obtaining sexual gratification or for the purpose of causing or encouraging the activity constituting the offence within subsection (1)(b) or the child's participation in it.
(4) A person guilty of an offence under this section is liable—
  (a) on summary conviction, to imprisonment for a term not exceeding 6 months or a fine not exceeding the statutory maximum or both;
  (b) on conviction on indictment, to imprisonment for a term not exceeding 14 years.

15. Meeting a child following sexual grooming etc.

(1) A person aged 18 or over (A) commits an offence if—
  (a) A has met or communicated with another person (B) on at least two occasions and subsequently—
    (i) A intentionally meets B,
    (ii) A travels with the intention of meeting B in any part of the world or arranges to meet B in any part of the world, or
    (iii) B travels with the intention of meeting A in any part of the world,
  (b) A intends to do anything to or in respect of B, during or after the meeting mentioned in paragraph (a)(i) to (iii) and in any part of the world, which if done will involve the commission by A of a relevant offence,
  (c) B is under 16, and
  (d) A does not reasonably believe that B is 16 or over.
(2) In subsection (1)—
  (a) the reference to A having met or communicated with B is a reference to A having met B in any part of the world or having communicated with B by any means from, to or in any part of the world;
  (b) 'relevant offence' means—
    (i) an offence under this Part,
    (ii) an offence within any of paragraphs 61 to 92 of Schedule 3, or
    (iii) anything done outside England and Wales and Northern Ireland which is not an offence within sub-paragraph (i) or (ii) but would be an offence within sub-paragraph (i) if done in England and Wales.
  …
(4) A person guilty of an offence under this section is liable—
  (a) on summary conviction, to imprisonment for a term not exceeding 6 months or a fine not exceeding the statutory maximum or both;
  (b) on conviction on indictment, to imprisonment for a term not exceeding 10 years.

30. Sexual activity with a person with a mental disorder impeding choice

(1) A person (A) commits an offence if—
  (a) he intentionally touches another person (B),

(b) the touching is sexual,
   (c) B is unable to refuse because of or for a reason related to a mental disorder, and
   (d) A knows or could reasonably be expected to know that B has a mental disorder and that because of it or for a reason related to it B is likely to be unable to refuse.
(2) B is unable to refuse if—
   (a) he lacks the capacity to choose whether to agree to the touching (whether because he lacks sufficient understanding of the nature or reasonably foreseeable consequences of what is being done, or for any other reason), or
   (b) he is unable to communicate such a choice to A.
(3) A person guilty of an offence under this section, if the touching involved—
   (a) penetration of B's anus or vagina with a part of A's body or anything else,
   (b) penetration of B's mouth with A's penis,
   (c) penetration of A's anus or vagina with a part of B's body, or
   (d) penetration of A's mouth with B's penis,
   is liable, on conviction on indictment, to imprisonment for life.
(4) Unless subsection (3) applies, a person guilty of an offence under this section is liable—
   (a) on summary conviction, to imprisonment for a term not exceeding 6 months or to a fine not exceeding the statutory maximum or both;
   (b) on conviction on indictment, to imprisonment for a term not exceeding 14 years.

31. Causing or inciting a person, with a mental disorder impeding choice, to engage in sexual activity

(1) A person (A) commits an offence if—
   (a) he intentionally causes or incites another person (B) to engage in an activity,
   (b) the activity is sexual,
   (c) B is unable to refuse because of or for a reason related to a mental disorder, and
   (d) A knows or could reasonably be expected to know that B has a mental disorder and that because of it or for a reason related to it B is likely to be unable to refuse.
(2) B is unable to refuse if—
   (a) he lacks the capacity to choose whether to agree to engaging in the activity caused or incited (whether because he lacks sufficient understanding of the nature or reasonably foreseeable consequences of the activity, or for any other reason), or
   (b) he is unable to communicate such a choice to A.
(3) A person guilty of an offence under this section, if the activity caused or incited involved—
   (a) penetration of B's anus or vagina,
   (b) penetration of B's mouth with a person's penis,
   (c) penetration of a person's anus or vagina with a part of B's body or by B with anything else, or
   (d) penetration of a person's mouth with B's penis,
   is liable, on conviction on indictment, to imprisonment for life.
(4) Unless subsection (3) applies, a person guilty of an offence under this section is liable—
   (a) on summary conviction, to imprisonment for a term not exceeding 6 months or to a fine not exceeding the statutory maximum or both;
   (b) on conviction on indictment, to imprisonment for a term not exceeding 14 years.

32. Engaging in sexual activity in the presence of a person with a mental disorder impeding choice

(1) A person (A) commits an offence if—
   (a) he intentionally engages in an activity,
   (b) the activity is sexual,
   (c) for the purpose of obtaining sexual gratification, he engages in it—
      (i) when another person (B) is present or is in a place from which A can be observed, and
      (ii) knowing or believing that B is aware, or intending that B should be aware, that he is engaging in it,
   (d) B is unable to refuse because of or for a reason related to a mental disorder, and
   (e) A knows or could reasonably be expected to know that B has a mental disorder and that because of it or for a reason related to it B is likely to be unable to refuse.

(2) B is unable to refuse if—
  (a) he lacks the capacity to choose whether to agree to being present (whether because he lacks sufficient understanding of the nature of the activity, or for any other reason), or
  (b) he is unable to communicate such a choice to A.
(3) A person guilty of an offence under this section is liable—
  (a) on summary conviction, to imprisonment for a term not exceeding 6 months or a fine not exceeding the statutory maximum or both;
  (b) on conviction on indictment, to imprisonment for a term not exceeding 10 years.

33. Causing a person, with a mental disorder impeding choice, to watch a sexual act

(1) A person (A) commits an offence if—
  (a) for the purpose of obtaining sexual gratification, he intentionally causes another person (B) to watch a third person engaging in an activity, or to look at an image of any person engaging in an activity,
  (b) the activity is sexual,
  (c) B is unable to refuse because of or for a reason related to a mental disorder, and
  (d) A knows or could reasonably be expected to know that B has a mental disorder and that because of it or for a reason related to it B is likely to be unable to refuse.
(2) B is unable to refuse if—
  (a) he lacks the capacity to choose whether to agree to watching or looking (whether because he lacks sufficient understanding of the nature of the activity, or for any other reason), or
  (b) he is unable to communicate such a choice to A.
(3) A person guilty of an offence under this section is liable—
  (a) on summary conviction, to imprisonment for a term not exceeding 6 months or a fine not exceeding the statutory maximum or both;
  (b) on conviction on indictment, to imprisonment for a term not exceeding 10 years.

47. Paying for sexual services of a child

(1) A person (A) commits an offence if—
  (a) he intentionally obtains for himself the sexual services of another person (B),
  (b) before obtaining those services, he has made or promised payment for those services to B or a third person, or knows that another person has made or promised such a payment, and
  (c) either—
    (i) B is under 18, and A does not reasonably believe that B is 18 or over, or
    (ii) B is under 13.
(2) In this section, 'payment' means any financial advantage, including the discharge of an obligation to pay or the provision of goods or services (including sexual services) gratuitously or at a discount.
(3) A person guilty of an offence under this section against a person under 13, where subsection (6) applies, is liable on conviction on indictment to imprisonment for life.
(4) Unless subsection (3) applies, a person guilty of an offence under this section against a person under 16 is liable—
  (a) where subsection (6) applies, on conviction on indictment, to imprisonment for a term not exceeding 14 years;
  (b) in any other case—
    (i) on summary conviction, to imprisonment for a term not exceeding 6 months or a fine not exceeding the statutory maximum or both;
    (ii) on conviction on indictment, to imprisonment for a term not exceeding 14 years.
(5) Unless subsection (3) or (4) applies, a person guilty of an offence under this section is liable—
  (a) on summary conviction, to imprisonment for a term not exceeding 6 months or a fine not exceeding the statutory maximum or both;
  (b) on conviction on indictment, to imprisonment for a term not exceeding 7 years.
(6) This subsection applies where the offence involved—
  (a) penetration of B's anus or vagina with a part of A's body or anything else,
  (b) penetration of B's mouth with A's penis,

(c) penetration of A's anus or vagina with a part of B's body or by B with anything else, or
(d) penetration of A's mouth with B's penis.

48. Causing or inciting child prostitution or pornography
(1) A person (A) commits an offence if—
   (a) he intentionally causes or incites another person (B) to become a prostitute, or to be involved in pornography, in any part of the world, and
   (b) either—
      (i) B is under 18, and A does not reasonably believe that B is 18 or over, or
      (ii) B is under 13.
(2) A person guilty of an offence under this section is liable—
   (a) on summary conviction, to imprisonment for a term not exceeding 6 months or a fine not exceeding the statutory maximum or both;
   (b) on conviction on indictment, to imprisonment for a term not exceeding 14 years.

49. Controlling a child prostitute or a child involved in pornography
(1) A person (A) commits an offence if—
   (a) he intentionally controls any of the activities of another person (B) relating to B's prostitution or involvement in pornography in any part of the world, and
   (b) either—
      (i) B is under 18, and A does not reasonably believe that B is 18 or over, or
      (ii) B is under 13.
(2) A person guilty of an offence under this section is liable—
   (a) on summary conviction, to imprisonment for a term not exceeding 6 months or a fine not exceeding the statutory maximum or both;
   (b) on conviction on indictment, to imprisonment for a term not exceeding 14 years.

50. Arranging or facilitating child prostitution or pornography
(1) A person (A) commits an offence if—
   (a) he intentionally arranges or facilitates the prostitution or involvement in pornography in any part of the world of another person (B), and
   (b) either—
      (i) B is under 18, and A does not reasonably believe that B is 18 or over, or
      (ii) B is under 13.
(2) A person guilty of an offence under this section is liable—
   (a) on summary conviction, to imprisonment for a term not exceeding 6 months or a fine not exceeding the statutory maximum or both;
   (b) on conviction on indictment, to imprisonment for a term not exceeding 14 years.

51. Sections 48 to 50: interpretation
(1) For the purposes of sections 48 to 50, a person is involved in pornography if an indecent image of that person is recorded; and similar expressions, and 'pornography', are to be interpreted accordingly.
(2) In those sections 'prostitute' means a person (A) who, on at least one occasion and whether or not compelled to do so, offers or provides sexual services to another person in return for payment or a promise of payment to A or a third person; and 'prostitution' is to be interpreted accordingly.
(3) In subsection (2), 'payment' means any financial advantage, including the discharge of an obligation to pay or the provision of goods or services (including sexual services) gratuitously or at a discount.

61. Administering a substance with intent
(1) A person commits an offence if he intentionally administers a substance to, or causes a substance to be taken by, another person (B)—
   (a) knowing that B does not consent, and
   (b) with the intention of stupefying or overpowering B, so as to enable any person to engage in a sexual activity that involves B.

(2) A person guilty of an offence under this section is liable—
   (a) on summary conviction, to imprisonment for a term not exceeding 6 months or a fine not exceeding the statutory maximum or both;
   (b) on conviction on indictment, to imprisonment for a term not exceeding 10 years.

62. Committing an offence with intent to commit a sexual offence

(1) A person commits an offence under this section if he commits any offence with the intention of committing a relevant sexual offence.
(2) In this section, 'relevant sexual offence' means any offence under this Part (including an offence of aiding, abetting, counselling or procuring such an offence).
(3) A person guilty of an offence under this section is liable on conviction on indictment, where the offence is committed by kidnapping or false imprisonment, to imprisonment for life.
(4) Unless subsection (3) applies, a person guilty of an offence under this section is liable—
   (a) on summary conviction, to imprisonment for a term not exceeding 6 months or a fine not exceeding the statutory maximum or both;
   (b) on conviction on indictment, to imprisonment for a term not exceeding 10 years.

63. Trespass with intent to commit a sexual offence

(1) A person commits an offence if—
   (a) he is a trespasser on any premises,
   (b) he intends to commit a relevant sexual offence on the premises, and
   (c) he knows that, or is reckless as to whether, he is a trespasser.
(2) In this section—
   'premises' includes a structure or part of a structure;
   'relevant sexual offence' has the same meaning as in section 62;
   'structure' includes a tent, vehicle or vessel or other temporary or movable structure.
(3) A person guilty of an offence under this section is liable—
   (a) on summary conviction, to imprisonment for a term not exceeding 6 months or a fine not exceeding the statutory maximum or both;
   (b) on conviction on indictment, to imprisonment for a term not exceeding 10 years.

72. Offences outside the United Kingdom

(1) If—
   (a) a United Kingdom national does an act in a country outside the United Kingdom, and
   (b) the act, if done in England and Wales or Northern Ireland, would constitute a sexual offence to which this section applies,
   the United Kingdom national is guilty in that part of the United Kingdom of that sexual offence.
(2) If—
   (a) a United Kingdom resident does an act in a country outside the United Kingdom,
   (b) the act constitutes an offence under the law in force in that country, and
   (c) the act, if done in England and Wales or Northern Ireland, would constitute a sexual offence to which this section applies,
   the United Kingdom resident is guilty in that part of the United Kingdom of that sexual offence.
(3) If—
   (a) a person does an act in a country outside the United Kingdom at a time when the person was not a United Kingdom national or a United Kingdom resident,
   (b) the act constituted an offence under the law in force in that country,
   (c) the act, if done in England and Wales or Northern Ireland, would have constituted a sexual offence to which this section applies, and
   (d) the person meets the residence or nationality condition at the relevant time,
   proceedings may be brought against the person in that part of the United Kingdom for that sexual offence as if the person had done the act there.
(4) The person meets the residence or nationality condition at the relevant time if the person is a United Kingdom national or a United Kingdom resident at the time when the proceedings are brought.

(5) An act punishable under the law in force in any country constitutes an offence under that law for the purposes of subsections (2) and (3) however it is described in that law.
(6) The condition in subsections (2)(b) or (3)(b) is to be taken to be met unless, not later than rules of court may provide, the defendant serves on the prosecution a notice—
    (a) stating that, on the facts as alleged with respect to the act in question, the condition is not in the defendant's opinion met,
    (b) showing the grounds for that opinion, and
    (c) requiring the prosecution to prove that it is met.
(7) But the court, if it thinks fit, may permit the defendant to require the prosecution to prove that the condition is met without service of a notice under subsection (6).
(8) In the Crown Court the question whether the condition is met is to be decided by the judge alone.
(9) In this section—
    'country' includes territory;
    'United Kingdom national' means an individual who is—
    (a) a British citizen, a British overseas territories citizen, a British National (Overseas) or a British Overseas citizen;
    (b) a person who under the British Nationality Act 1981 is a British subject; or
    (c) a British protected person within the meaning of that Act;
    'United Kingdom resident' means an individual who is resident in the United Kingdom.
(10) Schedule 2 lists the sexual offences to which this section applies.

73. Exceptions to aiding, abetting and counselling

(1) A person is not guilty of aiding, abetting or counselling the commission against a child of an offence to which this section applies if he acts for the purpose of—
    (a) protecting the child from sexually transmitted infection,
    (b) protecting the physical safety of the child,
    (c) preventing the child from becoming pregnant, or
    (d) promoting the child's emotional well-being by the giving of advice,
    and not for the purpose of obtaining sexual gratification or for the purpose of causing or encouraging the activity constituting the offence or the child's participation in it.
(2) This section applies to—
    (a) an offence under any of sections 5 to 7 (offences against children under 13);
    (b) an offence under section 9 (sexual activity with a child);
    (c) an offence under section 13 which would be an offence under section 9 if the offender were aged 18;
    (d) an offence under any of sections 16, 25, 30, 34 and 38 (sexual activity) against a person under 16.
(3) This section does not affect any other enactment or any rule of law restricting the circumstances in which a person is guilty of aiding, abetting or counselling an offence under this Part.

74. 'Consent'

For the purposes of this Part, a person consents if he agrees by choice, and has the freedom and capacity to make that choice.

75. Evidential presumptions about consent

(1) If in proceedings for an offence to which this section applies it is proved—
    (a) that the defendant did the relevant act,
    (b) that any of the circumstances specified in subsection (2) existed, and
    (c) that the defendant knew that those circumstances existed,
    the complainant is to be taken not to have consented to the relevant act unless sufficient evidence is adduced to raise an issue as to whether he consented, and the defendant is to be taken not to have reasonably believed that the complainant consented unless sufficient evidence is adduced to raise an issue as to whether he reasonably believed it.

(2) The circumstances are that—
   (a) any person was, at the time of the relevant act or immediately before it began, using violence against the complainant or causing the complainant to fear that immediate violence would be used against him;
   (b) any person was, at the time of the relevant act or immediately before it began, causing the complainant to fear that violence was being used, or that immediate violence would be used, against another person;
   (c) the complainant was, and the defendant was not, unlawfully detained at the time of the relevant act;
   (d) the complainant was asleep or otherwise unconscious at the time of the relevant act;
   (e) because of the complainant's physical disability, the complainant would not have been able at the time of the relevant act to communicate to the defendant whether the complainant consented;
   (f) any person had administered to or caused to be taken by the complainant, without the complainant's consent, a substance which, having regard to when it was administered or taken, was capable of causing or enabling the complainant to be stupefied or overpowered at the time of the relevant act.
(3) In subsection (2)(a) and (b), the reference to the time immediately before the relevant act began is, in the case of an act which is one of a continuous series of sexual activities, a reference to the time immediately before the first sexual activity began.

76. Conclusive presumptions about consent
(1) If in proceedings for an offence to which this section applies it is proved that the defendant did the relevant act and that any of the circumstances specified in subsection (2) existed, it is to be conclusively presumed—
   (a) that the complainant did not consent to the relevant act, and
   (b) that the defendant did not believe that the complainant consented to the relevant act.
(2) The circumstances are that—
   (a) the defendant intentionally deceived the complainant as to the nature or purpose of the relevant act;
   (b) the defendant intentionally induced the complainant to consent to the relevant act by impersonating a person known personally to the complainant.

77. Sections 75 and 76: relevant acts
In relation to an offence to which sections 75 and 76 apply, references in those sections to the relevant act and to the complainant are to be read as follows—

Offence	Relevant Act
An offence under section 1 (rape).	The defendant intentionally penetrating, with his penis, the vagina, anus or mouth of another person ('the complainant').
An offence under section 2 (assault by penetration).	The defendant intentionally penetrating, with a part of his body or anything else, the vagina or anus of another person ('the complainant'), where the penetration is sexual.
An offence under section 3 (sexual assault).	The defendant intentionally touching another person ('the complainant'), where the touching is sexual.
An offence under section 4 (causing a person to engage in sexual activity without consent).	The defendant intentionally causing another person ('the complainant') to engage in an activity, where the activity is sexual.

78. 'Sexual'
For the purposes of this Part (except section 71), penetration, touching or any other activity is sexual if a reasonable person would consider that—
   (a) whatever its circumstances or any person's purpose in relation to it, it is because of its nature sexual, or
   (b) because of its nature it may be sexual and because of its circumstances or the purpose of any person in relation to it (or both) it is sexual.

79. Part 1: general interpretation

(1) The following apply for the purposes of this Part.
(2) Penetration is a continuing act from entry to withdrawal.
(3) References to a part of the body include references to a part surgically constructed (in particular, through gender reassignment surgery).
(4) 'Image' means a moving or still image and includes an image produced by any means and, where the context permits, a three-dimensional image.
(5) References to an image of a person include references to an image of an imaginary person.
(6) 'Mental disorder' has the meaning given by section 1 of the Mental Health Act 1983.
(7) References to observation (however expressed) are to observation whether direct or by looking at an image.
(8) Touching includes touching—
   (a) with any part of the body,
   (b) with anything else,
   (c) through anything,
   and in particular includes touching amounting to penetration.
(9) 'Vagina' includes vulva.
(10) In relation to an animal, references to the vagina or anus include references to any similar part.

SCHEDULE 2 | SEXUAL OFFENCES TO WHICH SECTION 72 APPLIES

ENGLAND AND WALES

1   In relation to England and Wales, the following are sexual offences to which section 72 applies—
   (a) an offence under any of sections 5 to 19, 25 and 26 and 47 to 50;
   (b) an offence under any of sections 1 to 4, 30 to 41 and 61 where the victim of the offence was under 18 at the time of the offence;
   (c) an offence under sections 62 or 63 where the intended offence was an offence against a person under 18;
   (d) an offence under—
      (i) section 1 of the Protection of Children Act 1978 (indecent photographs of children), or
      (ii) section 160 of the Criminal Justice Act 1988 (possession of indecent photograph of child).

| STREET OFFENCES ACT 1959

1. Loitering or soliciting for purposes of prostitution

(1) It shall be an offence for a common prostitute (whether male or female) to loiter or solicit in a street or public place for the purpose of prostitution.
(2) A person guilty of an offence under this section shall be liable on summary conviction to a fine of an amount not exceeding level 2 on the standard scale or, for an offence committed after a previous conviction, to a fine of an amount not exceeding level 3 on that scale.
(4) For the purposes of this section 'street' includes any bridge, road, lane, footway, subway, square, court, alley or passage, whether a thoroughfare or not, which is for the time being open to the public; and the doorways and entrances of premises abutting on a street (as hereinbefore defined), and any ground adjoining and open to a street, shall be treated as forming part of the street.

SUICIDE ACT 1961

1. Suicide to cease to be a crime
The rule of law whereby it is a crime for a person to commit suicide is hereby abrogated.

2. Criminal liability for complicity in another's suicide
(1) A person who aids, abets, counsels or procures the suicide of another, or an attempt by another to commit suicide, shall be liable on conviction on indictment to imprisonment for a term not exceeding fourteen years.

(2) If on the trial of an indictment for murder or manslaughter it is proved that the accused aided, abetted, counselled or procured the suicide of the person in question, the jury may find him guilty of that offence.

...

(4) No proceedings shall be instituted for an offence under this section except by or with the consent of the Director of Public Prosecutions

SUPPRESSION OF TERRORISM ACT 1978

4. Jurisdiction in respect of offences committed outside United Kingdom
(1) If a person, whether a citizen of the United Kingdom and Colonies or not, does in a convention country any act which, if he had done it in a part of the United Kingdom, would have made him guilty in that part of the United Kingdom of—
   (a) an offence mentioned in paragraphs 1, 2, 4, 5, 10, 11B, 12, 13, 14 or 15 of Schedule 1 to this Act; or
   (b) an offence of attempting to commit any offence so mentioned,
   he shall, in that part of the United Kingdom, be guilty of the offence or offences aforesaid of which the act would have made him guilty if he had done it there.

(3) If a person who is a national of a convention country but not a citizen of the United Kingdom and Colonies does outside the United Kingdom and that convention country any act which makes him in that convention country guilty of an offence and which, if he had been a citizen of the United Kingdom and Colonies, would have made him in any part of the United Kingdom guilty of an offence mentioned in paragraphs 1, 2 or 13 of Schedule 1 to this Act, he shall, in any part of the United Kingdom, be guilty of the offence or offences aforesaid of which the act would have made him guilty if he had been such a citizen.

...

(7) For the purposes of this section any act done—
   (a) on board a ship registered in a convention country, being an act which, if the ship had been registered in the United Kingdom, would have constituted an offence within the jurisdiction of the Admiralty; or
   (b) on board an aircraft registered in a convention country while the aircraft is in flight elsewhere than in or over that country; or
   (c) on board a hovercraft registered in a convention country while the hovercraft is in journey elsewhere than in or over that country,
   shall be treated as done in that convention country; and subsection (4) of section 92 of the Civil Aviation Act 1982 (definition of 'in flight' or, as applied to hovercraft, 'in journey') shall apply for the purposes of this subsection as it applies for the purposes of that section.

8. Provisions as to interpretation and orders
(1) In this Act—
   'act' includes omission;

'convention country' means a country for the time being designated in an order made by the Secretary of State as a party to the European Convention on the Suppression of Terrorism signed at Strasbourg on the 27th January 1977;

'country' includes any territory;

...

(2) Except so far as the context otherwise requires, any reference in this Act to an enactment is a reference to it as amended by or under any other enactment, including this Act.

SCHEDULE 1

COMMON LAW OFFENCES

1. Murder.
2. Manslaughter or culpable homicide.
  ...
4. Kidnapping, abduction or plagium.
5. False imprisonment.

ABDUCTION

...

10. An offence under any of the following provisions of the Offences against the Person Act 1861—
    (a) section 55 (abduction of unmarried girl under 16);
    (b) section 56 (child-stealing or receiving stolen child).
11. An offence under section 20 of the Sexual Offences Act 1956 (abduction of unmarried girl under 16).

TAKING OF HOSTAGES

11B. An offence under section 2 of the Child Abduction Act 1984 (abduction of child by person other than parent etc.) or any corresponding provision in force in Northern Ireland.

EXPLOSIVES

12. An offence under any of the following provisions of the Offences against the Person Act 1861—
    (a) section 28 (causing bodily injury by gunpowder);
    (b) section 29 (causing gunpowder to explode etc. with intent to do grievous bodily harm);
    (c) section 30 (placing gunpowder near a building etc. with intent to cause bodily injury).
13. An offence under any of the following provisions of the Explosive Substances Act 1883—
    (a) section 2 (causing explosion likely to endanger life or property);
    (b) section 3 (doing any act with intent to cause such an explosion, conspiring to cause such an explosion, or making or possessing explosive with intent to endanger life or property).

FIREARMS

14. The following offences under the Firearms Act 1968—
    (a) an offence under section 16 (possession of firearm with intent to injure);
    (b) an offence under subsection (1) of section 17 (use of firearm or imitation firearm to resist arrest) involving the use or attempted use of a firearm within the meaning of that section.
    ...

TAKING OF HOSTAGES ACT 1982

1. Hostage-taking
(1) A person, whatever his nationality, who, in the United Kingdom or elsewhere—
  (a) detains any other person ('the hostage'), and
  (b) in order to compel a State, international governmental organisation or person to do or abstain from doing any act, threatens to kill, injure or continue to detain the hostage, commits an offence.
(2) A person guilty of an offence under this Act shall be liable, on conviction on indictment, to imprisonment for life.

TERRORISM ACT 2000

PART I INTRODUCTORY

1. Terrorism: interpretation
(1) In this Act 'terrorism' means the use or threat of action where—
  (a) the action falls within subsection (2),
  (b) the use or threat is designed to influence the government or an international governmental organisation or to intimidate the public or a section of the public, and
  (c) the use or threat is made for the purpose of advancing a political, religious or ideological cause.
(2) Action falls within this subsection if it—
  (a) involves serious violence against a person,
  (b) involves serious damage to property,
  (c) endangers a person's life, other than that of the person committing the action,
  (d) creates a serious risk to the health or safety of the public or a section of the public, or
  (e) is designed seriously to interfere with or seriously to disrupt an electronic system.
(3) The use or threat of action falling within subsection (2) which involves the use of firearms or explosives is terrorism whether or not subsection (1)(b) is satisfied.
(4) In this section—
  (a) 'action' includes action outside the United Kingdom,
  (b) a reference to any person or to property is a reference to any person, or to property, wherever situated,
  (c) a reference to the public includes a reference to the public of a country other than the United Kingdom, and
  (d) 'the government' means the government of the United Kingdom, of a part of the United Kingdom or of a country other than the United Kingdom.
(5) In this Act a reference to action taken for the purposes of terrorism includes a reference to action taken for the benefit of a proscribed organisation.

PART II PROSCRIBED ORGANISATIONS

3. Proscription
(1) For the purposes of this Act an organisation is proscribed if—
  (a) it is listed in Schedule 2, or
  (b) it operates under the same name as an organisation listed in that Schedule.
(2) Subsection (1)(b) shall not apply in relation to an organisation listed in Schedule 2 if its entry is the subject of a note in that Schedule.

11. Membership

(1) A person commits an offence if he belongs or professes to belong to a proscribed organisation.
(2) It is a defence for a person charged with an offence under subsection (1) to prove—
   (a) that the organisation was not proscribed on the last (or only) occasion on which he became a member or began to profess to be a member, and
   (b) that he has not taken part in the activities of the organisation at any time while it was proscribed.
(3) A person guilty of an offence under this section shall be liable—
   (a) on conviction on indictment, to imprisonment for a term not exceeding ten years, to a fine or to both, or
   (b) on summary conviction, to imprisonment for a term not exceeding six months, to a fine not exceeding the statutory maximum or to both.
(4) In subsection (2) 'proscribed' means proscribed for the purposes of any of the following—
   (a) this Act;
   (b) the Northern Ireland (Emergency Provisions) Act 1996;
   (c) the Northern Ireland (Emergency Provisions) Act 1991;
   (d) the Prevention of Terrorism (Temporary Provisions) Act 1989;
   (e) the Prevention of Terrorism (Temporary Provisions) Act 1984;
   (f) the Northern Ireland (Emergency Provisions) Act 1978;
   (g) the Prevention of Terrorism (Temporary Provisions) Act 1976;
   (h) the Prevention of Terrorism (Temporary Provisions) Act 1974;
   (i) the Northern Ireland (Emergency Provisions) Act 1973.

12. Support

(1) A person commits an offence if—
   (a) he invites support for a proscribed organisation, and
   (b) the support is not, or is not restricted to, the provision of money or other property (within the meaning of section 15).
(2) A person commits an offence if he arranges, manages or assists in arranging or managing a meeting which he knows is—
   (a) to support a proscribed organisation,
   (b) to further the activities of a proscribed organisation, or
   (c) to be addressed by a person who belongs or professes to belong to a proscribed organisation.
(3) A person commits an offence if he addresses a meeting and the purpose of his address is to encourage support for a proscribed organisation or to further its activities.
(4) Where a person is charged with an offence under subsection (2)(c) in respect of a private meeting it is a defence for him to prove that he had no reasonable cause to believe that the address mentioned in subsection (2)(c) would support a proscribed organisation or further its activities.
(5) In subsections (2) to (4)—
   (a) 'meeting' means a meeting of three or more persons, whether or not the public are admitted, and
   (b) a meeting is private if the public are not admitted.
(6) A person guilty of an offence under this section shall be liable—
   (a) on conviction on indictment, to imprisonment for a term not exceeding ten years, to a fine or to both, or
   (b) on summary conviction, to imprisonment for a term not exceeding six months, to a fine not exceeding the statutory maximum or to both.

13. Uniform

(1) A person in a public place commits an offence if he—
   (a) wears an item of clothing, or
   (b) wears, carries or displays an article,
   in such a way or in such circumstances as to arouse reasonable suspicion that he is a member or supporter of a proscribed organisation.
      …

(3) A person guilty of an offence under this section shall be liable on summary conviction to—
    (a) imprisonment for a term not exceeding six months,
    (b) a fine not exceeding level 5 on the standard scale, or
    (c) both.

PART III TERRORIST PROPERTY

14. Terrorist property
(1) In this Act 'terrorist property' means—
    (a) money or other property which is likely to be used for the purposes of terrorism (including any resources of a proscribed organisation),
    (b) proceeds of the commission of acts of terrorism, and
    (c) proceeds of acts carried out for the purposes of terrorism.
(2) In subsection (1)—
    (a) a reference to proceeds of an act includes a reference to any property which wholly or partly, and directly or indirectly, represents the proceeds of the act (including payments or other rewards in connection with its commission), and
    (b) the reference to an organisation's resources includes a reference to any money or other property which is applied or made available, or is to be applied or made available, for use by the organisation.

15. Fund-raising
(1) A person commits an offence if he—
    (a) invites another to provide money or other property, and
    (b) intends that it should be used, or has reasonable cause to suspect that it may be used, for the purposes of terrorism.
(2) A person commits an offence if he—
    (a) receives money or other property, and
    (b) intends that it should be used, or has reasonable cause to suspect that it may be used, for the purposes of terrorism.
(3) A person commits an offence if he—
    (a) provides money or other property, and
    (b) knows or has reasonable cause to suspect that it will or may be used for the purposes of terrorism.
(4) In this section a reference to the provision of money or other property is a reference to its being given, lent or otherwise made available, whether or not for consideration.

16. Use and possession
(1) A person commits an offence if he uses money or other property for the purposes of terrorism.
(2) A person commits an offence if he—
    (a) possesses money or other property, and
    (b) intends that it should be used, or has reasonable cause to suspect that it may be used, for the purposes of terrorism.

17. Funding arrangements
A person commits an offence if—
    (a) he enters into or becomes concerned in an arrangement as a result of which money or other property is made available or is to be made available to another, and
    (b) he knows or has reasonable cause to suspect that it will or may be used for the purposes of terrorism.

18. Money laundering
(1) A person commits an offence if he enters into or becomes concerned in an arrangement which facilitates the retention or control by or on behalf of another person of terrorist property—
    (a) by concealment,
    (b) by removal from the jurisdiction,
    (c) by transfer to nominees, or

(d) in any other way.
(2) It is a defence for a person charged with an offence under subsection (1) to prove that he did not know and had no reasonable cause to suspect that the arrangement related to terrorist property.

19. Disclosure of information: duty

(1) This section applies where a person—
    (a) believes or suspects that another person has committed an offence under any of sections 15 to 18, and
    (b) bases his belief or suspicion on information which comes to his attention in the course of a trade, profession, business or employment.
(1A) But this section does not apply if the information came to the person in the course of a business in the regulated sector.
(2) The person commits an offence if he does not disclose to a constable as soon as is reasonably practicable—
    (a) his belief or suspicion, and
    (b) the information on which it is based.
(3) It is a defence for a person charged with an offence under subsection (2) to prove that he had a reasonable excuse for not making the disclosure.
(4) Where—
    (a) a person is in employment,
    (b) his employer has established a procedure for the making of disclosures of the matters specified in subsection (2), and
    (c) he is charged with an offence under that subsection,
    it is a defence for him to prove that he disclosed the matters specified in that subsection in accordance with the procedure.
(5) Subsection (2) does not require disclosure by a professional legal adviser of—
    (a) information which he obtains in privileged circumstances, or
    (b) a belief or suspicion based on information which he obtains in privileged circumstances.
(6) For the purpose of subsection (5) information is obtained by an adviser in privileged circumstances if it comes to him, otherwise than with a view to furthering a criminal purpose—
    (a) from a client or a client's representative, in connection with the provision of legal advice by the adviser to the client,
    (b) from a person seeking legal advice from the adviser, or from the person's representative, or
    (c) from any person, for the purpose of actual or contemplated legal proceedings.
(7) For the purposes of subsection (1)(a) a person shall be treated as having committed an offence under one of sections 15 to 18 if—
    (a) he has taken an action or been in possession of a thing, and
    (b) he would have committed an offence under one of those sections if he had been in the United Kingdom at the time when he took the action or was in possession of the thing.
(7A) The reference to a business in the regulated sector must be construed in accordance with Schedule 3A.
(7B) The reference to a constable includes a reference to a member of the staff of the Serious Organised Crime Agency authorised for the purposes of this section by the Director General of that Agency.
(8) A person guilty of an offence under this section shall be liable—
    (a) on conviction on indictment, to imprisonment for a term not exceeding five years, to a fine or to both, or
    (b) on summary conviction, to imprisonment for a term not exceeding six months, or to a fine not exceeding the statutory maximum or to both.

21. Cooperation with police

(1) A person does not commit an offence under any of sections 15 to 18 if he is acting with the express consent of a constable.

(2) Subject to subsections (3) and (4), a person does not commit an offence under any of sections 15 to 18 by involvement in a transaction or arrangement relating to money or other property if he discloses to a constable—
   (a) his suspicion or belief that the money or other property is terrorist property, and
   (b) the information on which his suspicion or belief is based.
(3) Subsection (2) applies only where a person makes a disclosure—
   (a) after he becomes concerned in the transaction concerned,
   (b) on his own initiative, and
   (c) as soon as is reasonably practicable.
(4) Subsection (2) does not apply to a person if—
   (a) a constable forbids him to continue his involvement in the transaction or arrangement to which the disclosure relates, and
   (b) he continues his involvement.
(5) It is a defence for a person charged with an offence under any of sections 15(2) and (3) and 16 to 18 to prove that—
   (a) he intended to make a disclosure of the kind mentioned in subsections (2) and (3), and
   (b) there is reasonable excuse for his failure to do so.
(6) Where—
   (a) a person is in employment, and
   (b) his employer has established a procedure for the making of disclosures of the same kind as may be made to a constable under subsection (2),
   this section shall have effect in relation to that person as if any reference to disclosure to a constable included a reference to disclosure in accordance with the procedure.
(7) A reference in this section to a transaction or arrangement relating to money or other property includes a reference to use or possession.

21ZA. Arrangements with prior consent

(1) A person does not commit an offence under any of sections 15 to 18 by involvement in a transaction or an arrangement relating to money or other property if, before becoming involved, the person—
   (a) discloses to an authorised officer the person's suspicion or belief that the money or other property is terrorist property and the information on which the suspicion or belief is based, and
   (b) has the authorised officer's consent to becoming involved in the transaction or arrangement.
(2) A person is treated as having an authorised officer's consent if before the end of the notice period the person does not receive notice from an authorised officer that consent is refused.
(3) The notice period is the period of 7 working days starting with the first working day after the person makes the disclosure.
(4) A working day is a day other than a Saturday, a Sunday, Christmas Day, Good Friday or a day that is a bank holiday under the Banking and Financial Dealings Act 1971 in the part of the United Kingdom in which the person is when making the disclosure.
(5) In this section 'authorised officer' means a member of the staff of the Serious Organised Crime Agency authorised for the purposes of this section by the Director General of that Agency.
(6) The reference in this section to a transaction or arrangement relating to money or other property includes a reference to use or possession.

21ZB. Disclosure after entering into arrangements

(1) A person does not commit an offence under any of sections 15 to 18 by involvement in a transaction or an arrangement relating to money or other property if, after becoming involved, the person discloses to an authorised officer—
   (a) the person's suspicion or belief that the money or other property is terrorist property, and
   (b) the information on which the suspicion or belief is based.
(2) This section applies only where—
   (a) there is a reasonable excuse for the person's failure to make the disclosure before becoming involved in the transaction or arrangement, and
   (b) the disclosure is made on the person's own initiative and as soon as it is reasonably practicable for the person to make it.

(3) This section does not apply to a person if—
    (a) an authorised officer forbids the person to continue involvement in the transaction or arrangement to which the disclosure relates, and
    (b) the person continues that involvement.
(4) In this section 'authorised officer' means a member of the staff of the Serious Organised Crime Agency authorised for the purposes of this section by the Director General of that Agency.
(5) The reference in this section to a transaction or arrangement relating to money or other property includes a reference to use or possession.

21ZC. Reasonable excuse for failure to disclose
It is a defence for a person charged with an offence under any of sections 15 to 18 to prove that—
    (a) the person intended to make a disclosure of the kind mentioned in section 21ZA or 21ZB, and
    (b) there is a reasonable excuse for the person's failure to do so.

21A. Failure to disclose: regulated sector
(1) A person commits an offence if each of the following three conditions is satisfied.
(2) The first condition is that he—
    (a) knows or suspects, or
    (b) has reasonable grounds for knowing or suspecting, that another person has committed or attempted to commit an offence under any of sections 15 to 18.
(3) The second condition is that the information or other matter—
    (a) on which his knowledge or suspicion is based, or
    (b) which gives reasonable grounds for such knowledge or suspicion, came to him in the course of a business in the regulated sector.
(4) The third condition is that he does not disclose the information or other matter to a constable or a nominated officer as soon as is practicable after it comes to him.
(5) But a person does not commit an offence under this section if—
    (a) he has a reasonable excuse for not disclosing the information or other matter;
    (b) he is a professional legal adviser or relevant professional adviser and the information or other matter came to him in privileged circumstances; or
    (c) subsection (5A) applies to him
(5A) This subsection applies to a person if—
    (a) the person is employed by, or is in partnership with, a professional legal adviser or relevant professional adviser to provide the adviser with assistance or support,
    (b) the information or other matter comes to the person in connection with the provision of such assistance or support, and
    (c) the information or other matter came to the adviser in privileged circumstances.
(6) In deciding whether a person committed an offence under this section the court must consider whether he followed any relevant guidance which was at the time concerned—
    (a) issued by a supervisory authority or any other appropriate body,
    (b) approved by the Treasury, and
    (c) published in a manner it approved as appropriate in its opinion to bring the guidance to the attention of persons likely to be affected by it.
(7) A disclosure to a nominated officer is a disclosure which—
    (a) is made to a person nominated by the alleged offender's employer to receive disclosures under this section, and
    (b) is made in the course of the alleged offender's employment and in accordance with the procedure established by the employer for the purpose.
(8) Information or other matter comes to a professional legal adviser or relevant professional adviser in privileged circumstances if it is communicated or given to him—
    (a) by (or by a representative of) a client of his in connection with the giving by the adviser of legal advice to the client,
    (b) by (or by a representative of) a person seeking legal advice from the adviser, or
    (c) by a person in connection with legal proceedings or contemplated legal proceedings.
(9) But subsection (8) does not apply to information or other matter which is communicated or given with a view to furthering a criminal purpose.

(10) Schedule 3A has effect for the purpose of determining what is—
    (a) a business in the regulated sector;
    (b) a supervisory authority.
(11) For the purposes of subsection (2) a person is to be taken to have committed an offence there mentioned if—
    (a) he has taken an action or been in possession of a thing, and
    (b) he would have committed the offence if he had been in the United Kingdom at the time when he took the action or was in possession of the thing.
(12) A person guilty of an offence under this section is liable—
    (a) on conviction on indictment, to imprisonment for a term not exceeding five years or to a fine or to both;
    (b) on summary conviction, to imprisonment for a term not exceeding six months or to a fine not exceeding the statutory maximum or to both.
(13) An appropriate body is any body which regulates or is representative of any trade, profession, business or employment carried on by the alleged offender.
(14) The reference to a constable includes a reference to a member of the staff of the Serious Organised Crime Agency authorised for the purposes of this section by the Director General of that Agency.
(15) In this section 'relevant professional adviser' means an accountant, auditor or tax adviser who is a member of a professional body which is established for accountants, auditors or tax advisers (as the case may be) and which makes provision for—
    (a) testing the competence of those seeking admission to membership of such a body as a condition for such admission; and
    (b) imposing and maintaining professional and ethical standards for its members, as well as imposing sanctions for non-compliance with those standards.

21B. Protected disclosures

(1) A disclosure which satisfies the following three conditions is not to be taken to breach any restriction on the disclosure of information (however imposed).
(2) The first condition is that the information or other matter disclosed came to the person making the disclosure (the discloser) in the course of a business in the regulated sector.
(3) The second condition is that the information or other matter—
    (a) causes the discloser to know or suspect, or
    (b) gives him reasonable grounds for knowing or suspecting, that another person has committed or attempted to commit an offence under any of sections 15 to 18.
(4) The third condition is that the disclosure is made to a constable or a nominated officer as soon as is practicable after the information or other matter comes to the discloser.
(5) A disclosure to a nominated officer is a disclosure which—
    (a) is made to a person nominated by the discloser's employer to receive disclosures under this section, and
    (b) is made in the course of the discloser's employment and in accordance with the procedure established by the employer for the purpose.
(6) The reference to a business in the regulated sector must be construed in accordance with Schedule 3A.
(7) The reference to a constable includes a reference to a member of the staff of the Serious Organised Crime Agency authorised for the purposes of this section by the Director General of that Agency.

21C. Disclosures to SOCA

(1) Where a disclosure is made under a provision of this Part to a constable, the constable must disclose it in full as soon as practicable after it has been made to a member of staff of the Serious Organised Crime Agency authorised for the purposes of that provision by the Director General of that Agency.
(2) Where a disclosure is made under section 21 (cooperation with police) to a constable, the constable must disclose it in full as soon as practicable after it has been made to a member of staff of the Serious Organised Crime Agency authorised for the purposes of this subsection by

the Director General of that Agency.

21D. Tipping off: regulated sector

(1) A person commits an offence if—
    (a) the person discloses any matter within subsection (2);
    (b) the disclosure is likely to prejudice any investigation that might be conducted following the disclosure referred to in that subsection; and
    (c) the information on which the disclosure is based came to the person in the course of a business in the regulated sector.
(2) The matters are that the person or another person has made a disclosure under a provision of this Part—
    (a) to a constable,
    (b) in accordance with a procedure established by that person's employer for the making of disclosures under that provision,
    (c) to a nominated officer, or
    (d) to a member of staff of the Serious Organised Crime Agency authorised for the purposes of that provision by the Director General of that Agency,
    of information that came to that person in the course of a business in the regulated sector.
(3) A person commits an offence if—
    (a) the person discloses that an investigation into allegations that an offence under this Part has been committed is being contemplated or is being carried out;
    (b) the disclosure is likely to prejudice that investigation; and
    (c) the information on which the disclosure is based came to the person in the course of a business in the regulated sector.
(4) A person guilty of an offence under this section is liable—
    (a) on summary conviction to imprisonment for a term not exceeding three months, or to a fine not exceeding level 5 on the standard scale, or to both;
    (b) on conviction on indictment to imprisonment for a term not exceeding two years, or to a fine, or to both.
(5) This section is subject to—
    (a) section 21E (disclosures within an undertaking or group etc.),
    (b) section 21F (other permitted disclosures between institutions etc.), and
    (c) section 21G (other permitted disclosures etc.).

21E. Disclosures within an undertaking or group etc.

(1) An employee, officer or partner of an undertaking does not commit an offence under section 21D if the disclosure is to an employee, officer or partner of the same undertaking.
(2) A person does not commit an offence under section 21D in respect of a disclosure by a credit institution or a financial institution if—
    (a) the disclosure is to a credit institution or a financial institution,
    (b) the institution to whom the disclosure is made is situated in an EEA State or in a country or territory imposing equivalent money laundering requirements, and
    (c) both the institution making the disclosure and the institution to whom it is made belong to the same group.
(3) In subsection (2) 'group' has the same meaning as in Directive 2002/87/EC of the European Parliament and of the Council of 16th December 2002 on the supplementary supervision of credit institutions, insurance undertakings and investment firms in a financial conglomerate.
(4) A professional legal adviser or a relevant professional adviser does not commit an offence under section 21D if—
    (a) the disclosure is to a professional legal adviser or a relevant professional adviser,
    (b) both the person making the disclosure and the person to whom it is made carry on business in an EEA state or in a country or territory imposing equivalent money laundering requirements, and
    (c) those persons perform their professional activities within different undertakings that share common ownership, management or control.

21F. Other permitted disclosures between institutions etc.

(1) This section applies to a disclosure—
   (a) by a credit institution to another credit institution,
   (b) by a financial institution to another financial institution,
   (c) by a professional legal adviser to another professional legal adviser, or
   (d) by a relevant professional adviser of a particular kind to another relevant professional adviser of the same kind.
(2) A person does not commit an offence under section 21D in respect of a disclosure to which this section applies if—
   (a) the disclosure relates to—
      (i) a client or former client of the institution or adviser making the disclosure and the institution or adviser to whom it is made,
      (ii) a transaction involving them both, or
      (iii) the provision of a service involving them both;
   (b) the disclosure is for the purpose only of preventing an offence under this Part of this Act;
   (c) the institution or adviser to whom the disclosure is made is situated in an EEA State or in a country or territory imposing equivalent money laundering requirements; and
   (d) the institution or adviser making the disclosure and the institution or adviser to whom it is made are subject to equivalent duties of professional confidentiality and the protection of personal data (within the meaning of section 1 of the Data Protection Act 1998).

21G. Other permitted disclosures etc.

(1) A person does not commit an offence under section 21D if the disclosure is—
   (a) to the authority that is the supervisory authority for that person by virtue of the Money Laundering Regulations 2007 (S.I. 2007/2157); or
   (b) for the purpose of—
      (i) the detection, investigation or prosecution of a criminal offence (whether in the United Kingdom or elsewhere),
      (ii) an investigation under the Proceeds of Crime Act 2002, or
      (iii) the enforcement of any order of a court under that Act.
(2) A professional legal adviser or a relevant professional adviser does not commit an offence under section 21D if the disclosure—
   (a) is to the adviser's client, and
   (b) is made for the purpose of dissuading the client from engaging in conduct amounting to an offence.
(3) A person does not commit an offence under section 21D(1) if the person does not know or suspect that the disclosure is likely to have the effect mentioned in section 21D(1)(b).
(4) A person does not commit an offence under section 21D(3) if the person does not know or suspect that the disclosure is likely to have the effect mentioned in section 21D(3)(b).

21H. Interpretation of sections 21D to 21G

(1) The references in sections 21D to 21G—
   (a) to a business in the regulated sector, and
   (b) to a supervisory authority,
   are to be construed in accordance with Schedule 3A.
(2) In those sections—
   'credit institution' has the same meaning as in Schedule 3A;
   'financial institution' means an undertaking that carries on a business in the regulated sector by virtue of any of paragraphs (b) to (i) of paragraph 1(1) of that Schedule.
(3) References in those sections to a disclosure by or to a credit institution or a financial institution include disclosure by or to an employee, officer or partner of the institution acting on its behalf.
(4) For the purposes of those sections a country or territory imposes 'equivalent money laundering requirements' if it imposes requirements equivalent to those laid down in Directive 2005/60/EC of the European Parliament and of the Council of 26th October 2005 on the prevention of the use of the financial system for the purpose of money laundering and terrorist financing.

(5) In those sections 'relevant professional adviser' means an accountant, auditor or tax adviser who is a member of a professional body which is established for accountants, auditors or tax advisers (as the case may be) and which makes provision for—
   (a) testing the competence of those seeking admission to membership of such a body as a condition for such admission; and
   (b) imposing and maintaining professional and ethical standards for its members, as well as imposing sanctions for non-compliance with those standards.

39. Disclosure of information, etc.
(1) Subsection (2) applies where a person knows or has reasonable cause to suspect that a constable is conducting or proposes to conduct a terrorist investigation.
(2) The person commits an offence if he—
   (a) discloses to another anything which is likely to prejudice the investigation, or
   (b) interferes with material which is likely to be relevant to the investigation.
(3) Subsection (4) applies where a person knows or has reasonable cause to suspect that a disclosure has been or will be made under any of sections 19 to 21B or 38B.
(4) The person commits an offence if he—
   (a) discloses to another anything which is likely to prejudice an investigation resulting from the disclosure under that section, or
   (b) interferes with material which is likely to be relevant to an investigation resulting from the disclosure under that section.
(5) It is a defence for a person charged with an offence under subsection (2) or (4) to prove—
   (a) that he did not know and had no reasonable cause to suspect that the disclosure or interference was likely to affect a terrorist investigation, or
   (b) that he had a reasonable excuse for the disclosure or interference.
(6) Subsections (2) and (4) do not apply to a disclosure which is made by a professional legal adviser—
   (a) to his client or to his client's representative in connection with the provision of legal advice by the adviser to the client and not with a view to furthering a criminal purpose, or
   (b) to any person for the purpose of actual or contemplated legal proceedings and not with a view to furthering a criminal purpose.
(6A) Subsections (2) and (4) do not apply if—
   (a) the disclosure is of a matter within sections 21D(2) or (3)(a) (terrorist property: tipping off), and
   (b) the information on which the disclosure is based came to the person in the course of a business in the regulated sector.
(7) A person guilty of an offence under this section shall be liable—
   (a) on conviction on indictment, to imprisonment for a term not exceeding five years, to a fine or to both, or
   (b) on summary conviction, to imprisonment for a term not exceeding six months, to a fine not exceeding the statutory maximum or to both.
(8) For the purposes of this section—
   (a) a reference to conducting a terrorist investigation includes a reference to taking part in the conduct of, or assisting, a terrorist investigation, and
   (b) a person interferes with material if he falsifies it, conceals it, destroys it or disposes of it, or if he causes or permits another to do any of those things.
(9) The reference in subsection (6A) to a business in the regulated sector is to be construed in accordance with Schedule 3A.

48. Authorisations
(1) An authorisation under this section authorises any constable in uniform to prohibit or restrict the parking of vehicles on a road specified in the authorisation.
(2) An authorisation may be given only if the person giving it considers it expedient for the prevention of acts of terrorism.

(3) An authorisation may be given—
  (a) where the road specified is outside Northern Ireland and is wholly or partly within a police area other than one mentioned in paragraphs (b) or (c), by a police officer for the area who is of at least the rank of assistant chief constable;
  (b) where the road specified is wholly or partly in the metropolitan police district, by a police officer for the district who is of at least the rank of commander of the metropolitan police;
  (c) where the road specified is wholly or partly in the City of London, by a police officer for the City who is of at least the rank of commander in the City of London police force;
  (d) where the road specified is in Northern Ireland, by a member of the Royal Ulster Constabulary who is of at least the rank of assistant chief constable.
(4) If an authorisation is given orally, the person giving it shall confirm it in writing as soon as is reasonably practicable.

49. Exercise of power
(1) The power conferred by an authorisation under section 48 shall be exercised by placing a traffic sign on the road concerned.
(2) A constable exercising the power conferred by an authorisation under section 48 may suspend a parking place.
(3) Where a parking place is suspended under subsection (2), the suspension shall be treated as a restriction imposed by virtue of section 48—
  (a) for the purposes of section 99 of the Road Traffic Regulation Act 1984 (removal of vehicles illegally parked, etc.) and of any regulations in force under that section, and
  ...

51. Offences
(1) A person commits an offence if he parks a vehicle in contravention of a prohibition or restriction imposed by virtue of section 48.
(2) A person commits an offence if—
  (a) he is the driver or other person in charge of a vehicle which has been permitted to remain at rest in contravention of any prohibition or restriction imposed by virtue of section 48, and
  (b) he fails to move the vehicle when ordered to do so by a constable in uniform.
(3) It is a defence for a person charged with an offence under this section to prove that he had a reasonable excuse for the act or omission in question.
(4) Possession of a current disabled person's badge shall not itself constitute a reasonable excuse for the purposes of subsection (3).
(5) A person guilty of an offence under subsection (1) shall be liable on summary conviction to a fine not exceeding level 4 on the standard scale.
(6) A person guilty of an offence under subsection (2) shall be liable on summary conviction to—
  (a) imprisonment for a term not exceeding three months,
  (b) a fine not exceeding level 4 on the standard scale, or
  (c) both.

52. Interpretation
In sections 48 to 51—
  'disabled person's badge' means a badge issued, or having effect as if issued, under any regulations for the time being in force under section 21 of the Chronically Sick and Disabled Persons Act 1970 (in relation to England and Wales and Scotland) ...;
  'driver' means, in relation to a vehicle which has been left on any road, the person who was driving it when it was left there;
  'parking' means leaving a vehicle or permitting it to remain at rest;
  'traffic sign' has the meaning given in section 142(1) of the Road Traffic Regulation Act 1984 (in relation to England and Wales and Scotland) ...;
  'vehicle' has the same meaning as in section 99(5) of the Road Traffic Regulation Act 1984 (in relation to England and Wales and Scotland) ...

PART VI MISCELLANEOUS

54. Weapons training
(1) A person commits an offence if he provides instruction or training in the making or use of—
   (a) firearms,
   (aa) radioactive material or weapons designed or adapted for the discharge of any radioactive material,
   (b) explosives, or
   (c) chemical, biological or nuclear weapons.
(2) A person commits an offence if he receives instruction or training in the making or use of—
   (a) firearms,
   (aa) radioactive material or weapons designed or adapted for the discharge of any radioactive material,
   (b) explosives, or
   (c) chemical, biological or nuclear weapons.
(3) A person commits an offence if he invites another to receive instruction or training and the receipt—
   (a) would constitute an offence under subsection (2), or
   (b) would constitute an offence under subsection (2) but for the fact that it is to take place outside the United Kingdom.
(4) For the purpose of subsections (1) and (3)—
   (a) a reference to the provision of instruction includes a reference to making it available either generally or to one or more specific persons, and
   (b) an invitation to receive instruction or training may be either general or addressed to one or more specific persons.
(5) It is a defence for a person charged with an offence under this section in relation to instruction or training to prove that his action or involvement was wholly for a purpose other than assisting, preparing for or participating in terrorism.
(6) A person guilty of an offence under this section shall be liable—
   (a) on conviction on indictment, to imprisonment for a term not exceeding ten years, to a fine or to both, or
   (b) on summary conviction, to imprisonment for a term not exceeding six months, to a fine not exceeding the statutory maximum or to both.
(7) A court by or before which a person is convicted of an offence under this section may order the forfeiture of anything which the court considers to have been in the person's possession for purposes connected with the offence.
   ...

55. Weapons training: interpretation
In section 54—
   'biological weapon' means a biological agent or toxin (within the meaning of the Biological Weapons Act 1974) in a form capable of use for hostile purposes or anything to which section 1(1)(b) of that Act applies,
   'chemical weapon' has the meaning given by section 1 of the Chemical Weapons Act 1996, and
   'radioactive material' means radioactive material capable of endangering life or causing harm to human health.

56. Directing terrorist organisation
(1) A person commits an offence if he directs, at any level, the activities of an organisation which is concerned in the commission of acts of terrorism.
(2) A person guilty of an offence under this section is liable on conviction on indictment to imprisonment for life.

57. Possession for terrorist purposes
(1) A person commits an offence if he possesses an article in circumstances which give rise to a reasonable suspicion that his possession is for a purpose connected with the commission, preparation or instigation of an act of terrorism.

(2) It is a defence for a person charged with an offence under this section to prove that his possession of the article was not for a purpose connected with the commission, preparation or instigation of an act of terrorism.
(3) In proceedings for an offence under this section, if it is proved that an article—
    (a) was on any premises at the same time as the accused, or
    (b) was on premises of which the accused was the occupier or which he habitually used otherwise than as a member of the public,
    the court may assume that the accused possessed the article, unless he proves that he did not know of its presence on the premises or that he had no control over it.
(4) A person guilty of an offence under this section shall be liable—
    (a) on conviction on indictment, to imprisonment for a term not exceeding 15 years, to a fine or to both, or
    (b) on summary conviction, to imprisonment for a term not exceeding six months, to a fine not exceeding the statutory maximum or to both.

58. Collection of information

(1) A person commits an offence if—
    (a) he collects or makes a record of information of a kind likely to be useful to a person committing or preparing an act of terrorism, or
    (b) he possesses a document or record containing information of that kind.
(2) In this section 'record' includes a photographic or electronic record.
(3) It is a defence for a person charged with an offence under this section to prove that he had a reasonable excuse for his action or possession.
(4) A person guilty of an offence under this section shall be liable—
    (a) on conviction on indictment, to imprisonment for a term not exceeding 15 years, to a fine or to both, or
    (b) on summary conviction, to imprisonment for a term not exceeding six months, to a fine not exceeding the statutory maximum or to both.
(5) A court by or before which a person is convicted of an offence under this section may order the forfeiture of any document or record containing information of the kind mentioned in subsection (1)(a).

...

59. England and Wales

(1) A person commits an offence if—
    (a) he incites another person to commit an act of terrorism wholly or partly outside the United Kingdom, and
    (b) the act would, if committed in England and Wales, constitute one of the offences listed in subsection (2).
(2) Those offences are—
    (a) murder,
    (b) an offence under section 18 of the Offences against the Person Act 1861 (wounding with intent),
    (c) an offence under sections 23 or 24 of that Act (poison),
    (d) an offence under sections 28 or 29 of that Act (explosions), and
    (e) an offence under section 1(2) of the Criminal Damage Act 1971 (endangering life by damaging property).
(3) A person guilty of an offence under this section shall be liable to any penalty to which he would be liable on conviction of the offence listed in subsection (2) which corresponds to the act which he incites.
(4) For the purposes of subsection (1) it is immaterial whether or not the person incited is in the United Kingdom at the time of the incitement.
(5) Nothing in this section imposes criminal liability on any person acting on behalf of, or holding office under, the Crown.

62. Terrorist bombing: jurisdiction

(1) If—
    (a) a person does anything outside the United Kingdom as an act of terrorism or for the purposes of terrorism, and
    (b) his action would have constituted the commission of one of the offences listed in subsection (2) if it had been done in the United Kingdom,
    he shall be guilty of the offence.
(2) The offences referred to in subsection (1)(b) are—
    (a) an offence under sections 2, 3 or 5 of the Explosive Substances Act 1883 (causing explosions & c),
    (b) an offence under section 1 of the Biological Weapons Act 1974 (biological weapons), and
    (c) an offence under section 2 of the Chemical Weapons Act 1996 (chemical weapons).

PART VIII GENERAL

117. Consent to prosecution

(1) This section applies to an offence under any provision of this Act other than an offence under—
    (a) section 36,
    (b) section 51,
    (c) paragraph 18 of Schedule 7,
    (d) paragraph 12 of Schedule 12, or
    (e) Schedule 13.
(2) Proceedings for an offence to which this section applies—
    (a) shall not be instituted in England and Wales without the consent of the Director of Public Prosecutions, and
    (b) ...
(3) Where it appears to the Director of Public Prosecutions ... that an offence to which this section applies is committed for a purpose connected with the affairs of a country other than the United Kingdom—
    (a) subsection (2) shall not apply, and
    (b) proceedings for the offence shall not be instituted without the consent of the Attorney General...

118. Defences

(1) Subsection (2) applies where in accordance with a provision mentioned in subsection (5) it is a defence for a person charged with an offence to prove a particular matter.
(2) If the person adduces evidence which is sufficient to raise an issue with respect to the matter the court or jury shall assume that the defence is satisfied unless the prosecution proves beyond reasonable doubt that it is not.
(3) Subsection (4) applies where in accordance with a provision mentioned in subsection (5) a court—
    (a) may make an assumption in relation to a person charged with an offence unless a particular matter is proved, or
    (b) may accept a fact as sufficient evidence unless a particular matter is proved.
(4) If evidence is adduced which is sufficient to raise an issue with respect to the matter mentioned in subsection (3)(a) or (b) the court shall treat it as proved unless the prosecution disproves it beyond reasonable doubt.
(5) The provisions in respect of which subsections (2) and (4) apply are—
    (a) sections 12(4), 39(5)(a), 54, 57, 58, 77 and 103 of this Act, and
    ...

121. Interpretation

In this Act—
    'act' and 'action' include omission,
    'article' includes substance and any other thing,

'British Transport Police Force' means the constables appointed under section 53 of the British Transport Commission Act 1949,

'customs officer' means an officer of Revenue and Customs,

'dwelling' means a building or part of a building used as a dwelling, and a vehicle which is habitually stationary and which is used as a dwelling,

'explosive' means—
(a) an article or substance manufactured for the purpose of producing a practical effect by explosion,
(b) materials for making an article or substance within paragraph (a),
(c) anything used or intended to be used for causing or assisting in causing an explosion, and
(d) a part of anything within paragraph (a) or (c),

'firearm' includes an air gun or air pistol,

'immigration officer' means a person appointed as an immigration officer under paragraph 1 of Schedule 2 to the Immigration Act 1971,

'the Islands' means the Channel Islands and the Isle of Man,

'organisation' includes any association or combination of persons,

'police premises', in relation to England and Wales, has the meaning given by section 53(3) of the British Transport Commissions Act 1949 …

'premises', except in section 63D, includes any place and in particular includes—
(a) a vehicle,
(b) an offshore installation within the meaning given in section 44 of the Petroleum Act 1998, and
(c) a tent or moveable structure,

'property' includes property wherever situated and whether real or personal, heritable or moveable, and things in action and other intangible or incorporeal property,

'public place' means a place to which members of the public have or are permitted to have access, whether or not for payment,

'road' has the same meaning as in the Road Traffic Act 1988 (in relation to England and Wales), … and includes part of a road, and

'vehicle', except in sections 48 to 52 and Schedule 7, includes an aircraft, hovercraft, train or vessel.

[Note: the text of Schedule 2 of the Act is available on the accompanying website, www.unlockingthelaw.co.uk/keystatutes.]

TERRORISM ACT 2006

PART 1 OFFENCES

1. Encouragement of terrorism

(1) This section applies to a statement that is likely to be understood by some or all of the members of the public to whom it is published as a direct or indirect encouragement or other inducement to them to the commission, preparation or instigation of acts of terrorism or Convention offences.

(2) A person commits an offence if—
    (a) he publishes a statement to which this section applies or causes another to publish such a statement; and
    (b) at the time he publishes it or causes it to be published, he—
        (i) intends members of the public to be directly or indirectly encouraged or otherwise induced by the statement to commit, prepare or instigate acts of terrorism or Convention offences; or
        (ii) is reckless as to whether members of the public will be directly or indirectly encouraged or otherwise induced by the statement to commit, prepare or instigate such acts or offences.

(3) For the purposes of this section, the statements that are likely to be understood by members of the public as indirectly encouraging the commission or preparation of acts of terrorism or Convention offences include every statement which—
   (a) glorifies the commission or preparation (whether in the past, in the future or generally) of such acts or offences; and
   (b) is a statement from which those members of the public could reasonably be expected to infer that what is being glorified is being glorified as conduct that should be emulated by them in existing circumstances.
(4) For the purposes of this section the questions how a statement is likely to be understood and what members of the public could reasonably be expected to infer from it must be determined having regard both—
   (a) to the contents of the statement as a whole; and
   (b) to the circumstances and manner of its publication.
(5) It is irrelevant for the purposes of subsections (1) to (3)—
   (a) whether anything mentioned in those subsections relates to the commission, preparation or instigation of one or more particular acts of terrorism or Convention offences, of acts of terrorism or Convention offences of a particular description or of acts of terrorism or Convention offences generally; and,
   (b) whether any person is in fact encouraged or induced by the statement to commit, prepare or instigate any such act or offence.
(6) In proceedings for an offence under this section against a person in whose case it is not proved that he intended the statement directly or indirectly to encourage or otherwise induce the commission, preparation or instigation of acts of terrorism or Convention offences, it is a defence for him to show—
   (a) that the statement neither expressed his views nor had his endorsement (whether by virtue of section 3 or otherwise); and
   (b) that it was clear, in all the circumstances of the statement's publication, that it did not express his views and (apart from the possibility of his having been given and failed to comply with a notice under subsection (3) of that section) did not have his endorsement.
(7) A person guilty of an offence under this section shall be liable—
   (a) on conviction on indictment, to imprisonment for a term not exceeding 7 years or to a fine, or to both;
   (b) on summary conviction in England and Wales, to imprisonment for a term not exceeding 12 months or to a fine not exceeding the statutory maximum, or to both;
   ...
(8) In relation to an offence committed before the commencement of section 154(1) of the Criminal Justice Act 2003, the reference in subsection (7)(b) to 12 months is to be read as a reference to 6 months.

2. Dissemination of terrorist publications

(1) A person commits an offence if he engages in conduct falling within subsection (2) and, at the time he does so—
   (a) he intends an effect of his conduct to be a direct or indirect encouragement or other inducement to the commission, preparation or instigation of acts of terrorism;
   (b) he intends an effect of his conduct to be the provision of assistance in the commission or preparation of such acts; or
   (c) he is reckless as to whether his conduct has an effect mentioned in paragraph (a) or (b).
(2) For the purposes of this section a person engages in conduct falling within this subsection if he—
   (a) distributes or circulates a terrorist publication;
   (b) gives, sells or lends such a publication;
   (c) offers such a publication for sale or loan;
   (d) provides a service to others that enables them to obtain, read, listen to or look at such a publication, or to acquire it by means of a gift, sale or loan;
   (e) transmits the contents of such a publication electronically; or
   (f) has such a publication in his possession with a view to its becoming the subject of conduct falling within any of paragraphs (a) to (e).

(3) For the purposes of this section a publication is a terrorist publication, in relation to conduct falling within subsection (2), if matter contained in it is likely—
   (a) to be understood, by some or all of the persons to whom it is or may become available as a consequence of that conduct, as a direct or indirect encouragement or other inducement to them to the commission, preparation or instigation of acts of terrorism; or
   (b) to be useful in the commission or preparation of such acts and to be understood, by some or all of those persons, as contained in the publication, or made available to them, wholly or mainly for the purpose of being so useful to them.
(4) For the purposes of this section matter that is likely to be understood by a person as indirectly encouraging the commission or preparation of acts of terrorism includes any matter which—
   (a) glorifies the commission or preparation (whether in the past, in the future or generally) of such acts; and
   (b) is matter from which that person could reasonably be expected to infer that what is being glorified is being glorified as conduct that should be emulated by him in existing circumstances.
(5) For the purposes of this section the question whether a publication is a terrorist publication in relation to particular conduct must be determined—
   (a) as at the time of that conduct; and
   (b) having regard both to the contents of the publication as a whole and to the circumstances in which that conduct occurs.
(6) In subsection (1) references to the effect of a person's conduct in relation to a terrorist publication include references to an effect of the publication on one or more persons to whom it is or may become available as a consequence of that conduct.
(7) It is irrelevant for the purposes of this section whether anything mentioned in subsections (1) to (4) is in relation to the commission, preparation or instigation of one or more particular acts of terrorism, of acts of terrorism of a particular description or of acts of terrorism generally.
(8) For the purposes of this section it is also irrelevant, in relation to matter contained in any article whether any person—
   (a) is in fact encouraged or induced by that matter to commit, prepare or instigate acts of terrorism; or
   (b) in fact makes use of it in the commission or preparation of such acts.
(9) In proceedings for an offence under this section against a person in respect of conduct to which subsection (10) applies, it is a defence for him to show—
   (a) that the matter by reference to which the publication in question was a terrorist publication neither expressed his views nor had his endorsement (whether by virtue of section 3 or otherwise); and
   (b) that it was clear, in all the circumstances of the conduct, that that matter did not express his views and (apart from the possibility of his having been given and failed to comply with a notice under subsection (3) of that section) did not have his endorsement.
(10) This subsection applies to the conduct of a person to the extent that—
   (a) the publication to which his conduct related contained matter by reference to which it was a terrorist publication by virtue of subsection (3)(a); and
   (b) that person is not proved to have engaged in that conduct with the intention specified in subsection (1)(a).
(11) A person guilty of an offence under this section shall be liable—
   (a) on conviction on indictment, to imprisonment for a term not exceeding 7 years or to a fine, or to both;
   (b) on summary conviction in England and Wales, to imprisonment for a term not exceeding 12 months or to a fine not exceeding the statutory maximum, or to both;
   (c) on summary conviction in Scotland or Northern Ireland, to imprisonment for a term not exceeding 6 months or to a fine not exceeding the statutory maximum, or to both.
(12) In relation to an offence committed before the commencement of section 154(1) of the Criminal Justice Act 2003, the reference in subsection (11)(b) to 12 months is to be read as a reference to 6 months.
(13) In this section—
   'lend' includes let on hire, and 'loan' is to be construed accordingly;

'publication' means an article or record of any description that contains any of the following, or any combination of them—
(a) matter to be read;
(b) matter to be listened to;
(c) matter to be looked at or watched.

3. Application of sections 1 and 2 to internet activity etc.

(1) This section applies for the purposes of sections 1 and 2 in relation to cases where—
    (a) a statement is published or caused to be published in the course of, or in connection with, the provision or use of a service provided electronically; or
    (b) conduct falling within section 2(2) was in the course of, or in connection with, the provision or use of such a service.
(2) The cases in which the statement, or the article or record to which the conduct relates, is to be regarded as having the endorsement of a person (the relevant person) at any time include a case in which—
    (a) a constable has given him a notice under subsection (3);
    (b) that time falls more than 2 working days after the day on which the notice was given; and
    (c) the relevant person has failed, without reasonable excuse, to comply with the notice.
(3) A notice under this subsection is a notice which—
    (a) declares that, in the opinion of the constable giving it, the statement or the article or record is unlawfully terrorism-related;
    (b) requires the relevant person to secure that the statement or the article or record, so far as it is so related, is not available to the public or is modified so as no longer to be so related;
    (c) warns the relevant person that a failure to comply with the notice within 2 working days will result in the statement, or the article or record, being regarded as having his endorsement; and
    (d) explains how, under subsection (4), he may become liable by virtue of the notice if the statement, or the article or record, becomes available to the public after he has complied with the notice.
(4) Where—
    (a) a notice under subsection (3) has been given to the relevant person in respect of a statement, or an article or record, and he has complied with it, but
    (b) he subsequently publishes or causes to be published a statement which is, or is for all practical purposes, the same or to the same effect as the statement to which the notice related, or to matter contained in the article or record to which it related, (a 'repeat statement');
    the requirements of subsection (2)(a) to (c) shall be regarded as satisfied in the case of the repeat statement in relation to the times of its subsequent publication by the relevant person.
(5) In proceedings against a person for an offence under sections 1 or 2 the requirements of subsection (2)(a) to (c) are not, in his case, to be regarded as satisfied in relation to any time by virtue of subsection (4) if he shows that he—
    (a) has, before that time, taken every step he reasonably could to prevent a repeat statement from becoming available to the public and to ascertain whether it does; and
    (b) was, at that time, a person to whom subsection (6) applied.
(6) This subsection applies to a person at any time when he—
    (a) is not aware of the publication of the repeat statement; or
    (b) having become aware of its publication, has taken every step that he reasonably could to secure that it either ceased to be available to the public or was modified as mentioned in subsection (3)(b).
(7) For the purposes of this section a statement or an article or record is unlawfully terrorism-related if it constitutes, or if matter contained in the article or record constitutes—
    (a) something that is likely to be understood, by any one or more of the persons to whom it has or may become available, as a direct or indirect encouragement or other inducement to the commission, preparation or instigation of acts of terrorism or Convention offences; or
    (b) information which—
        (i) is likely to be useful to any one or more of those persons in the commission or preparation of such acts; and

(ii) is in a form or context in which it is likely to be understood by any one or more of those persons as being wholly or mainly for the purpose of being so useful.
(8) The reference in subsection (7) to something that is likely to be understood as an indirect encouragement to the commission or preparation of acts of terrorism or Convention offences includes anything which is likely to be understood as—
   (a) the glorification of the commission or preparation (whether in the past, in the future or generally) of such acts or such offences; and
   (b) a suggestion that what is being glorified is being glorified as conduct that should be emulated in existing circumstances.
(9) In this section 'working day' means any day other than—
   (a) a Saturday or a Sunday;
   (b) Christmas Day or Good Friday; or
   (c) a day which is a bank holiday under the Banking and Financial Dealings Act 1971 in any part of the United Kingdom.

4. Giving of notices under section 3

(1) Except in a case to which any of subsections (2) to (4) applies, a notice under section 3(3) may be given to a person only—
   (a) by delivering it to him in person; or
   (b) by sending it to him, by means of a postal service providing for delivery to be recorded, at his last known address.
(2) Such a notice may be given to a body corporate only—
   (a) by delivering it to the secretary of that body in person; or
   (b) by sending it to the appropriate person, by means of a postal service providing for delivery to be recorded, at the address of the registered or principal office of the body.
(3) Such a notice may be given to a firm only—
   (a) by delivering it to a partner of the firm in person;
   (b) by so delivering it to a person having the control or management of the partnership business; or
   (c) by sending it to the appropriate person, by means of a postal service providing for delivery to be recorded, at the address of the principal office of the partnership.
(4) Such a notice may be given to an unincorporated body or association only—
   (a) by delivering it to a member of its governing body in person; or
   (b) by sending it to the appropriate person, by means of a postal service providing for delivery to be recorded, at the address of the principal office of the body or association.
(5) In the case of—
   (a) a company registered outside the United Kingdom,
   (b) a firm carrying on business outside the United Kingdom, or
   (c) an unincorporated body or association with offices outside the United Kingdom,
   the references in this section to its principal office include references to its principal office within the United Kingdom (if any).
(6) In this section 'the appropriate person' means—
   (a) in the case of a body corporate, the body itself or its secretary;
   (b) in the case of a firm, the firm itself or a partner of the firm or a person having the control or management of the partnership business; and
   (c) in the case of an unincorporated body or association, the body or association itself or a member of its governing body.
(7) For the purposes of section 3 the time at which a notice under subsection (3) of that section is to be regarded as given is—
   (a) where it is delivered to a person, the time at which it is so delivered; and
   (b) where it is sent by a postal service providing for delivery to be recorded, the time recorded as the time of its delivery.
(8) In this section 'secretary', in relation to a body corporate, means the secretary or other equivalent officer of the body.

5. Preparation of terrorist acts

(1) A person commits an offence if, with the intention of—
   (a) committing acts of terrorism, or
   (b) assisting another to commit such acts,
   he engages in any conduct in preparation for giving effect to his intention.
(2) It is irrelevant for the purposes of subsection (1) whether the intention and preparations relate to one or more particular acts of terrorism, acts of terrorism of a particular description or acts of terrorism generally.
(3) A person guilty of an offence under this section shall be liable, on conviction on indictment, to imprisonment for life.

6. Training for terrorism

(1) A person commits an offence if—
   (a) he provides instruction or training in any of the skills mentioned in subsection (3); and
   (b) at the time he provides the instruction or training, he knows that a person receiving it intends to use the skills in which he is being instructed or trained—
      (i) for or in connection with the commission or preparation of acts of terrorism or Convention offences; or
      (ii) for assisting the commission or preparation by others of such acts or offences.
(2) A person commits an offence if—
   (a) he receives instruction or training in any of the skills mentioned in subsection (3); and
   (b) at the time of the instruction or training, he intends to use the skills in which he is being instructed or trained—
      (i) for or in connection with the commission or preparation of acts of terrorism or Convention offences; or
      (ii) for assisting the commission or preparation by others of such acts or offences.
(3) The skills are—
   (a) the making, handling or use of a noxious substance, or of substances of a description of such substances;
   (b) the use of any method or technique for doing anything else that is capable of being done for the purposes of terrorism, in connection with the commission or preparation of an act of terrorism or Convention offence or in connection with assisting the commission or preparation by another of such an act or offence; and
   (c) the design or adaptation for the purposes of terrorism, or in connection with the commission or preparation of an act of terrorism or Convention offence, of any method or technique for doing anything.
(4) It is irrelevant for the purposes of subsections (1) and (2)—
   (a) whether any instruction or training that is provided is provided to one or more particular persons or generally;
   (b) whether the acts or offences in relation to which a person intends to use skills in which he is instructed or trained consist of one or more particular acts of terrorism or Convention offences, acts of terrorism or Convention offences of a particular description or acts of terrorism or Convention offences generally; and
   (c) whether assistance that a person intends to provide to others is intended to be provided to one or more particular persons or to one or more persons whose identities are not yet known.
(5) A person guilty of an offence under this section shall be liable—
   (a) on conviction on indictment, to imprisonment for a term not exceeding 10 years or to a fine, or to both;
   (b) on summary conviction in England and Wales, to imprisonment for a term not exceeding 12 months or to a fine not exceeding the statutory maximum, or to both;
   ...
(6) In relation to an offence committed before the commencement of section 154(1) of the Criminal Justice Act 2003, the reference in subsection (5)(b) to 12 months is to be read as a reference to 6 months.

(7) In this section—
'noxious substance' means—
   (a) a dangerous substance within the meaning of Part 7 of the Anti-terrorism, Crime and Security Act 2001; or
   (b) any other substance which is hazardous or noxious or which may be or become hazardous or noxious only in certain circumstances;
'substance' includes any natural or artificial substance (whatever its origin or method of production and whether in solid or liquid form or in the form of a gas or vapour) and any mixture of substances.

8. Attendance at a place used for terrorist training

(1) A person commits an offence if—
   (a) he attends at any place, whether in the United Kingdom or elsewhere;
   (b) while he is at that place, instruction or training of the type mentioned in section 6(1) of this Act or section 54(1) of the Terrorism Act 2000 (weapons training) is provided there;
   (c) that instruction or training is provided there wholly or partly for purposes connected with the commission or preparation of acts of terrorism or Convention offences; and
   (d) the requirements of subsection (2) are satisfied in relation to that person.
(2) The requirements of this subsection are satisfied in relation to a person if—
   (a) he knows or believes that instruction or training is being provided there wholly or partly for purposes connected with the commission or preparation of acts of terrorism or Convention offences; or
   (b) a person attending at that place throughout the period of that person's attendance could not reasonably have failed to understand that instruction or training was being provided there wholly or partly for such purposes.
(3) It is immaterial for the purposes of this section—
   (a) whether the person concerned receives the instruction or training himself; and
   (b) whether the instruction or training is provided for purposes connected with one or more particular acts of terrorism or Convention offences, acts of terrorism or Convention offences of a particular description or acts of terrorism or Convention offences generally.
(4) A person guilty of an offence under this section shall be liable—
   (a) on conviction on indictment, to imprisonment for a term not exceeding 10 years or to a fine, or to both;
   (b) on summary conviction in England and Wales, to imprisonment for a term not exceeding 12 months or to a fine not exceeding the statutory maximum, or to both;
   …
(5) In relation to an offence committed before the commencement of section 154(1) of the Criminal Justice Act 2003, the reference in subsection (4)(b) to 12 months is to be read as a reference to 6 months.
(6) References in this section to instruction or training being provided include references to its being made available.

9. Making and possession of devices or materials

(1) A person commits an offence if—
   (a) he makes or has in his possession a radioactive device, or
   (b) he has in his possession radioactive material,
with the intention of using the device or material in the course of or in connection with the commission or preparation of an act of terrorism or for the purposes of terrorism, or of making it available to be so used.
(2) It is irrelevant for the purposes of subsection (1) whether the act of terrorism to which an intention relates is a particular act of terrorism, an act of terrorism of a particular description or an act of terrorism generally.
(3) A person guilty of an offence under this section shall be liable, on conviction on indictment, to imprisonment for life.
(4) In this section—
'radioactive device' means—

(a) a nuclear weapon or other nuclear explosive device;
(b) a radioactive material dispersal device;
(c) a radiation-emitting device;
'radioactive material' means nuclear material or any other radioactive substance which—
(a) contains nuclides that undergo spontaneous disintegration in a process accompanied by the emission of one or more types of ionising radiation, such as alpha radiation, beta radiation, neutron particles or gamma rays; and
(b) is capable, owing to its radiological or fissile properties, of—
   (i) causing serious bodily injury to a person;
   (ii) causing serious damage to property;
   (iii) endangering a person's life; or
   (iv) creating a serious risk to the health or safety of the public.

(5) In subsection (4)—
'device' includes any of the following, whether or not fixed to land, namely, machinery, equipment, appliances, tanks, containers, pipes and conduits;
'nuclear material' has the same meaning as in the Nuclear Material (Offences) Act 1983 (see section 6 of that Act).

10. Misuse of devices or material and misuse and damage of facilities

(1) A person commits an offence if he uses—
   (a) a radioactive device, or
   (b) radioactive material,
in the course of or in connection with the commission of an act of terrorism or for the purposes of terrorism.

(2) A person commits an offence if, in the course of or in connection with the commission of an act of terrorism or for the purposes of terrorism, he uses or damages a nuclear facility in a manner which—
   (a) causes a release of radioactive material; or
   (b) creates or increases a risk that such material will be released.

(3) A person guilty of an offence under this section shall be liable, on conviction on indictment, to imprisonment for life.

(4) In this section—
'nuclear facility' means—
a nuclear reactor, including a reactor installed in or on any transportation device for use as an energy source in order to propel it or for any other purpose; or
a plant or conveyance being used for the production, storage, processing or transport of radioactive material;
'radioactive device' and 'radioactive material' have the same meanings as in section 9.

(5) In subsection (4)—
'nuclear reactor' has the same meaning as in the Nuclear Installations Act 1965 (see section 26 of that Act);
'transportation device' means any vehicle or any space object (within the meaning of the Outer Space Act 1986.

11. Terrorist threats relating to devices, materials or facilities

(1) A person commits an offence if, in the course of or in connection with the commission of an act of terrorism or for the purposes of terrorism—
   (a) he makes a demand—
      (i) for the supply to himself or to another of a radioactive device or of radioactive material;
      (ii) for a nuclear facility to be made available to himself or to another; or
      (iii) for access to such a facility to be given to himself or to another;
   (b) he supports the demand with a threat that he or another will take action if the demand is not met; and
   (c) the circumstances and manner of the threat are such that it is reasonable for the person to whom it is made to assume that there is real risk that the threat will be carried out if the demand is not met.

(2) A person also commits an offence if—
   (a) he makes a threat falling within subsection (3) in the course of or in connection with the commission of an act of terrorism or for the purposes of terrorism; and
   (b) the circumstances and manner of the threat are such that it is reasonable for the person to whom it is made to assume that there is real risk that the threat will be carried out, or would be carried out if demands made in association with the threat are not met.
(3) A threat falls within this subsection if it is—
   (a) a threat to use radioactive material;
   (b) a threat to use a radioactive device; or
   (c) a threat to use or damage a nuclear facility in a manner that releases radioactive material or creates or increases a risk that such material will be released.
(4) A person guilty of an offence under this section shall be liable, on conviction on indictment, to imprisonment for life.
(5) In this section—
   'nuclear facility' has the same meaning as in section 10;
   'radioactive device' and 'radioactive material' have the same meanings as in section 9.

17. Commission of offences abroad

(1) If—
   (a) a person does anything outside the United Kingdom, and
   (b) his action, if done in a part of the United Kingdom, would constitute an offence falling within subsection (2),
   he shall be guilty in that part of the United Kingdom of the offence.
(2) The offences falling within this subsection are—
   (a) an offence under section 1 or 6 of this Act so far as it is committed in relation to any statement, instruction or training in relation to which that section has effect by reason of its relevance to the commission, preparation or instigation of one or more Convention offences;
   (b) an offence under any of sections 8 to 11 of this Act;
   (c) an offence under section 11(1) of the Terrorism Act 2000 (membership of proscribed organisations);
   (d) an offence under section 54 of that Act (weapons training);
   (e) conspiracy to commit an offence falling within this subsection;
   (f) inciting a person to commit such an offence;
   (g) attempting to commit such an offence;
   (h) aiding, abetting, counselling or procuring the commission of such an offence.
(3) Subsection (1) applies irrespective of whether the person is a British citizen or, in the case of a company, a company incorporated in a part of the United Kingdom.
(4) In the case of an offence falling within subsection (2) which is committed wholly or partly outside the United Kingdom—
   (a) proceedings for the offence may be taken at any place in the United Kingdom; and
   (b) the offence may for all incidental purposes be treated as having been committed at any such place.
(5) In section 3(1)(a) and (b) of the Explosive Substances Act 1883 (offences committed in preparation for use of explosives with intent to endanger life or property in the United Kingdom or the Republic of Ireland), in each place, for 'the Republic of Ireland' substitute 'elsewhere'.
   ...

18. Liability of company directors etc.

(1) Where an offence under this Part is committed by a body corporate and is proved to have been committed with the consent or connivance of—
   (a) a director, manager, secretary or other similar officer of the body corporate, or
   (b) a person who was purporting to act in any such capacity,
   he (as well as the body corporate) is guilty of that offence and shall be liable to be proceeded against and punished accordingly.
   ...

(3) In this section 'director', in relation to a body corporate whose affairs are managed by its members, means a member of the body corporate.

19. Consents to prosecutions

(1) Proceedings for an offence under this Part—
   (a) may be instituted in England and Wales only with the consent of the Director of Public Prosecutions; and
   (b) ...
(2) But if it appears to the Director of Public Prosecutions... that an offence under this Part has been committed for a purpose wholly or partly connected with the affairs of a country other than the United Kingdom, his consent for the purposes of this section may be given only with the permission—
   (a) in the case of the Director of Public Prosecutions, of the Attorney General;
   ...

20. Interpretation of Part 1

(1) Expressions used in this Part and in the Terrorism Act 2000 have the same meanings in this Part as in that Act.
(2) In this Part—
   'act of terrorism' includes anything constituting an action taken for the purposes of terrorism, within the meaning of the Terrorism Act 2000 (see section 1(5) of that Act);
   'article' includes anything for storing data;
   'Convention offence' means an offence listed in Schedule 1 or an equivalent offence under the law of a country or territory outside the United Kingdom;
   'glorification' includes any form of praise or celebration, and cognate expressions are to be construed accordingly;
   'public' is to be construed in accordance with subsection (3);
   'publish' and cognate expressions are to be construed in accordance with subsection (4);
   'record' means a record so far as not comprised in an article, including a temporary record created electronically and existing solely in the course of, and for the purposes of, the transmission of the whole or a part of its contents;
   'statement' is to be construed in accordance with subsection (6).
(3) In this Part references to the public—
   (a) are references to the public of any part of the United Kingdom or of a country or territory outside the United Kingdom, or any section of the public; and
   (b) except in section 9(4), also include references to a meeting or other group of persons which is open to the public (whether unconditionally or on the making of a payment or the satisfaction of other conditions).
(4) In this Part references to a person's publishing a statement are references to—
   (a) his publishing it in any manner to the public;
   (b) his providing electronically any service by means of which the public have access to the statement; or
   (c) his using a service provided to him electronically by another so as to enable or to facilitate access by the public to the statement;
   but this subsection does not apply to the references to a publication in section 2.
(5) In this Part references to providing a service include references to making a facility available; and references to a service provided to a person are to be construed accordingly.
(6) In this Part references to a statement are references to a communication of any description, including a communication without words consisting of sounds or images or both.
(7) In this Part references to conduct that should be emulated in existing circumstances include references to conduct that is illustrative of a type of conduct that should be so emulated.
(8) In this Part references to what is contained in an article or record include references—
   (a) to anything that is embodied or stored in or on it; and
   (b) to anything that may be reproduced from it using apparatus designed or adapted for the purpose.

(9) The Secretary of State may by order made by statutory instrument—
   (a) modify Schedule 1 so as to add an offence to the offences listed in that Schedule;
   (b) modify that Schedule so as to remove an offence from the offences so listed;
   (c) make supplemental, incidental, consequential or transitional provision in connection with the addition or removal of an offence.
(10) An order under subsection (9) may add an offence in or as regards Scotland to the offences listed in Schedule 1 to the extent only that a provision creating the offence would be outside the legislative competence of the Scottish Parliament.
(11) The Secretary of State must not make an order containing (with or without other provision) any provision authorised by subsection (9) unless a draft of the order has been laid before Parliament and approved by a resolution of each House.

THEFT ACT 1968

1. Basic definition of theft

(1) A person is guilty of theft if he dishonestly appropriates property belonging to another with the intention of permanently depriving the other of it; and 'thief' and 'steal' shall be construed accordingly.
(2) It is immaterial whether the appropriation is made with a view to gain, or is made for the thief's own benefit.
(3) The five following sections of this Act shall have effect as regards the interpretation and operation of this section (and, except as otherwise provided by this Act, shall apply only for purposes of this section).

2. 'Dishonestly'

(1) A person's appropriation of property belonging to another is not to be regarded as dishonest—
   (a) if he appropriates the property in the belief that he has in law the right to deprive the other of it, on behalf of himself or of a third person; or
   (b) if he appropriates the property in the belief that he would have the other's consent if the other knew of the appropriation and the circumstances of it; or
   (c) (except where the property came to him as trustee or personal representative) if he appropriates the property in the belief that the person to whom the property belongs cannot be discovered by taking reasonable steps.
(2) A person's appropriation of property belonging to another may be dishonest notwithstanding that he is willing to pay for the property.

3. 'Appropriates'

(1) Any assumption by a person of the rights of an owner amounts to an appropriation, and this includes, where he has come by the property (innocently or not) without stealing it, any later assumption of a right to it by keeping or dealing with it as owner.
(2) Where property or a right or interest in property is or purports to be transferred for value to a person acting in good faith, no later assumption by him of rights which he believed himself to be acquiring shall, by reason of any defect in the transferor's title, amount to theft of the property.

4. 'Property'

(1) 'Property' includes money and all other property, real or personal, including things in action and other intangible property.
(2) A person cannot steal land, or things forming part of land and severed from it by him or by his directions, except in the following cases, that it to say—
   (a) when he is a trustee or personal representative, or is authorised by power of attorney, or as liquidator of a company, or otherwise, to sell or dispose of land belonging to another, and he appropriates the land or anything forming part of it by dealing with it in breach of the confidence reposed in him; or

(b) when he is not in possession of the land and appropriates anything forming part of the land by severing it or causing it to be severed, or after it has been severed; or
(c) when, being in possession of the land under a tenancy, he appropriates the whole or part of any fixture or structure let to be used with the land.

For purposes of this subsection 'land' does not include incorporeal hereditaments; 'tenancy' means a tenancy for years or any less period and includes an agreement for such a tenancy, but a person who after the end of a tenancy remains in possession as statutory tenant or otherwise is to be treated as having possession under the tenancy, and 'let' shall be construed accordingly.

(3) A person who picks mushrooms growing wild on any land, or who picks flowers, fruit or foliage from a plant growing wild on any land, does not (although not in possession of the land) steal what he picks, unless he does it for reward or for sale or other commercial purpose.

For purposes of this subsection 'mushroom' includes any fungus, and 'plant' includes any shrub or tree.

(4) Wild creatures, tamed or untamed, shall be regarded as property; but a person cannot steal a wild creature not tamed nor ordinarily kept in captivity, or the carcass of any such creature, unless either it has been reduced into possession by or on behalf of another person and possession of it has not since been lost or abandoned, or another person is in course of reducing it into possession.

5. 'Belonging to another'

(1) Property shall be regarded as belonging to any person having possession or control of it, or having in it any proprietary right or interest (not being an equitable interest arising only from an agreement to transfer or grant an interest).
(2) Where property is subject to a trust, the persons to whom it belongs shall be regarded as including any person having a right to enforce the trust, and an intention to defeat the trust shall be regarded accordingly as an intention to deprive of the property any person having that right.
(3) Where a person receives property from or on account of another, and is under an obligation to the other to retain and deal with that property or its proceeds in a particular way, the property or proceeds shall be regarded (as against him) as belonging to the other.
(4) Where a person gets property by another's mistake, and is under an obligation to make restoration (in whole or in part) of the property or its proceeds or of the value thereof, then to the extent of that obligation the property or proceeds shall be regarded (as against him) as belonging to the person entitled to restoration, and an intention not to make restoration shall be regarded accordingly as an intention to deprive that person of the property or proceeds.
(5) Property of a corporation sole shall be regarded as belonging to the corporation notwithstanding a vacancy in the corporation.

6. 'With the intention of permanently depriving the other of it'

(1) A person appropriating property belonging to another without meaning the other permanently to lose the thing itself is nevertheless to be regarded as having the intention of permanently depriving the other of it if his intention is to treat the thing as his own to dispose of regardless of the other's rights; and a borrowing or lending of it may amount to so treating it if, but only if, the borrowing or lending is for a period and in circumstances making it equivalent to an outright taking or disposal.
(2) Without prejudice to the generality of subsection (1) above, where a person, having possession or control (lawfully or not) of property belonging to another, parts with the property under a condition as to its return which he may not be able to perform, this (if done for purposes of his own and without the other's authority) amounts to treating the property as his own to dispose of regardless of the other's rights.

7. Theft

A person guilty of theft shall on conviction on indictment be liable to imprisonment for a term not exceeding seven years.

8. Robbery

(1) A person is guilty of robbery if he steals, and immediately before or at the time of doing so, and in order to do so, he uses force on any person or puts or seeks to put any person in fear of being then and there subjected to force.
(2) A person guilty of robbery, or of an assault with intent to rob, shall on conviction on indictment be liable to imprisonment for life.

9. Burglary

(1) A person is guilty of burglary if—
   (a) he enters any building or part of a building as a trespasser and with intent to commit any such offence as is mentioned in subsection (2) below; or
   (b) having entered any building or part of a building as a trespasser he steals or attempts to steal anything in the building or that part of it or inflicts or attempts to inflict on any person therein any grievous bodily harm.
(2) The offences referred to in subsection (1)(a) above are offences of stealing anything in the building or part of a building in question, of inflicting on any person therein any grievous bodily harm therein, and of doing unlawful damage to the building or anything therein.
(3) A person guilty of burglary shall on conviction on indictment be liable to imprisonment for a term not exceeding—
   (a) where the offence was committed in respect of a building or part of a building which is a dwelling, fourteen years;
   (b) in any other case, ten years.
(4) References in subsections (1) and (2) above to a building, and the reference in subsection (3) above to a building which is a dwelling, shall apply also to an inhabited vehicle or vessel, and shall apply to any such vehicle or vessel at times when the person having a habitation in it is not there as well as at times when he is.

10. Aggravated burglary

(1) A person is guilty of aggravated burglary if he commits any burglary and at the time has with him any firearm or imitation firearm, any weapon of offence, or any explosive; and for this purpose—
   (a) 'firearm' includes an airgun or air pistol, and 'imitation firearm' means anything which has the appearance of being a firearm, whether capable of being discharged or not; and
   (b) 'weapon of offence' means any article made or adapted for use for causing injury to or incapacitating a person, or intended by the person having it with him for such use; and
   (c) 'explosive' means any article manufactured for the purpose of producing a practical effect by explosion, or intended by the person having it with him for that purpose.
(2) A person guilty of aggravated burglary shall on conviction on indictment be liable to imprisonment for life.

12. Taking motor vehicle or other conveyance without authority

(1) Subject to subsections (5) and (6) below, a person shall be guilty of an offence if, without having the consent of the owner or other lawful authority, he takes any conveyance for his own or another's use or, knowing that any conveyance has been taken without such authority, drives it or allows himself to be carried in or on it.
(2) A person guilty of an offence under subsection (1) above shall be liable on summary conviction to a fine not exceeding level 5 on the standard scale, to imprisonment for a term not exceeding six months, or to both.
(4) If on the trial of an indictment for theft the jury are not satisfied that the accused committed theft, but it is proved that the accused committed an offence under subsection (1) above, the jury may find him guilty of the offence under subsection (1) and if he is found guilty of it, he shall be liable as he would have been liable under subsection (2) above on summary conviction.
(4A) Proceedings for an offence under subsection (1) above (but not proceedings of a kind falling within subsection (4) above) in relation to a mechanically propelled vehicle—
   (a) shall not be commenced after the end of the period of three years beginning with the day on which the offence was committed; but

(b) subject to that, may be commenced at any time within the period of six months beginning with the relevant day.

(4B) In subsection (4A)(b) above 'the relevant day' means—
  (a) in the case of a prosecution for an offence under subsection (1) above by a public prosecutor, the day on which sufficient evidence to justify the proceedings came to the knowledge of any person responsible for deciding whether to commence any such prosecution;
  (b) in the case of a prosecution for an offence under subsection (1) above which is commenced by a person other than a public prosecutor after the discontinuance of a prosecution falling within paragraph (a) above which relates to the same facts, the day on which sufficient evidence to justify the proceedings came to the knowledge of the person who has decided to commence the prosecution or (if later) the discontinuance of the other prosecution;
  (c) in the case of any other prosecution for an offence under subsection (1) above, the day on which sufficient evidence to justify the proceedings came to the knowledge of the person who has decided to commence the prosecution.

(4C) For the purposes of subsection (4A)(b) above a certificate of a person responsible for deciding whether to commence a prosecution of a kind mentioned in subsection (4B)(a) above as to the date on which such evidence as is mentioned in the certificate came to the knowledge of any person responsible for deciding whether to commence any such prosecution shall be conclusive evidence of that fact.

(5) Subsection (1) above shall not apply in relation to pedal cycles; but, subject to subsection (6) below, a person who, without having the consent of the owner or other lawful authority, takes a pedal cycle for his own or another's use, or rides a pedal cycle knowing it to have been taken without such authority, shall on summary conviction be liable to a fine not exceeding level 3 on the standard scale.

(6) A person does not commit an offence under this section by anything done in the belief that he has lawful authority to do it or that he would have the owner's consent if the owner knew of his doing it and the circumstances of it.

(7) For purposes of this section—
  (a) 'conveyance' means any conveyance constructed or adapted for the carriage of a person or persons whether by land, water or air, except that it does not include a conveyance constructed or adapted for use only under the control of a person not carried in or on it, and 'drive' shall be construed accordingly; and
  (b) 'owner', in relation to a conveyance which is the subject of a hiring agreement or hire-purchase agreement, means the person in possession of the conveyance under that agreement.

12A. Aggravated vehicle-taking

(1) Subject to subsection (3) below, a person is guilty of aggravated taking of a vehicle if—
  (a) he commits an offence under section 12(1) above (in this section referred to as a 'basic offence') in relation to a mechanically propelled vehicle; and
  (b) it is proved that, at any time after the vehicle was unlawfully taken (whether by him or another) and before it was recovered, the vehicle was driven, or injury or damage was caused, in one or more of the circumstances set out in paragraphs (a) to (d) of subsection (2) below.

(2) The circumstances referred to in subsection (1)(b) above are—
  (a) that the vehicle was driven dangerously on a road or other public place;
  (b) that, owing to the driving of the vehicle, an accident occurred by which injury was caused to any person;
  (c) that, owing to the driving of the vehicle, an accident occurred by which damage was caused to any property, other than the vehicle;
  (d) that damage was caused to the vehicle.

(3) A person is not guilty of an offence under this section if he proves that, as regards any such proven driving, injury or damage as is referred to in subsection (1)(b) above, either—
  (a) the driving, accident or damage referred to in subsection (2) above occurred before he committed the basic offence; or

(b) he was neither in nor on nor in the immediate vicinity of the vehicle when that driving, accident or damage occurred.
(4) A person guilty of an offence under this section shall be liable on conviction on indictment to imprisonment for a term not exceeding two years or, if it is proved that, in circumstances falling within subsection (2)(b) above, the accident caused the death of the person concerned, fourteen years.
(5) If a person who is charged with an offence under this section is found not guilty of that offence but it is proved that he committed a basic offence, he may be convicted of the basic offence.
(6) If by virtue of subsection (5) above a person is convicted of a basic offence before the Crown Court, that court shall have the same powers and duties as a magistrates' court would have had on convicting him of such an offence.
(7) For the purposes of this section a vehicle is driven dangerously if—
 (a) it is driven in a way which falls far below what would be expected of a competent and careful driver; and
 (b) it would be obvious to a competent and careful driver that driving the vehicle in that way would be dangerous.
(8) For the purposes of this section a vehicle is recovered when it is restored to its owner or to other lawful possession or custody; and in this subsection 'owner' has the same meaning as in section 12 above.

13. Abstracting of electricity

A person who dishonestly uses without due authority, or dishonestly causes to be wasted or diverted, any electricity shall on conviction on indictment be liable to imprisonment for a term not exceeding five years.

17. False accounting

(1) Where a person dishonestly, with a view to gain for himself or another or with intent to cause loss to another,—
 (a) destroys, defaces, conceals or falsifies any account or any record or document made or required for any accounting purpose; or
 (b) in furnishing information for any purpose produces or makes use of any account, or any such record or document as aforesaid, which to his knowledge is or may be misleading, false or deceptive in a material particular;
he shall, on conviction on indictment, be liable to imprisonment for a term not exceeding seven years.
(2) For purposes of this section a person who makes or concurs in making in an account or other document an entry which is or may be misleading, false or deceptive in a material particular, or who omits or concurs in omitting a material particular from an account or other document, is to be treated as falsifying the account or document.

18. Liability of company officers for certain offences by company

(1) Where an offence committed by a body corporate under section 17 of this Act is proved to have been committed with the consent or connivance of any director, manager, secretary or other similar officer of the body corporate, or any person who was purporting to act in any such capacity, he as well as the body corporate shall be guilty of that offence, and shall be liable to be proceeded against and punished accordingly.
(2) Where the affairs of a body corporate are managed by its members, this section shall apply in relation to the acts and defaults of a member in connection with his functions of management as if he were a director of the body corporate.

19. False statements by company directors, etc.

(1) Where an officer of a body corporate or unincorporated association (or person purporting to act as such), with intent to deceive members or creditors of the body corporate or association about its affairs, publishes or concurs in publishing a written statement or account which to his knowledge is or may be misleading, false or deceptive in a material particular, he shall on conviction on indictment be liable to imprisonment for a term not exceeding seven years.

(2) For purposes of this section a person who has entered into a security for the benefit of a body corporate or association is to be treated as a creditor of it.
(3) Where the affairs of a body corporate or association are managed by its members, this section shall apply to any statement which a member publishes or concurs in publishing in connection with his functions of management as if he were an officer of the body corporate or association.

20. Suppression, etc. of documents
(1) A person who dishonestly, with a view to gain for himself or another or with intent to cause loss to another, destroys, defaces or conceals any valuable security, any will or other testamentary document or any original document of or belonging to, or filed or deposited in, any court of justice or any government department shall on conviction on indictment be liable to imprisonment for a term not exceeding seven years.
(3) For the purposes of this section 'valuable security' means any document creating, transferring, surrendering or releasing any right to, in or over property, or authorising the payment of money or delivery of any property, or evidencing the creation, transfer, surrender or release of any such right, or the payment of money or delivery of any property, or the satisfaction of any obligation.

21. Blackmail
(1) A person is guilty of blackmail if, with a view to gain for himself or another or with intent to cause loss to another, he makes any unwarranted demand with menaces; and for this purpose a demand with menaces is unwarranted unless the person making it does so in the belief—
(a) that he has reasonable grounds for making the demand; and
(b) that the use of the menaces is a proper means of reinforcing the demand.
(2) The nature of the act or omission demanded is immaterial, and it is also immaterial whether the menaces relate to action to be taken by the person making the demand.
(3) A person guilty of blackmail shall on conviction on indictment be liable to imprisonment for a term not exceeding fourteen years.

22. Handling stolen goods
(1) A person handles stolen goods if (otherwise than in the course of the stealing) knowing or believing them to be stolen goods he dishonestly receives the goods, or dishonestly undertakes or assists in their retention, removal, disposal or realisation by or for the benefit of another person, or if he arranges to do so.
(2) A person guilty of handling stolen goods shall on conviction on indictment be liable to imprisonment for a term not exceeding fourteen years.

23. Advertising rewards for return of goods stolen or lost
Where any public advertisement of a reward for the return of any goods which have been stolen or lost uses any words to the effect that no questions will be asked, or that the person producing the goods will be safe from apprehension or inquiry, or that any money paid for the purchase of the goods or advanced by way of loan on them will be repaid, the person advertising the reward and any person who prints or publishes the advertisement shall on summary conviction be liable to a fine not exceeding level 3 on the standard scale.

24. Scope of offences relating to stolen goods
(1) The provisions of this Act relating to goods which have been stolen shall apply whether the stealing occurred in England or Wales or elsewhere, and whether it occurred before or after the commencement of this Act, provided that the stealing (if not an offence under this Act) amounted to an offence where and at the time when the goods were stolen; and references to stolen goods shall be construed accordingly.
(2) For purposes of those provisions references to stolen goods shall include, in addition to the goods originally stolen and parts of them (whether in their original state or not),—
(a) any other goods which directly or indirectly represent or have at any time represented the stolen goods in the hands of the thief as being the proceeds of any disposal or realisation of the whole or part of the goods stolen or of goods so representing the stolen goods; and
(b) any other goods which directly or indirectly represent or have at any time represented the stolen goods in the hands of a handler of the stolen goods or any part of them as being the

proceeds of any disposal or realisation of the whole or part of the stolen goods handled by him or of goods so representing them.
(3) But no goods shall be regarded as having continued to be stolen goods after they have been restored to the person from whom they were stolen or to other lawful possession or custody, or after that person and any other person claiming through him have otherwise ceased as regards those goods to have any right to restitution in respect of the theft.
(4) For purposes of the provisions of this Act relating to goods which have been stolen (including subsections (1) to (3) above) goods obtained in England or Wales or elsewhere either by blackmail or, subject to subsection (5) below, by fraud (within the meaning of the Fraud Act 2006) shall be regarded as stolen; and 'steal', 'theft' and 'thief' shall be construed accordingly.
(5) Subsection (1) above applies in relation to goods obtained by fraud as if—
    (a) the reference to the commencement of this Act were a reference to the commencement of the Fraud Act 2006, and
    (b) the reference to an offence under this Act were a reference to an offence under section 1 of that Act.

24A. Dishonestly retaining a wrongful credit

(1) A person is guilty of an offence if—
    (a) a wrongful credit has been made to an account kept by him or in respect of which he has any right or interest;
    (b) he knows or believes that the credit is wrongful; and
    (c) he dishonestly fails to take such steps as are reasonable in the circumstances to secure that the credit is cancelled.
(2) References to a credit are to a credit of an amount of money.
(2A) A credit to an account is wrongful to the extent that it derives from—
    (a) theft;
    (b) blackmail;
    (c) fraud (contrary to section 1 of the Fraud Act 2006); or
    (d) stolen goods.
(5) In determining whether a credit to an account is wrongful, it is immaterial (in particular) whether the account is overdrawn before or after the credit is made.
(6) A person guilty of an offence under this section shall be liable on conviction on indictment to imprisonment for a term not exceeding ten years.
(7) Subsection (8) below applies for purposes of provisions of this Act relating to stolen goods (including subsection (2A) above).
(8) References to stolen goods include money which is dishonestly withdrawn from an account to which a wrongful credit has been made, but only to the extent that the money derives from the credit.
(9) 'Account' means an account kept with—
    (a) a bank;
    (b) a person carrying on a business which falls within subsection (10) below; or
    (c) an issuer of electronic money (as defined for the purposes of Part 2 of the Financial Services and Markets Act 2000).
(10) A business falls within this subsection if—
    (a) in the course of the business money received by way of deposit is lent to others; or
    (b) any other activity of the business is financed, wholly or to any material extent, out of the capital of or the interest on money received by way of deposit.
(11) References in subsection (10) above to a deposit must be read with—
    (a) section 22 of the Financial Services and Markets Act 2000;
    (b) any relevant order under that section; and
    (c) Schedule 2 to that Act;
    but any restriction on the meaning of deposit which arises from the identity of the person making it is to be disregarded.
(12) For the purposes of subsection (10) above—
    (a) all the activities which a person carries on by way of business shall be regarded as a single business carried on by him; and

(b) 'money' includes money expressed in a currency other than sterling.

25. Going equipped for stealing, etc.
(1) A person shall be guilty of an offence if, when not at his place of abode, he has with him any article for use in the course of or in connection with any burglary or theft.
(2) A person guilty of an offence under this section shall on conviction on indictment be liable to imprisonment for a term not exceeding three years.
(3) Where a person is charged with an offence under this section, proof that he had with him any article made or adapted for use in committing a burglary or theft shall be evidence that he had it with him for such use.
(5) For the purposes of this section an offence under section 12(1) of this Act of taking a conveyance shall be treated as theft.

30. Spouses and civil partners
(1) This Act shall apply in relation to the parties to a marriage, and to property belonging to the wife or husband whether or not by reason of an interest derived from the marriage, as it would apply if they were not married and any such interest subsisted independently of the marriage.
(2) Subject to subsection (4) below, a person shall have the same right to bring proceedings against that person's wife or husband for any offence (whether under this Act or otherwise) as if they were not married, and a person bringing any such proceedings shall be competent to give evidence for the prosecution at every stage of the proceedings.
(4) Proceedings shall not be instituted against a person for any offence of stealing or doing unlawful damage to property which at the time of the offence belongs to that person's wife or husband, or civil partner or for any attempt or conspiracy to commit such an offence, unless the proceedings are instituted by or with the consent of the Director of Public Prosecutions: Provided that—
   (a) this subsection shall not apply to proceedings against a person for an offence—
      (i) if that person is charged with committing the offence jointly with the wife or husband or civil partner;
      (ii) if by virtue of any judicial decree or order (wherever made) that person and the wife or husband are at the time of the offence under no obligation to cohabit; or
      (iii) an order (wherever made) is in force providing for the separation of that person and his or her civil partner.
(5) Notwithstanding section 6 of the Prosecution of Offences Act 1979 subsection (4) of this section shall apply—
   (a) to an arrest (if without warrant) made by the wife or husband or civil partner, and
   (b) to a warrant of arrest issued on an information laid by the wife or husband or civil partner.

34. Interpretation
(1) Sections 4(1) and 5(1) of this Act shall apply generally for purposes of this Act as they apply for purposes of section 1.
(2) For purposes of this Act—
   (a) 'gain' and 'loss' are to be construed as extending only to gain or loss in money or other property, but as extending to any such gain or loss whether temporary or permanent; and—
      (i) 'gain' includes a gain by keeping what one has, as well as a gain by getting what one has not; and
      (ii) 'loss' includes a loss by not getting what one might get, as well as a loss by parting with what one has;
   (b) 'goods', except in so far as the context otherwise requires, includes money and every other description of property except land, and includes things severed from the land by stealing; and.
   (c) 'mail bag' and 'postal packet' have the meanings given by section 125(1) of the Postal Services Act 2000.

THEFT ACT 1978

3. Making off without payment

(1) Subject to subsection (3) below, a person who, knowing that payment on the spot for any goods supplied or service done is required or expected from him, dishonestly makes off without having paid as required or expected and with intent to avoid payment of the amount due shall be guilty of an offence.

(2) For purposes of this section 'payment on the spot' includes payment at the time of collecting goods on which work has been done or in respect of which service has been provided.

(3) Subsection (1) above shall not apply where the supply of the goods or the doing of the service is contrary to law, or where the service done is such that payment is not legally enforceable.

4. Punishments

(1) Offences under this Act shall be punishable either on conviction on indictment or on summary conviction.

(2) A person convicted on indictment shall be liable—
   (b) for an offence under section 3 of this Act, to imprisonment for a term not exceeding two years.

(3) A person convicted summarily of any offence under this Act shall be liable—
   (a) to imprisonment for a term not exceeding six months; or
   (b) to a fine not exceeding the prescribed sum for the purposes of section 32 of the Magistrates' Courts Act 1980 (punishment on summary conviction of offences triable either way: £1,000 or other sum substituted by order under that Act),
   or to both.

TREASURE ACT 1996

8. Duty of finder to notify coroner

(1) A person who finds an object which he believes or has reasonable grounds for believing is treasure must notify the coroner for the district in which the object was found before the end of the notice period.

(2) The notice period is fourteen days beginning with—
   (a) the day after the find; or
   (b) if later, the day on which the finder first believes or has reason to believe the object is treasure.

(3) Any person who fails to comply with subsection (1) is guilty of an offence and liable on summary conviction to—
   (a) imprisonment for a term not exceeding three months;
   (b) a fine of an amount not exceeding level 5 on the standard scale; or
   (c) both.

(4) In proceedings for an offence under this section, it is a defence for the defendant to show that he had, and has continued to have, a reasonable excuse for failing to notify the coroner.

(5) If the office of coroner for a district is vacant, the person acting as coroner for that district is the coroner for the purposes of subsection (1).

TRIAL OF LUNATICS ACT 1883

2. Special verdict where accused found guilty, but insane at date of act or omission charged, and orders thereupon

(1) Where in any indictment or information any act or omission is charged against any person as an offence, and it is given in evidence on the trial of such person for that offence that he was insane, so as not to be responsible, according to law, for his actions at the time when the act was done or omission made, then, if it appears to the jury before whom such person is tried that he did the act or made the omission charged, but was insane as aforesaid at the time when he did or made the same, the jury shall return a special verdict that the accused is not guilty by reason of insanity.

UK BORDERS ACT 2007

22. Assaulting an immigration officer: offence

(1) A person who assaults an immigration officer commits an offence.
(2) A person guilty of an offence under this section shall be liable on summary conviction to—
 (a) imprisonment for a period not exceeding 51 weeks,
 (b) a fine not exceeding level 5 on the standard scale, or
 (c) both.
 ...
(5) In relation to an offence committed before the commencement of section 281(5) of the Criminal Justice Act 2003 (51 week maximum term of sentences) the reference in subsection (2)(a) to 51 weeks shall be treated as a reference to 6 months.

VIOLENT CRIME REDUCTION ACT 2006

28. Using someone to mind a weapon

(1) A person is guilty of an offence if—
 (a) he uses another to look after, hide or transport a dangerous weapon for him; and
 (b) he does so under arrangements or in circumstances that facilitate, or are intended to facilitate, the weapon's being available to him for an unlawful purpose.
(2) For the purposes of this section the cases in which a dangerous weapon is to be regarded as available to a person for an unlawful purpose include any case where—
 (a) the weapon is available for him to take possession of it at a time and place; and
 (b) his possession of the weapon at that time and place would constitute, or be likely to involve or to lead to, the commission by him of an offence.
(3) In this section 'dangerous weapon' means—
 (a) a firearm other than an air weapon or a component part of, or accessory to, an air weapon; or
 (b) a weapon to which section 141 or 141A of the Criminal Justice Act 1988 applies (specified offensive weapons, knives and bladed weapons).
 ...

36. Manufacture, import and sale of realistic imitation firearms

(1) A person is guilty of an offence if—
 (a) he manufactures a realistic imitation firearm;
 (b) he modifies an imitation firearm so that it becomes a realistic imitation firearm;

(c) he sells a realistic imitation firearm; or
(d) he brings a realistic imitation firearm into Great Britain or causes one to be brought into Great Britain.
(2) Subsection (1) has effect subject to the defences in section 37.
(3) The Secretary of State may by regulations—
  (a) provide for exceptions and exemptions from the offence under subsection (1); and
  (b) provide for it to be a defence in proceedings for such an offence to show the matters specified or described in the regulations.
(4) Regulations under subsection (3) may—
  (a) frame any exception, exemption or defence by reference to an approval or consent given in accordance with the regulations;
  (b) provide for approvals and consents to be given in relation to particular cases or in relation to such descriptions of case as may be specified or described in the regulations; and
  (c) confer the function of giving approvals or consents on such persons specified or described in the regulations as the Secretary of State thinks fit.
(5) The power of the Secretary of State to make regulations under subsection (3) shall be exercisable by statutory instrument subject to annulment in pursuance of a resolution of either House of Parliament.
(6) That power includes power—
  (a) to make different provision for different cases;
  (b) to make provision subject to such exemptions and exceptions as the Secretary of State thinks fit; and
  (c) to make such incidental, supplemental, consequential and transitional provision as he thinks fit.
(7) A realistic imitation firearm brought into Great Britain shall be liable to forfeiture under the customs and excise Acts.
(8) In subsection (7) 'the customs and excise Acts' has the meaning given by section 1 of the Customs and Excise Management Act 1979.
(9) An offence under this section shall be punishable, on summary conviction—
  (a) in England and Wales, with imprisonment for a term not exceeding 51 weeks or with a fine not exceeding level 5 on the standard scale, or with both; and
  ...
(10) In relation to an offence committed before the commencement of section 281(5) of the Criminal Justice Act 2003, the reference in subsection (9)(a) of this section to 51 weeks is to be read as a reference to 6 months.
(11) In this section 'realistic imitation firearm' has the meaning given by section 38.

37. Specific defences applying to the offence under section 36

(1) It shall be a defence for a person charged with an offence under section 36 in respect of any conduct to show that the conduct was for the purpose only of making the imitation firearm in question available for one or more of the purposes specified in subsection (2).
(2) Those purposes are—
  (a) the purposes of a museum or gallery;
  (b) the purposes of theatrical performances and of rehearsals for such performances;
  (c) the production of films (within the meaning of Part 1 of the Copyright, Designs and Patents Act 1988 (see section 5B of that Act);
  (d) the production of television programmes (within the meaning of the Communications Act 2003 (see section 405(1) of that Act);
  (e) the organisation and holding of historical re-enactments organised and held by persons specified or described for the purposes of this section by regulations made by the Secretary of State;
  (f) the purposes of functions that a person has in his capacity as a person in the service of Her Majesty.
(3) It shall also be a defence for a person charged with an offence under section 36 in respect of conduct falling within subsection (1)(d) of that section to show that the conduct—
  (a) was in the course of carrying on any trade or business; and

(b) was for the purpose of making the imitation firearm in question available to be modified in a way which would result in its ceasing to be a realistic imitation firearm.
(4) For the purposes of this section a person shall be taken to have shown a matter specified in subsection (1) or (3) if—
   (a) sufficient evidence of that matter is adduced to raise an issue with respect to it; and
   (b) the contrary is not proved beyond a reasonable doubt.
(5) The power of the Secretary of State to make regulations under this section shall be exercisable by statutory instrument subject to annulment in pursuance of a resolution of either House of Parliament.
(6) That power includes power—
   (a) to make different provision for different cases;
   (b) to make provision subject to such exemptions and exceptions as the Secretary of State thinks fit; and
   (c) to make such incidental, supplemental, consequential and transitional provision as he thinks fit.
(7) In this section—
   'historical re-enactment' means any presentation or other event held for the purpose of re-enacting an event from the past or of illustrating conduct from a particular time or period in the past;
   'museum or gallery' includes any institution which—
   (a) has as its purpose, or one of its purposes, the preservation, display and interpretation of material of historical, artistic or scientific interest; and
   (b) gives the public access to it.

38. Meaning of 'realistic imitation firearm'

(1) In sections 36 and 37 'realistic imitation firearm' means an imitation firearm which—
   (a) has an appearance that is so realistic as to make it indistinguishable, for all practical purposes, from a real firearm; and
   (b) is neither a de-activated firearm nor itself an antique.
(2) For the purposes of this section, an imitation firearm is not (except by virtue of subsection (3)(b)) to be regarded as distinguishable from a real firearm for any practical purpose if it could be so distinguished only—
   (a) by an expert;
   (b) on a close examination; or
   (c) as a result of an attempt to load or to fire it.
(3) In determining for the purposes of this section whether an imitation firearm is distinguishable from a real firearm—
   (a) the matters that must be taken into account include any differences between the size, shape and principal colour of the imitation firearm and the size, shape and colour in which the real firearm is manufactured; and
   (b) the imitation is to be regarded as distinguishable if its size, shape or principal colour is unrealistic for a real firearm.
(4) The Secretary of State may by regulations provide that, for the purposes of subsection (3)(b)—
   (a) the size of an imitation firearm is to be regarded as unrealistic for a real firearm only if the imitation firearm has dimensions that are less than the dimensions specified in the regulations; and
   (b) a colour is to be regarded as unrealistic for a real firearm only if it is a colour specified in the regulations.
(5) The power of the Secretary of State to make regulations under this section shall be exercisable by statutory instrument subject to annulment in pursuance of a resolution of either House of Parliament.
(6) That power includes power—
   (a) to make different provision for different cases;
   (b) to make provision subject to such exemptions and exceptions as the Secretary of State thinks fit; and

    (c) to make such incidental, supplemental, consequential and transitional provision as he thinks fit.
(7) In this section—
'colour' is to be construed in accordance with subsection (9);
'de-activated firearm' means an imitation firearm that consists in something which—
    (a) was a firearm; but
    (b) has been so rendered incapable of discharging a shot, bullet or other missile as no longer to be a firearm;
'real firearm' means—
    (a) a firearm of an actual make or model of modern firearm (whether existing or discontinued); or
    (b) something falling within a description which could be used for identifying, by reference to their appearance, the firearms falling within a category of actual modern firearms which, even though they include firearms of different makes or models (whether existing or discontinued) or both, all have the same or a similar appearance.
(8) In subsection (7) 'modern firearm' means any firearm other than one the appearance of which would tend to identify it as having a design and mechanism of a sort first dating from before the year 1870.
(9) References in this section, in relation to an imitation firearm or a real firearm, to its colour include references to its being made of transparent material.
(10) Section 8 of the Firearms (Amendment) Act 1988 (under which firearms are deemed to be deactivated if they are appropriately marked) applies for the purposes of this section as it applies for the purposes of the 1968 Act.

55. Continuity of sexual offences law

(1) This section applies where, in any proceedings—
    (a) a person ('the defendant') is charged in respect of the same conduct both with an offence under the Sexual Offences Act 2003 ('the 2003 Act offence') and with an offence specified in subsection (2) ('the pre-commencement offence');
    (b) the only thing preventing the defendant from being found guilty of the 2003 Act offence is the fact that it has not been proved beyond a reasonable doubt that the time when the conduct took place was after the coming into force of the enactment providing for the offence; and
    (c) the only thing preventing the defendant from being found guilty of the pre-commencement offence is the fact that it has not been proved beyond a reasonable doubt that that time was before the coming into force of the repeal of the enactment providing for the offence.
(2) The offences referred to in subsection (1)(a) are—
    (a) any offence under the Sexual Offences Act 1956;
    (b) an offence under section 4 of the Vagrancy Act 1824 (obscene exposure);
    (c) an offence under section 28 of the Town Police Clauses Act 1847 (indecent exposure);
    (d) an offence under sections 61 or 62 of the Offences against the Person Act 1861 (buggery etc.);
    (e) an offence under section 128 of the Mental Health Act 1959 (sexual intercourse with patients);
    (f) an offence under section 1 of the Indecency with Children Act 1960 (indecency with children);
    (g) an offence under sections 4 or 5 of the Sexual Offences Act 1967 (procuring a man to commit buggery and living on the earnings of male prostitution);
    (h) an offence under section 9 of the Theft Act 1968 (burglary, including entering premises with intent to commit rape);
    (i) an offence under section 54 of the Criminal Law Act 1977 (incitement of girl under 16 to commit incest);
    (j) an offence under section 1 of the Protection of Children Act 1978 (indecent photographs of children);
    (k) an offence under section 3 of the Sexual Offences (Amendment) Act 2000 (abuse of position of trust);

(l) an offence under section 145 of the Nationality, Immigration and Asylum Act 2002 (traffic in prostitution).
(3) For the purpose of determining the guilt of the defendant it shall be conclusively presumed that the time when the conduct took place was—
   (a) if the maximum penalty for the pre-commencement offence is less than the maximum penalty for the 2003 Act offence, a time before the coming into force of the repeal of the enactment providing for the pre-commencement offence; and
   (b) in any other case, a time after the coming into force of the enactment providing for the 2003 Act offence.
(4) In subsection (3) the reference, in relation an offence, to the maximum penalty is a reference to the maximum penalty by way imprisonment or other detention that could be imposed on the defendant on conviction of the offence in the proceedings in question.
(5) A reference in this section to an offence under the Sexual Offences Act 2003 or to an offence specified in subsection (2) includes a reference to—
   (a) inciting the commission of that offence;
   (b) conspiracy to commit that offence; and
   (c) attempting to commit that offence;
and, in relation to an offence falling within paragraphs (a) to (c), a reference in this section to the enactment providing for the offence so falling has effect as a reference to the enactment providing for the offence under that Act or, as the case may be, for the offence so specified.
(6) This section applies to any proceedings, whenever commenced, other than proceedings in which the defendant has been convicted or acquitted of the 2003 Act offence or the pre-commencement offence before the commencement of this section.

WATER RESOURCES ACT 1991

85. Offences of polluting controlled waters

(1) A person contravenes this section if he causes or knowingly permits any poisonous, noxious or polluting matter or any solid waste matter to enter any controlled waters.
   …
(3) A person contravenes this section if he causes or knowingly permits any trade effluent or sewage effluent to be discharged—
   (a) into any controlled waters; or
   (b) from land in England and Wales, through a pipe, into the sea outside the seaward limits of controlled waters.
   …
(5) A person contravenes this section if he causes or knowingly permits any matter whatever to enter any inland freshwaters so as to tend (either directly or in combination with other matter which he or another person causes or permits to enter those waters) to impede the proper flow of the waters in a manner leading, or likely to lead, to a substantial aggravation of—
   (a) pollution due to other causes; or
   (b) the consequences of such pollution.
(6) Subject to the following provisions of this Chapter, a person who contravenes this section or the conditions of any consent given under this Chapter for the purposes of this section shall be guilty of an offence and liable—
   (a) on summary conviction, to imprisonment for a term not exceeding three months or to a fine not exceeding £20,000 or to both;
   (b) on conviction on indictment, to imprisonment for a term not exceeding two years or to a fine or to both.
(7) For the purpose of subsection (1) 'waste', in the term 'wastematter' includes anything that is waste for the purpose of Directive 2006/12/EC of the European Parliament and of the Council of 5 April 2006 on Waste, and that is not excluded from the scope of that Directive by Article 2(1) of that Directive.

89. Other defences to principal offences

(1) A person shall not be guilty of an offence under section 85 above in respect of the entry of any matter into any waters or any discharge if—
  (a) the entry is caused or permitted, or the discharge is made, in an emergency in order to avoid danger to life or health;
  (b) that person takes all such steps as are reasonably practicable in the circumstances for minimising the extent of the entry or discharge and of its polluting effects; and
  (c) particulars of the entry or discharge are furnished to the Agency as soon as reasonably practicable after the entry occurs.
(2) A person shall not be guilty of an offence under section 85 above by reason of his causing or permitting any discharge of trade or sewage effluent from a vessel.
(3) A person shall not be guilty of an offence under section 85 above by reason only of his permitting water from an abandoned mine or an abandoned part of a mine to enter controlled waters.
  ...
(4) A person shall not, otherwise than in respect of the entry of any poisonous, noxious or polluting matter into any controlled waters, be guilty of an offence under section 85 above by reason of his depositing the solid refuse of a mine or quarry on any land so that it falls or is carried into inland freshwaters if—
  (a) he deposits the refuse on the land with the consent of the Agency;
  (b) no other site for the deposit is reasonably practicable; and
  (c) he takes all reasonably practicable steps to prevent the refuse from entering those inland freshwaters.
  ...
(6) In this section 'mine' and 'quarry' have the same meanings as in the Mines and Quarries Act 1954.

WIRELESS TELEGRAPHY ACT 2006

47. Misleading messages

(1) A person commits an offence if, by means of wireless telegraphy, he sends or attempts to send a message to which this section applies.
(2) This section applies to a message which, to the person's knowledge—
  (a) is false or misleading; and
  (b) is likely to prejudice the efficiency of a safety of life service or to endanger the safety of a person or of a ship, aircraft or vehicle.
(3) This section applies in particular to a message which, to the person's knowledge, falsely suggests that a ship or aircraft—
  (a) is in distress or in need of assistance; or
  (b) is not in distress or not in need of assistance.
(4) A person who commits an offence under this section is liable—
  (a) on summary conviction, to imprisonment for a term not exceeding 12 months or to a fine not exceeding the statutory maximum or to both;
  (b) on conviction on indictment, to imprisonment for a term not exceeding two years or to a fine or to both.
  ...

Part 2

BILLS BEFORE PARLIAMENT (2007–2008) SESSION

COUNTER TERRORISM BILL 2006-07 (COMMONS VERSION 13/06/2008)

1. Power to remove documents for examination
(1) This section applies to a search under any of the following provisions—
   (a) section 43(1) of the Terrorism Act 2000 (search of suspected terrorist);
   (b) section 43(2) of that Act (search of person arrested under section 41 on suspicion of being a terrorist);
   (c) paragraph 1, 3, 11, 15, 28 or 31 of Schedule 5 to that Act (terrorist investigations);
   (d) section 52(1) or (3)(b) of the Anti-terrorism, Crime and Security Act 2001 (search for evidence of commission of weapons-related offences);
   (e) section 7A, 7B or 7C of the Prevention of Terrorism Act 2005) (searches in connection with control orders);
   (f) section 28 of the Terrorism Act 2006 (search for terrorist publications).
(2) A constable who carries out a search to which this section applies may, for the purpose of ascertaining whether a document is one that may be seized, remove the document to another place for examination and retain it there until the examination is completed.
(3) Where a constable carrying out a search to which this section applies has power to remove a document by virtue of this section, and the document—
   (a) consists of information that is stored in electronic form, and
   (b) is accessible from the premises being searched,
   the constable may require the document to be produced in a form in which it can be taken away, and in which it is visible and legible or from which it can readily be produced in a visible and legible form.
(4) Where a document is removed under this section a constable has the same powers of seizure as if it had not been removed and any matters discovered on examination after removal had been discovered before its removal.

2. Offence of obstruction
(1) A person who wilfully obstructs a constable in the exercise of the power conferred by section 1 commits an offence.
(2) A person guilty of an offence under this section is liable on summary conviction—
   (a) in England and Wales, to imprisonment for a term not exceeding 51 weeks or a fine not exceeding level 5 on the standard scale, or both;
   ...
(3) In subsection (2)(a) as it applies in relation to an offence committed before section 281(5) of the Criminal Justice Act 2003 comes into force, for '51 weeks' substitute 'six months'.

3. Items subject to legal privilege
(1) Section 1 does not authorise a constable to remove a document if the constable has reasonable cause to believe—
   (a) it is an item subject to legal privilege, or
   (b) it has an item subject to legal privilege comprised in it.
(2) Subsection (1)(b) does not prevent the removal of a document if it is not reasonably practicable for the item subject to legal privilege to be separated from the rest of the document without prejudicing any use of the rest of the document that would be lawful if it were subsequently seized.
(3) If, after a document has been removed under section 1, it is discovered that—
   (a) it is an item subject to legal privilege, or
   (b) it has an item subject to legal privilege comprised in it,
   the document must be returned forthwith.
(4) Subsection (3)(b) does not require the return of a document if it is not reasonably practicable for the item subject to legal privilege to be separated from the rest of the document without

prejudicing any use of the rest of the document that would be lawful if it were subsequently seized.
(5) Where an item subject to legal privilege is removed under subsection (2) or retained under subsection (4), it must not be examined or put to any other use except to the extent necessary for facilitating the examination of the rest of the document.
(6) For the purposes of this section 'item subject to legal privilege'—
    (a) in England and Wales, has the same meaning as in the Police and Criminal Evidence Act 1984;
    …

83. Offences relating to information about members of armed forces etc
(1) After section 58 of the Terrorism Act 2000 (collection of information) insert—

'58A Eliciting, publishing or communicating information about members of armed forces
(1) A person commits an offence who—
    (a) elicits or attempts to elicit information about an individual who is or has been a
        (i) a member of Her Majesty's Armed Forces,
        (ii) a member of any of the intelligence services, or
        (iii) a constable,
        which is of a kind likely to be useful to a person committing or preparing an act of terrorism, or
    (b) publishes or communicates any such information.
(2) It is a defence for a person charged with an offence under this section to prove that they had a reasonable excuse for their action.
(3) A person guilty of an offence under this section is liable—
    (a) on conviction on indictment, to imprisonment for a term not exceeding 10 years or to a fine, or to both;
    (b) on summary conviction—
        (i) in England and Wales or Scotland, to imprisonment for a term not exceeding 12 months or to a fine not exceeding the statutory maximum, or to both;
(4) In this section 'the intelligence services' means the Security Services, the Secret Intelligence Service and GCHQ (within the meaning of section 3 of the Intelligence Services Act 1994).
(5) Schedule 8A to this Act contains supplementary provisions relating to the offence under this section.'.
(2) In the application of section 58A in England and Wales in relation to an offence committed before the commencement of section 154(1) of the Criminal Justice Act 2003 the reference in subsection (3)(b)(i) to 12 months is to be read as a reference to 6 months.
(3) In section 118 of the Terrorism Act 2000 (defences), in subsection (5)(a) after '58,' insert '58A,'.
(4) After Schedule 8 to the Terrorism Act 2000 insert the Schedule set out in Schedule 7 to this Act.

84. Terrorist property: disclosure of information about possible offences
(1) Part 3 of the Terrorism Act 2000 (terrorist property) is amended as follows.
(2) In section 19(1) (duty to disclose belief or suspicion that offence committed), in paragraph (b) for 'comes to his attention in the course of a trade, profession, business or employment' substitute—'comes to his attention—
        (i) in the course of a trade, profession or business, or
        (ii) in the course of his employment (whether or not in the course of a trade, profession or business).'.
(3) After section 22 insert—

'22A Meaning of 'employment'
In sections 19 to 21B—
    (a) 'employment' means any employment (whether paid or unpaid) and includes—
        (i) work under a contract for services or as an office-holder,
        (ii) work experience provided pursuant to a training course or programme or in the course of training for employment, and
        (iii) voluntary work;

(b) 'employer' has a corresponding meaning.'.

(4) So far as the amendment in subsection (3) above extends any provision of sections 19 to 21B of the Terrorism Act 2000 involving belief or suspicion to cases to which that provision did not previously apply, that provision applies where the belief or suspicion is held after subsection (3) above comes into force even if based on information that came to the person's attention before that subsection was in force.

In any such case sections 19(2), 21(3) and 21A(4) of that Act (duty to make disclosure as soon as is reasonably practicable) are to be read as requiring the person to act as soon as is reasonably practicable after subsection (3) above comes into force.

98. Meaning of 'terrorism'
In this Act 'terrorism' has the same meaning as in the Terrorism Act 2000 (see section 1 of that Act).

99. Meaning of offence having a 'terrorist connection'
For the purposes of this Act an offence has a terrorist connection if the offence—
- (a) is, or takes place in the course of, an act of terrorism, or
- (b) is committed for the purposes of terrorism.

DRUGS (RECLASSIFICATION) BILL 2007–08 (COMMONS VERSION 19/02/2008)

1. Amendment of the Misuse of Drugs Act 1971
(1) Schedule 2 (controlled drugs) of the Misuse of Drugs Act 1971 is amended as follows.

(2) In Part 2 (which specifies the drugs which are subject to control under that Act as Class B drugs), in paragraph (1)(a) after 'Amphetamine' insert 'Cannabinol; Cannabinol derivatives; Cannabis and cannabis resin'.

(3) In Part 3 (which specifies the drugs which are subject to control under that Act as Class C drugs), in paragraph (1)(a) omit 'Cannabinol; Cannabinol derivatives; Cannabis and cannabis resin'.

2. Short title
(1) This Act may be cited as the Drugs (Reclassification) Act 2008.

ILLEGALLY LOGGED TIMBER (PROHIBITION OF SALE AND DISTRIBUTION) BILL 2007–08 (COMMONS VERSION 03/04/2008)

1. Interpretation
In this Act—

'distributor' means any person who, for professional and commercial purposes, irrespective of the selling technique used—
(a) manufactures and sells wood,
(b) sells wood manufactured by another person, or
(c) imports or exports wood into the United Kingdom;

'importer' means any person established within the United Kingdom who is responsible for the physical introduction for commercial purposes of wood or wood products into the United Kingdom;

'person' includes any individual or organisation of any kind subject to any jurisdiction in the United Kingdom;
'wood' means any timber, bamboo or rattan and products thereof.

2. Prohibited acts

A distributor or importer who—
- (a) sells, or offers for sale, any wood that has been—
    - (i) harvested, sold, taken or possessed illegally in the country from which the wood was orginally harvested, or
    - (ii) exported illegally from a country from which it was originally harvested or imported illegally into a country through which it passed or was transhipped,
- (b) attempts to commit any act falling within paragraph (a),
- (c) commits any act falling within paragraph (a) not knowingly but recklessly and where he should have known that such an act was being committed,
- (d) commits any act falling within paragraph (a) in good faith, or
- (e) falsifies labels or records in connection with the acts falling within paragraph (a),

is guilty of an offence.

3. Penalties, forfeiture, etc.

(1) A distributor or importer guilty of an offence under—
- (a) section 2(a) or (b) shall be liable on conviction on indictment to imprisonment for a term not exceeding 5 years or a fine not exceeding £100,000, or both,
- (b) section 2(c) shall be liable on conviction on indictment to imprisonment for a term not exceeding 1 year or a fine not exceeding £50,000, or both,
- (c) section 2(d) shall be liable on summary conviction to a fine not exceeding level 5 on the standard scale,
- (d) section 2(e) shall be liable on conviction on indictment to imprisonment for a term not exceeding 1 year or a fine not exceeding £10,000, or both.

…

HUMAN FERTILISATION AND EMBRYOLOGY BILL 2007–08 (HOUSE OF LORDS VERSION 13/06/2008)

ACTIVITIES GOVERNED BY THE HUMAN FERTILISATION AND EMBRYOLOGY ACT 1990

3. Prohibitions in connection with embryos

(1) Section 3 of the 1990 Act (prohibitions in connection with embryos) is amended as follows.

(2) For subsection (2) substitute—
  '(2) No person shall place in a woman—
  (a) an embryo other than a permitted embryo (as defined by section 3ZA), or
  (b) any gametes other than permitted eggs or permitted sperm (as so defined).'

(3) In subsection (3)—
  (a) at the end of paragraph (b), insert 'or', and
  (b) omit paragraph (d) and the word 'or' immediately before it.

(4) In subsection (4), for 'the day when the gametes are mixed' substitute 'the day on which the process of creating the embryo began'.

(5) After section 3 insert—

'3ZA. Permitted eggs, permitted sperm and permitted embryos
(1) This section has effect for the interpretation of section 3(2).
(2) A permitted egg is one—
   (a) which has been produced by or extracted from the ovaries of a woman, and
   (b) whose nuclear or mitochondrial DNA has not been altered.
(3) Permitted sperm are sperm—
   (a) which have been produced by or extracted from the testes of a man, and
   (b) whose nuclear or mitochondrial DNA has not been altered.
(4) An embryo is a permitted embryo if—
   (a) it has been created by the fertilisation of a permitted egg by permitted sperm,
   (b) no nuclear or mitochondrial DNA of any cell of the embryo has been altered, and
   (c) no cell has been added to it other than by division of the embryo's own cells.
(5) Regulations may provide that—]
   (a) an egg can be a permitted egg, or
   (b) an embryo can be a permitted embryo,
   even though the egg or embryo has had applied to it in prescribed circumstances a prescribed process designed to prevent the transmission of serious mitochondrial disease.
(6) In this section—
   (a) 'woman' and 'man' include respectively a girl and a boy (from birth), and
   (b) 'prescribed' means prescribed by regulations.'
(6) The Human Reproductive Cloning Act 2001 (which is superseded by the preceding provisions of this section) ceases to have effect.

4. Prohibitions in connection with genetic material not of human origin
(1) In section 4 of the 1990 Act (prohibitions in connection with gametes)—
   (a) in subsection (1), omit—
      (i) paragraph (c), and
      (ii) the word 'or' immediately before it, and
   (b) in subsection (5), after 'section 3' insert 'or 4A'.
(2) After section 4 of the 1990 Act insert—

'4A. Prohibitions in connection with genetic material not of human origin
(1) No person shall place in a woman—
   (a) a human admixed embryo,
   (b) any other embryo that is not a human embryo, or
   (c) any gametes other than human gametes.
(2) No person shall—
   (a) mix human gametes with animal gametes,
   (b) bring about the creation of a human admixed embryo, or
   (c) keep or use a human admixed embryo,
   except in pursuance of a licence.
(3) A licence cannot authorise the keeping or using of a human admixed embryo after the earliest of the following—
   (a) the appearance of the primitive streak, or
   (b) the end of the period of 14 days beginning with the day on which the process of creating the human admixed embryo began, but not counting any time during which the human admixed embryo is stored.
(4) A licence cannot authorise placing a human admixed embryo in an animal.
(5) A license cannot authorise keeping or using a human admixed embryo in any circumstances in which regulations prohibit its keeping or use.
(6) For the purposes of this Act a human admixed embryo is—
   (a) an embryo created by replacing the nucleus of an animal egg or of an animal cell, or two animal pronuclei, with—
      (i) two human pronuclei,
      (ii) one nucleus of a human gamete or of any other human cell, or
      (iii) one human gamete or other human cell,

(b) any other embryo created by using—
  (i) human gametes and animal gametes, or
  (ii) one human pronucleus and one animal pronucleus,
(c) a human embryo that has been altered by the introduction of any sequence of nuclear or mitochondrial DNA of an animal into one or more cells of the embryo,
(d) a human embryo that has been altered by the introduction of one or more animal cells, or
(e) any embryo not falling within paragraphs (a) to (d) which contains both nuclear or mitochondrial DNA or a human and nuclear or mitochondrial DNA of an animal ('animal DNA') but in which the animal DNA is not predominant.
(7) In subsection (6)—
  (a) references to animal cells are to cells of an animal or of an animal embryo, and
  (b) references to human cells are to cells of a human or of a human embryo.
(8) For the purposes of this section an 'animal' is an animal other than man.
(9) In this section 'embryo' means a live embryo, including an egg that is in the process of fertilisation or is undergoing any other process capable of resulting in an embryo.
(10) In this section—
  (a) references to eggs are to live eggs, including cells of the female germ line at any stage of maturity, but not including eggs that are in the process of fertilisation or are undergoing any other process capable of resulting in an embryo, and
  (b) references to gametes are to eggs (as so defined) or to live sperm, including cells of the male germ line at any stage of maturity.
(11) If it appears to the Secretary of State necessary or desirable to do so in the light of developments in science or medicine, regulations may—
  (a) amend (but not repeal) paragraphs (a) to (e) of subsection (6);
  (b) provide that in this section 'embryo', 'eggs' or 'gametes' includes things specified in the regulations which would not otherwise fall within the definition.
(12) Regulations made by virtue of subsection (10)(a) may make any amendment of subsection (6) that appears to the Secretary of State to be appropriate in consequence of any amendment of subsection (5).'

STATUTE LAW (REPEALS) BILL 2007-2008 (HOUSE OF LORDS VERSION 03/06/2008)

SCHEDULE 1 PART 3 | CRIMINAL LAW

Reference	Extent of repeal
Sexual Offences Act 1956	In section 35(2), the words from '(whether' to '1885)'.
	In section 35(3), the words from 'or was so convicted' to 'commencement of this Act,' and from 'or under subsection (1)' to the end.